Lecture Notes in Economics and Mathematical Systems

Armin Schmutzler

Flexibility and Adjustment to Information in Sequential Decision Problems

A Systematic Approach

Springer-Verlag
Berlin Heidelberg New York
London Paris Tokyo
Hong Kong Barcelona
Budapest

Author

Armin Schmutzler
Alfred-Weber-Institut, Universität Heidelberg
Grabengasse 14, W-6900 Heidelberg, FRG

ISBN 3-540-54645-6 Springer-Verlag Berlin Heidelberg New York
ISBN 0-387-54645-6 Springer-Verlag New York Berlin Heidelberg

Printed in Germany

Typesetting: Camera ready by author
Printing and binding: Druckhaus Beltz, Hemsbach/Bergstr.
42/3140-543210 - Printed on acid-free paper

PREFACE

In many different areas of economics, intertemporal modelling has gained importance during the last one or two decades. A great number of sophisticated mathematical models has been produced. Given this development, we feel that attempts to unify different approaches may be helpful to increase the transparency of economic research in the field. This monograph attempts to provide a framework in which such a unification can take place.

I would like to appreciate the advice and help of many friends and colleagues, such as Switgard Feuerstein, Alexander Gerybadze, Stefan Huschens, Hans-Jürgen Jaksch, Frank Jöst, Marco Lehmann-Waffenschmidt, Rainer Leisten, Jürgen Malzacher, Peter Michaelis, Georg Müller, John Proops, Carla Rathgeber, Brigitte Rüger, Gunther Stephan and Gerhard Wagenhals. My wife Chrittie read the entire manuscript and made helpful stylistic suggestions. In particular, however, I would like to thank Malte Faber for the supervision of the Ph.D.-thesis from which this book resulted. His supportive attitude towards my work was a great help.

CONTENTS

INTRODUCTION

For an appropriate treatment of dynamic economic problems, a thorough understanding of intertemporal decisions of economic agents is necessary. To obtain such an understanding, it is helpful to identify typical elements of economic decision situations.

A simple but important observation is that many economic decisions affect the future well-being of the agent. For example, tomorrow's consumption possibilities of households depend on today's consumption and savings decisions, and tomorrow's production possibilities of firms depend on today's investment decisions. However, the precise nature of the relation between present decisions and future well-being is usually unknown. The impact of consumption and savings decisions on the future position of households depends, among other things, on future income streams and future preferences, which will generally not be known to the agent. Similarly, the effects of investment decisions on the future position of firms depend on the speed and nature of technical progress, on political factors (e.g. new environmental laws) and on consumer preferences.

Hence, economic agents have to make decisions without knowing the exact effects of these decisions on their future position. So much is hardly debatable. Disagreement among economists usually starts when it comes to adequate ways of treating this kind of uncertainty in microeconomic models. A view which appears to be more common among applied economists than among economic theorists is that in most relevant cases the decision situations are too complex to be modelled using the common abstractions of rational economic agents who maximize some kind of objective function. Nevertheless, this view also enjoys some support among theorists who are influenced by the work of scholars like KNIGHT (1921), KEYNES (1957) and SHACKLE (1958).

Contrary to this view is the standard approach of modelling microeconomic behaviour as maximization of an expected utility function subject to certain constraints. To use the expected utility approach in sequential decision problems, one usually makes the following assumptions:

(a) The set of choice sequences is known to the agent; in particular, he/she knows how decisions today affect choice possibilities tomorrow.

(b) The effects of a certain choice sequence on his/her well-being depend on a state of the world, an unknown element of a known set.

(c) The agent behaves in accordance with rationality axioms which imply that his/her behaviour can be described as maximization of an expected utility function with respect to certain objective or subjective probability distributions.

(d) In his/her decision, the agent does not consider whether or not a decision allows him/her to react to information that will be received in the future. In other words, flexibility considerations are not an issue.

Though modelling on the basis of these assumptions is still more common than any other procedure, there have been various attempts to extend this approach by using less restrictive assumptions about the agent's behaviour. Two of them will only be mentioned briefly, a third one will be the main subject of this study.

The first approach deals with decision situations where the agent chooses from a given set, but is not required to have a probability distribution on the set of states of the world (cf. e.g. ARROW/HURWICZ 1972, MASKIN 1979).

A second, more recent, approach has taken up the experimental observation by scholars like ALLAIS (1953) and ELLSBERG (1961) that the empirical foundations of expected utility theory are somewhat shaky. In particular, the independence axiom (cf. SINN 1980, p.28) has been subjected to criticism. This axiom is responsible for the linearity of the expected utility function in probabilities. Recent attempts to change the system of axioms in a fashion that is consistent with empirical observations therefore lead to "non-linear utility theories" (MACHINA 1982, 1987, 1989, FISHBURN 1985, CHEW/EPSTEIN 1989).

The main purpose of the third approach is to pay tribute to the fact that the knowledge of economic agents changes over time. Unlike the other two approaches, which are applicable to one-shot decisions, the third approach is relevant only when successive decisions are made.

It is the last approach that this study will deal with. We shall consider sequential decision problems where the agent

(a) knows that present decisions affect future well-being,
(b) is uncertain about the precise nature of the relation between present decisions and future well-being,
(c) receives additional information about this relation before taking the second decision of the sequence.

This allows to incorporate the idea into the model that agents expect to learn about the effect of their decisions and that the quality of a decision depends, among other things, on the extent to which it allows the agent to adapt to new information, information about his own preferences as well as information about exogenous factors, such as technology, market conditions and the like.

However, what is <u>not</u> included in our analysis is learning about events which the agent does not even conceive of when he takes his first decision, but which nevertheless happen. Such events are relevant in many parts of economic life. For instance, investment decisions of business firms have to be based on assumptions on technological development. But even though firms will generally be able to make some predictions as to the possible events that may occur, they are ignorant in a fundamental way. They may not only find it hard to say which element of a given set of events (e.g. invention of new techniques) turns out to be true, they will in general not even be able to name the complete set of possible events. For instance, a firm may realize that a new technique is invented, which it did not even think of a few years before. The failure to conceive of this possibility in advance may just be a problem of the particular firm - other more imaginative firms may have recognized the possibility at a much earlier point of time, but it may also be a case of "social ignorance"[1]; i.e. all the firms of an economy may be unaware of the possible occurrence of the event.

The importance of such considerations notwithstanding, they will not be included in this study. The goal of the study is to improve the understanding of flexibility considerations, i.e. of ex ante preparations for different events that may occur in the future. Though such flexibility considerations are a way of adjusting to uncertainty, to judge whether a certain choice is flexible one needs at least some knowledge as to the future. If literally nothing is known about an event in advance, it may certainly be possible to react to it when it happens, but there is no way to prepare for it.

Therefore, we restrict our considerations to learning processes that take the form of observing an element of a <u>known</u> set of possible events. We shall show that even in this rudimentary form the inclusion of the expectation of learning can improve both descriptive and normative economic analysis.

As to descriptive analysis, the inclusion of learning helps to understand economic phenomena that do not make sense within the usual framework of expected utility maximization without flexibility considerations. The phenomena we are thinking of relate to the fact that, in many decision problems, some choices imply less commitment to a particular course of action than others. This may be desirable in a world where additional information is received over time.

For instance, this is relevant to financial decisions. Certain assets, most notably money, have the property that holding them allows to react to a variety of different signals, e.g. to changes in income streams and prices of capital goods and assets, because

[1] cf. FABER/MANSTETTEN/PROOPS(1990) for a more detailed treatment of different types of ignorance.

they can be exchanged for consumption goods or other financial assets at low costs at any moment of time. In many cases, the relative ease with which two assets can be transformed into other assets or into consumption goods is important to determine which of the two is preferred in different situations. This kind of phenomenon can only be addressed formally if the model treats the arrival of new information in an adequate manner.

Similar considerations hold for real investment decisions. For instance, the idea that firms are reluctant to invest in particularly "uncertain" times because they would like to wait for the resolution of uncertainty can also be understood with the kind of framework we shall be working with. Again, this idea is not amenable to a method that uses expected utility maximization but ignores the fact that agents learn over time.

The extent to which different alternatives adapt to future information is not only pertinent to the decision whether investment should take place at all. It is also the choice of capital good for a particular purpose which should be influenced by such considerations.

For instance, the last decade has seen a growing inclination of firms to invest into "flexible manufacturing systems". One of the supposed advantages of these systems is that they adapt readily to changing environmental conditions, including changes in the demand for different, but similar products. In other words, they give the agent the opportunity to adjust his future decisions to new information that he may receive.

But it is not only descriptive analysis that appears to benefit from an appropriate treatment of learning and flexibility issues, these issues are also relevant to normative analysis. For instance, a standard tool in cost-benefit analysis is the net present value method (cf. IRVIN 1978). This method evaluates projects by maximization of the expected value of the discounted net benefits, the "net present value". It does not discriminate between alternatives on the grounds that one or the other allows for a better usage of future information. This drawback is particularly significant in situations where the project under investigation is expected to lead to irreversible destruction of natural resources. Whenever a project leads to such damage, choosing it means giving up the option to use future information about the usefulness of the resource before deciding whether to invest or not. The net present value method gives a misleading picture because it systematically ignores this "option value" of abstaining from investment (cf. ARROW/FISHER 1974, HENRY 1974, HANEMANN 1989).

Summing up, there is a variety of issues that crop up in economic analysis and are hard to treat with expected utility maximization in its simplest fashion, because this approach does not allow for flexibility considerations.

However, these shortcomings can not be ascribed to intrinsic problems of the approach. Mild generalizations of familiar concepts are enough to gain at least some understanding about flexibility and learning. This insight is not new; cf. e.g. ARROW/FISHER 1974, HENRY 1974, BERNANKE 1983, JONES/OSTROY 1984. Unfortunately, the literature on the subject is somewhat disperse. Furthermore, it is often rather technical. Therefore, it is often difficult to see the relation between different contributions to the subject. The main goal of the present study is to change this state of affairs by giving a systematic treatment of decision problems with irreversibility, uncertainty and learning. This will serve two purposes.

Firstly, and most obviously, it helps to understand decision problems where agents are modelled as adjusting to uncertainty (in the sense of a significant difference between present and expected future knowledge). In particular, the comparative statics of such situations can be investigated. How does an increase in the extent to which the agent expects to learn influence his optimal choice? Is it true that agents abstain from irreversible choices like investment projects when there is great uncertainty? In short, the first purpose of our approach is to answer the question: How does an increase in uncertainty affect the optimal decision for an agent who takes flexibility considerations into account?

Secondly, one can obtain some insight into the problem of the interpretation of results that are obtained from models in which agents do not take flexibility considerations into account. Accepting that simplicity may sometimes demand the use of models without flexibility considerations, it is advisable to ask in which way this kind of simplification may be misleading. This can help the model builder to evaluate how useful his results in the simplified case are. For instance, it can be shown that in many examples the neglect of flexibility considerations implies a systematic bias towards irreversible decisions. In other words, whatever the optimal choice of an agent in a model without flexibility considerations, it has to be expected to be "at least as irreversible" and possibly "more irreversible" than in the more appropriate but more complex case with flexibility considerations. Similarly, one can ask whether there are decision situations where the assumption of ordinary expected utility maximization (or even more drastic simplifications, like myopic maximization, i.e. maximization of short-term utility functions) does not give misleading conclusions. In short, the second purpose of our approach is to answer the question: How is the optimal choice of an agent affected if flexibility considerations are ignored?

It will turn out that, from a mathematical point of view, the two questions "how does an increase in uncertainty affect the optimal decision for an agent who takes flexibility considerations into account?" and "how is the optimal choice of an agent affected when flexibility considerations are ignored?" are actually different aspects of one problem.

To see this and to provide answers to these questions, we shall deal with an abstract choice theoretical framework which, on the one hand, has sufficient structure to contain all the above elements (irreversibility, uncertainty and learning), but, on the other hand, has no superfluous structure, or as RASMUSEN (1989, p.14) puts it, "no fat".

The whole study centres around this model. Before treating the general version, we shall approach the problem from two sides. In chapter 1, we shall treat familiar examples from economic theory and reality which help to get a first idea of what an adequate choice-theoretic treatment of irreversibility and learning should look like. In chapter 2, the model will then be introduced step by step. We devote considerable space to a simple version of the model in which uncertainty is not treated and the focus is on irreversibility. This is a preparation for the answer to the two above-mentioned questions. Later in the chapter, uncertainty and learning are introduced. The presentation in chapter 2, though rather formal, is still not guided by systematic considerations but rather by the goal to improve the intuition for the problems one can expect. Systematic considerations are the objective of chapter 3, where we shall reduce all the topics treated in this introduction to the question: How does the optimal choice in an appropriate sequential decision problem depend on the structure of the problem? Here the structure reflects the set of feasible choices of the agent, his choice criterion and the extent to which he expects to learn.

Chapter 4 contains an extension of the model to more than two periods, which will then be applied to discuss familiar tenets from the theory of money demand in a consistent formal framework in chapter 5. We note that section 3 of chapter 4 involves a slight digression. It deals with an alternative treatment of sequential decision making under uncertainty. Though related to our general discussion, it is not necessary for an understanding of our main line of thought. With minor exceptions, this is also true for section 4.2.

Therefore, a possible alternative to reading the book from cover to cover is to read chapters 1-3, 4.1 and 5. The reader who is already familiar with the issues raised in the introduction and, in particular, with the article by JONES/OSTROY (1984) and the option value literature may find it sufficient to restrict his attention to chapter 3. Finally, for a reader who is only interested in the basic ideas, it may be sufficient to read chapters 1 and 2 only.

The study contains a considerable number of concepts, propositions and examples which, to the author's knowledge, can not be found in the literature. However, the main objective of the study is not to prove new results but is to give a systematic treatment of an area where results are scattered all over the literature. Therefore, several results from the literature are included. This is particularly true for some of the work of JONES/OSTROY (1984), from which we take the two-period model (with minor modifications) and their central result.

Though mathematical terminology is used throughout the book, we have tried to keep the presentation as self-contained as possible. We hope that this helps to convey our central message: that in a field where great numbers of different models are produced, it may be expedient to search for general principles. This book is no more than a step in this direction, but we feel that it is a step worth taking.

Chapter 1

THE IMPORTANCE OF IRREVERSIBILITY AND LEARNING - FAMILIAR EXAMPLES REVISITED

In the introduction, we formulated what we want to investigate in this book. To get an idea how to do this, we shall have a look at well-known economic examples in chapter 1. This will give us some clues as to the structure that a model should have in order to be useful for our purposes. One of the sections of this chapter deals with a well-known theoretical edifice, the second one with a real-world issue.

The first section of this chapter, 1.1, is a brief review of neoclassical investment theory, which helps to understand how the nature of models is changed when irreversibility is taken into account in an adequate fashion.[1]

Section 1.2 contains a brief summary of recent developments in the manufacturing industry and serves to illustrate how the desire to avoid irreversible commitment in order to wait for future information can have a profound impact on industrial organization.

This chapter should not be expected to contain fundamentally new economic insights; it merely serves as a motivation for some of the abstract concepts that will be introduced in future chapters.

1.1 Neoclassical Investment Models: A Brief Survey

We start with a brief review of a simple dynamic neoclassical model of investment (cf. JORGENSON 1967) and several of its more recent variants. The discussion is by no means complete, and the emphasis is on those aspects of the model that relate to our general approach.

---

[1] For a review that covers similar topics with a different objective cf. WODOPIA (1986, p.23-47).

Though time is formally included in the simplest version of the neoclassical model, it plays only a very limited role. The assumptions of the model on markets for real capital are such that stock variables can be manipulated arbitrarily. Both buying and selling of capital are "timeless" matters, which implies for instance that investors never have to look into the future when they make decisions because immediate adjustment to changes in their environment is possible.

The assumptions of the model are therefore not only unrealistic, they also lead to rather implausible conclusions. Thus, it is not surprising that the original model was subjected to various modifications, thereby leading to more satisfactory results about the investment behaviour of firms. The underlying idea in all these modifications is to change the structure of the model to reflect the fact that today's decisions affect the future position of the firm. There are at least three ways how this can be achieved.

The first approach uses adjustment costs (cf. EISNER/STROTZ 1963, LUCAS 1967, GOULD 1968). It retains the assumption that capital can be bought and sold in arbitrary quantities at any moment of time, but claims that adjustment of capital stocks is more costly if it is to be achieved rapidly.

The second approach (cf. ARROW 1968, MARTIRENA-MARTEL 1971, NICKELL 1974a,b, PINDYCK 1988) emphasizes the fact that capital goods, once bought, cannot readily be resold, which is called the irreversibility of investment.

The third approach stresses the fact that capital stocks are generally not available immediately after they have been ordered, in other words, that decision makers have to consider delivery lags (NICKELL 1974a, 1977).

We shall start with a brief review of the simplest version of the neoclassical model in 1.1.1 and point out its merits and weak sides. In sections 1.1.2 - 1.1.4, we shall discuss the three above-mentioned modifications of the model. Adjustment costs will be treated in section 1.1.2; 1.1.3 deals with irreversibility and 1.1.4 with delivery lags.

1.1.1 The Standard Neoclassical Investment Theory Model

The starting point of our discussion is a model of a competitive firm that maximizes the present value of its profits in a world of perfect markets.

In particular, the firm is assumed to operate on a perfect capital market, so that at any moment t of time it can borrow and lend as much as it wishes at the going rate of interest R(t).

Furthermore, the firm is assumed to know all exogenous variables with certainty.

The technology of the firm is given by a neo-classical single output, two factor production function F(K(t),L(t))[2].

The output is assumed to be instantaneously available for sale. Capital is assumed to be homogeneous, but deteriorates at a constant rate δ.

The firm operates on perfect markets for factors and goods, which implies that it can buy and sell any quantity of capital at any moment of time and use it immediately.

Adjustment of capital stocks causes no costs apart from the mere costs of purchase.

Finally, it is assumed that there are no taxes.

The decision problem of the firm can then be summarized as follows.

Suppose given the price p(t) of the output, the price q(t) of the capital good, the wage rate w(t) and the interest rate R(t) for every $t \in R_+$. Then the firm chooses the capital stock K(t), the labour input L(t) and the investment I(t) so as to maximize the present value of the income stream,

---

2 By this we mean that F is twice differentiable with $F_K, F_L > 0$, $F_{KK}, F_{LL} < 0$.

$$V=\int_0^{\infty} \exp\left(-R(t)\right)[p(t)F(K(t),L(t))-w(t)L(t)-q(t)I(t)]dt$$

subject to $dK(t)/dt = I(t)-\delta K(t)$ and a given initial capital stock $K(0)$.

From the necessary conditions for this problem the investment behaviour of the firm can be derived. Thanks to the drastic simplifications of the model, these derivations are not very difficult. The price that has to be paid for this simplicity is that the results of the model are somewhat peculiar. For instance, it turns out that the firm loses nothing if it disregards the future in its decisions and maximizes instantaneous profit in each period. In other words, the optimal behaviour is myopic (cf. chapter 2.1.1).

A more appealing characteristic of the model is the reaction of the capital stock to a change of an important parameter, the cost of capital $c(t)=q(t)\{r(t)+\delta-\dot{q}(t)/q(t)\}$. The name "cost of capital" is justified because $c(t)$ contains $q(t)r(t)$, the interest charge on $q(t)$ for one (marginal) period, the depreciation charge $q(t)\delta$ and, with a negative sign, the capital gain $\dot{q}(t)$, which accrues to the owner of a unit of capital if he sells it after a marginal unit of time. The capital stock in each period can be seen to depend negatively on the cost of capital in that period, which is what one would expect (cf. NICKELL 1978, p.12).

A result that is only partly convincing concerns the behaviour of the capital stock when sudden changes of the interest rate are anticipated. For instance, a discontinuous fall in the interest rate can be seen to lead to an upward jump of the capital stock in the very moment the fall is expected (cf. NICKELL 1978, p.12; similar results hold for discontinuous changes of the other parameters). While the direction of this adjustment is not unreasonable, its instantaneous nature is, because adjustments of capital stocks to exogenous shocks take time.

The most serious defect of the model, however, becomes apparent when relatively rapid changes in the price of capital are expected. If, for instance, a rapid rise of this price in a certain time interval is expected, while all the other prices are expected to remain constant, the firm will buy a huge block of capital at the beginning of the interval and resell it towards the end. Indeed, if the price rise takes place during a very short interval, i.e. if it approaches a discontinuous jump, the amount of capital the firm buys (and sells soon afterwards) rises above all bounds. The reason for this unappealing result is that the firm will receive capital gains by exploiting the difference between present and future prices in very much the same way that speculators on paper asset markets do - the only difference being that the firms in the model can be absolutely sure to make these gains because there is no uncertainty).

All the above-mentioned deficiencies are quite obviously caused by the simplifying assumptions on the process of capital adjustment. It is not misleading to illustrate the structure of the model with the following example:

"... a restaurateur from this particular world who had more customers on weekends as opposed to weekdays would be observed to buy a small restaurant for weekdays but would sell it on Friday nights and purchase a large restaurant for the weekend, reselling it on Monday mornings." (NICKELL 1978, p.9)

In other words, the formulation of the model creates the illusion of an enormous flexibility of the firm, which is completely independent of its actions. It is this element of the model, the "total reversibility" (cf. chapter 2.1.1), that needs to be given up to get a better understanding of the investment decisions of firms.

1.1.2 The Investment Model with Adjustment Costs

In this section, the assumption that the firm can purchase or sell any amount of capital at any moment of time is not yet given up. However, an additional cost factor is introduced. While so far it was assumed that investment caused no costs over and above the mere costs of purchase, it is now supposed that changes in the capital stock cause additional costs which are related to the sale, the purchase or the implementation of capital goods and are not reflected in the buying price of these goods. That such "adjustment costs" exist can hardly be doubted; in general, new machinery can only be utilized after a certain amount of reorganization and retraining.

Such costs can be introduced into the model through an additional cost term C(I), where I denotes investment. For the moment, we may tentatively assume that these costs make rapid adjustment more costly than slow adjustment so that they grow more than proportionately with the investment level. This assumption is reflected in a strictly convex adjustment cost function C(I).

As an example of such a model, GOULD (1968) considered a firm with strictly convex adjustment costs and constant returns to scale. From the necessary conditions of this model, it follows readily that present value maximization is no longer guaranteed by the myopic rule "maximize short-term profit". This is hardly surprising: when rapid investment is overly costly, it is advisable to look into the future when choosing one's capital stock, so that the need for investment is anticipated.

This principle is also responsible for the fact that the effects of changes in exogenous parameters turn out to be more credible than in the case without adjustment costs. Anticipated changes of such parameters (e.g. of interest rates) lead to a gradual adjustment of the capital stock as opposed to the discontinuous adjustment in the earlier case.

The model with strictly convex adjustment costs therefore leads to more plausible results than the simpler "totally reversible" version of the model. However, these results depend on the strict convexity assumption, which was only casually justified by arguing that rapid adjustment is more costly than slow adjustment. While this argument appears to be reasonable for some ranges of I, it can hardly be claimed to be of general validity. As NICKELL (1978, p.37) puts it,

"it is probably cheaper to install a new production line in a month than in a day. But it is not clear that it is more expensive in terms of adjustment costs to install a new production line in a month than to install it in fifty years, which is the implication of strict convexity."

One would therefore want to test whether alternative assumptions can replace strictly convex adjustment costs.

As we shall show in the following two sections, this is indeed the case. Both the upward and the downward adjustment of capital stocks are severely limited in reality, which has significant effects on investment behaviour. We shall start with the limits to downward adjustment.

1.1.3 The Irreversibility of Investment

Most capital goods cannot easily be sold. While there may be a significant second-hand market for vehicles and certain types of buildings such as offices, many factories are of such a specific nature that they can be regarded as unsaleable. This kind of irreversibility can be introduced into the model by assuming that $I(t) \geq 0$ (cf. ARROW 1968). Hence, rapid downward adjustment of the capital stock is impossible, while rapid upward adjustment is not yet assumed to cause any problem.

Therefore, a reformulation of the model of section 1.1.1 that allows for irreversible investment will have no effect whatsoever in situations where the unconstrained firm, i.e. the firm that is allowed to choose $I(t) < 0$, would not consider such disinvestment. Hence, certain unsatisfactory results of the original model carry over to the modified version. For instance, the reaction to a single discontinuous downward shift of the rate of interest will still be a discontinuous upward jump of the capital stock: the structure of the model does not prohibit rapid adjustments as long as $I(t) \geq 0$. When, however, a rapid downward shift is optimal in the unconstrained case, the irreversibility of investment will change the optimal policy.

To bring out this point more clearly, it is useful to consider a firm under imperfect competition (cf. NICKELL 1974b). Suppose this firm faces a downward sloping demand function of the separable form $z(p(t))\beta(t)$, where the time-dependent parameter $\beta(t)$ is useful to model shifts in demand: an upward shift corresponds to a greater value of ß and vice versa.

Suppose now that the firm expects a rapid fall in ß, i.e. a severe slump in demand, between periods t_0 and t_1. Suppose the fall is so rapid that the rate of deterioration of the capital stock is smaller than the rate of decline of demand. Then the optimal unconstrained behaviour of the firm will lead to disinvestment in this interval. With the constraint, however, disinvestment is not feasible. Instead, the optimal policy is to stop investment <u>before</u> the beginning of the demand slump and not start investment again until after the end of the slump (cf. NICKELL 1974a).

Consequently, the decision-maker can no longer behave myopically. He has to anticipate future demand slumps so that he can adjust his capital stock early enough.

Before finishing this section, we note that the term "irreversibility of investment", which we used in this section (and which is frequently used in the literature) is a special case of the notion of irreversibility that we shall use in the rest of this thesis. In general, we call a decision (partially) irreversible if it makes some future choices impossible that would have been possible a priori, cf. chapter 2.1.1. The example at hand is a special case of this because the "irreversibility of investment" means that the choice of a certain capital stock today has the effect that the capital stock tomorrow cannot drop below certain bounds.

1.1.4 Delivery Lags

Through the introduction of the non-negativity constraint for investment, extreme downward shifts of the capital stock are excluded from the model. Sudden upward shifts, however, are still allowed.

Rapid upward shifts can be excluded by introducing the highly realistic assumption that, because of delivery lags, a considerable amount of time, say m time units, will elapse between the decision to invest and the moment of time when the first unit of output is produced with the new capital good.

As long as there is no uncertainty, the introduction of delivery lags does not make a great difference. If the decision-maker is sure about the behaviour of the exogenous variables, the investment path will be the same as before - the only difference being that, if investment is to take place at some moment t, an action, the ordering of the capital goods, has to take place at t-m. Hence, with delivery lags myopic behaviour is no longer appropriate.

To obtain more interesting results, one has to include uncertainty. As an intermediate case between certainty and uncertainty, consider a firm that believes firmly in a certain path of development of the exogenous parameters, but finds that it is wrong at some moment t_0 in time. More specifically, suppose the firm is in the (imperfectly competitive) situation of the last section, with the irreversibility constraint being replaced by the delivery lag condition. Furthermore, suppose it expects static demand conditions, i.e. constant β, to persist indefinitely. Finally, suppose that, contrary to its expectations, demand increases unexpectedly at t_0.

If capital stocks could be adjusted in no time, the firm would react to the increase in demand by investing immediately after it finds that its expectations are wrong. With delivery lags, however, this need not be the case. The reaction of the firm depends strongly on the way in which the recognition of its mistake influences future expectations. For instance, the firm may believe that the boom is only of a temporary nature and demand will be back at the expected level sooner than newly ordered capital goods can be delivered, i.e. less than m periods after the beginning of the unexpected temporary boom. Then there is no point in any additional investment at all, because the new capital good would only be available after the end of the boom period. Only if the boom is expected to be of a more permanent nature, the firm will decide to invest.

Hence, one may tentatively argue that the existence of delivery lags has a stabilizing effect on the investment behaviour of the firm, because it reduces the influence of unexpected demand fluctuations.

Again, this is a general principle: if a problem is rigid in the sense that there is a great time lag between a decision and its consequences, then the arrival of information may have little or no effect on the optimal behaviour. This resembles a result which will be proved as proposition 3.5 for our abstract model.

This point can be reinforced by allowing for ex ante uncertainty. It can then be shown that shifts of certain exogenous parameters, the precise date of which are not known, will not lead to the kind of rapid adjustment we observed in the original model, but instead to a smoother kind of adjustment.

More precisely, suppose the firm still operates in an imperfectly competitive environment. Suppose further that it expects a shift in one of the exogenous variables and is uncertain at which time the shift will take place.

Suppose, however, that it is sure that the shift will take place in some closed time interval [a,b] and that it has a subjective probability distribution as to which will be the precise moment of the jump.

Then it can be shown that the choice of a firm that maximizes the expected present value of its payoffs is significantly different than in the case without delivery lags. We shall briefly summarize the results, without giving proofs (cf. NICKELL 1977).

To understand the difference, consider the two situations where no jump in demand conditions occurs and β_0 and β_1 ($\beta_0 < \beta_1$) are the respective parameters. In other words, the firm operates under perfect certainty and the demand function is of the form $z(p(t))\beta_0$ in the first case, $z(p(t))\beta_1$ in the second case. The optimal accumulation path for β_0, the "lower trend path", can be seen to lie strictly below the corresponding path for β_1, the "upper trend path", as in figure 1.1.

In the case without delivery lags, the firm will stick to the lower trend path until the jump occurs and then adjust its capital stock to the higher trend value, cf. the "zero lag path" in figure 1.1.

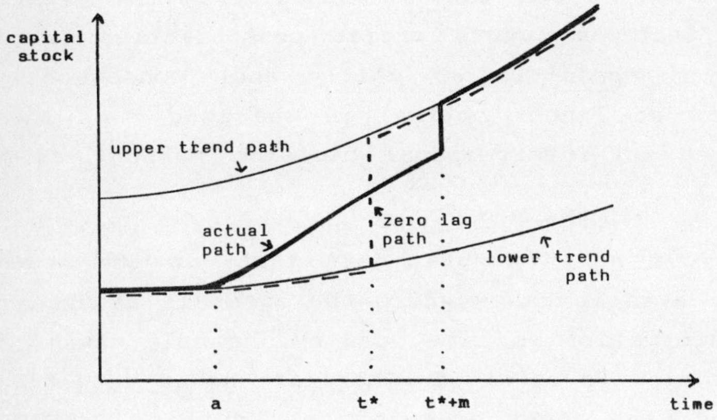

Figure 1.1: The Influence of Delivery Lags on the Investment Path

When there are delivery lags, this policy is not feasible. Suppose the firm abstains from investment until t*, when it observes the jump. Then, it will not be able to reach the upper trend path before period t*+m, even if it reacts immediately. It turns out (cf. NICKELL 1977) that the firm should start ordering the capital good at a−m and gradually move towards the upper trend path, with the size of investment around t depending on the probability that the event occurs around t+m. In the moment the jump occurs the firm will order the amount of capital needed to reach the upper trend path. This purchase, however, will generally be considerably smaller than in the case without delivery lags because the capital stock will, in general, already have left the lower trend path (cf. figure 1.1).

Summing up, the original neoclassical investment theory model (cf. section 1.1.1) has very little to commend itself to the observer. It leads to rather peculiar results which can be attributed to the fact that it makes adjustments of the capital stock too easy. If one changes this by including adjustment costs, an irreversibility constraint or delivery lags, more realistic investment patterns are obtained.[3]

In abstract terms, the reason for the improvement is the same in all three cases. As soon as one takes into account that present decisions have an effect on future choice possibilities, rapid change becomes either impossible or costly and, consequently, myopic optimization is no longer optimal in the long run. These are general principles of intertemporal decision making, as we shall see in chapter 2.1.

Before proceeding to our next example, note that, in the models used in this section, even in cases where the agent is assumed to receive additional information as time goes by, he only uses this fact after the information is received. There are no ex ante flexibility considerations; the agent does not ask to which extent a certain choice allows him to react to information that is received over time. Such considerations will be the subject of the next section.

Before concluding this section, it should be pointed out that the importance of upward and downward irreversibility of capital stocks is emphasized by Neo-Austrian Capital Theory, cf. e.g. STEPHAN 1988, 1989. Here "gestation periods" of capital goods are the reason for upward irreversibility.

1.2 Flexible Manufacturing Systems

In the preceding section, we saw how the occurrence of irreversibility affects optimal investment decisions in abstract models. In the models we discussed, choice is only between different quantities of investment. In real world investment decisions, choice is also between different types of capital goods. Different types of capital goods may mean smaller or greater degrees of future

---

[3] of course, one can also combine several of these elements (cf. CABALLERO 1991).

commitment, or, in other words, greater or smaller degrees of flexibility. More precisely, recent technological developments in the manufacturing industry suggest that similar tasks may be fulfilled by a variety of capital goods, some of which strongly restrict the firms future options, while others adapt to a large number of different situations in a flexible manner. More specifically, we shall argue that recent developments in the manufacturing industry can at least partly be attributed to a desire to stay flexible in times of high uncertainty.

In this section, we shall deal with this topic in somewhat more detail. This serves two purposes. Firstly, we find it illuminating to have a closer look at the "black box" that determines the choice possibilities of an agent for a specific choice problem. In particular, we would like to find out what kind of factors determine the flexibility of different choices. Secondly, we want to show by way of example how important economic developments can be understood as attempts to avoid irreversible commitment in situations where future information is relevant. This will help us to get some ideas as to the appropriate way of modelling choice problems where flexibility matters.

We shall start by giving some basic facts about manufacturing in section 1.2.1. In 1.2.2, we shall discuss the determinants of the flexibility of manufacturing systems. Finally, in 1.2.3, we shall relate our findings to the main theme of this thesis. We show how the investment decisions of firms that expect to receive new information can be treated formally in a multiperiod choice framework.

1.2.1 Some Basic Facts about Manufacturing

Until the nineteen sixties, there were essentially two complementary principles in the manufacturing industry. For the production of large quantities of identical products, the benefits of increasing returns to scale provided by automatic transfer lines were (and still are) exploited . Transfer lines consist of several specialized machine tools that are coupled together by a transport system which transfers the components from one machine to the other in an unchangeable sequence.

Transfer lines have a variety of unfavourable characteristics. Apart from the fact that they only allow for the production of large numbers of identical goods, they are highly dependent on the well-functioning of every single element of the system: the breakdown of one machine can cause the halt of the entire system, at least when the transfer line works as a continuous flow.

The corresponding system for small volume and large variety has traditionally been job shop production: the manufacturing system consists of different job shops, every one of which is responsible for one type of machining operation (drilling, milling, etc.). These operations are usually carried out by general-purpose machines that are capable of performing all variants of a given type of operation (EBERWEIN 1989, p.27).

The most significant disadvantage of job shop production is that it does not exploit economies of scale and therefore leads to high unit costs compared with transfer lines. Furthermore, the distance between different job shops causes high transport and control costs (EBERWEIN 1989, p.29-31). One advantage of job shops is that a large spectrum of product variants can be produced because general-purpose machines are available.

During the last twenty years, the polarity between large volume/small variety and small volume/large variety production has started to become obsolete. The advance in information technologies has allowed the introduction of manufacturing systems that, according to their proponents, combine the advantages of both polar cases: though allowing for a considerable degree of variety in production, they exploit the merits of automation. Generally speaking, such "flexible manufacturing systems" (FMS) consist of computerized numerically controlled (CNC) machine tools that are connected by a transport system and coordinated by an information system.

GERWIN (1985, p.444) describes the merits of FMS as follows:

"With an FMS it is possible to automatically produce a mix of related parts, change the components of the mix over time, reroute production if a machine breaks down, handle engineering design changes for a certain part and machine different parts in random order.
An FMS is a highly customized manufacturing system which typically has several general-purpose and specialized machine tools, an automated material handling system and a central computer. The parts to be machined are fixtured and loaded onto vehicles which are individually routed through the system by the computer. When a machining destination is reached the part is transferred and the designated operations are performed under computer control."

To see why such systems are called flexible, we want to discuss the flexibility of manufacturing systems in more general terms.

1.2.2 The Determinants of the Flexibility of Manufacturing Systems

Building up a capital stock is always a partially irreversible decision. In particular, any choice of a manufacturing system restricts future options.

As an extreme example, if only one product can be produced with a transfer line, the firm cannot switch to other goods when it receives the information that demand for its product has dropped. Similarly, if production is organized in a continuous flow, the firm cannot reroute production as a reaction to the information that one part of the system has broken down.

More generally, the ability of manufacturing systems to adjust to new information depends, among other things, on the following factors (cf. BESSANT/HAYWOOD 1986, p.469, EBERWEIN 1989, p.8-14, GERWIN 1985, p.445):

- the ability to adjust the aggregate amount of production of the process to changes in demand ("volume flexibility");
- the ability to switch between the production of different versions of products ("modification flexibility");
- the ability to alter the sequence of machines through which a given component passes ("rerouting flexibility");

- the ability to cope with differences in the quality of the inputs ("material flexibility").

Flexible manufacturing systems are often claimed to perform well with respect to the first three points. For instance, the use of CNC-machines in flexible manufacturing systems allows for a high degree of modification flexibility because only minor reprogramming and refixturing activities are necessary to handle design changes (GERWIN 1985, p.447, EBERWEIN 1989, p.54). Similarly, volume flexibility of FMS is generally considered to be very high. Furthermore, FMS can relatively easily be adapted to new tasks, at least in those cases where the CNC-machine tools of the system are built in a modular fashion, i.e. they consist of standardized parts: it has been estimated that, in value terms, 50-80% of the parts of such a machine tool can on average be used again when the system is refitted to new tasks (cf. WILDEMANN 1984, p.10).

An entirely different matter is the question whether these advantages are significant enough to justify the introduction of FMS. We leave this subject to the experts in the field, but not without mentioning that the amount of flexibility provided by an FMS is not merely a technological matter. It has been pointed out repeatedly (cf. GERWIN 1985, BESSANT/HAYWOOD 1986, BÜHNER 1986), that the success of Computer Aided Manufacturing also depends on organizational issues: due to what is sometimes called the "organizational lag" (DAMANPOUR/EVAN 1984), the slow adjustment of administrative processes (e.g. accounting, maintenance, quality control) to technological change, it may happen that potential advantages of flexible manufacturing systems do not actually materialize.

For our purposes, it is not important to judge whether flexible manufacturing systems actually deserve their name and solve the "dilemma of rationalization" (WILDEMANN 1987, p.209) by achieving productivity and flexibility at the same time, as their proponents claim. It is sufficient to know that they are advocated because of supposed flexibility advantages. If sufficiently many investors are convinced by these flexibility arguments, it is reasonable to assume that the choice of manufacturing systems is influenced by considerations about the extent to which competing systems can make use of future information.

Before showing how such considerations can help us to find the right structure for our general choice model, we note that the issues we are talking about are not merely problems of individual firms. In fact, it has been argued by AOKI (1990) that the competitive position of entire industries is strongly influenced by the extent to which firms arrange the structure of their production, and not just the technology, in a manner that allows to incorporate future information. Specifically, he argues that the recent success of Japanese firms can be explained by their flexible production structure that gives them the ability to react more rapidly to changing demand conditions. This would also explain why Japanese competitive advantages are felt most strongly in sectors where small and medium-batch production of varieties of products is common. A high degree of specialization of machinery and personnel (and hence little scope to react to new information) which, according to AOKI (1990), is typical of the Western firm, is of no harm in stable sectors where standardized products are produced at a large scale. However, small scale production in rapidly changing sectors requires an organisation of the production process that allows to cope with a great number of situations. To this end, the Japanese mode of production and, in particular, its emphasis on horizontal cooperation that is based on informal sharing of information, appears to be particularly suitable.

Summing up, empirical evidence suggests that the relative ability to react to new information is of central importance for the decisions of firms. This ability depends on the choice of manufacturing system, the organisational structure and various other factors.

We shall now move on to see what we can infer from this section for our general approach.

1.2.3 Manufacturing as a Multiperiod Choice Problem

We now have enough information about manufacturing systems at hand to see how the choice of a manufacturing system and its subsequent utilization can be interpreted as a multiperiod choice problem. Rather than going into every detail, we shall just sketch how this can be done.

First of all, one should specify what the objects of choice in this model are. We suppose that in period 1 the firm takes an action a_1: it chooses a certain manufacturing system from a set A_1 of techniques available for the firm. This set should be thought of as containing e.g. transfer lines, various methods of job shop production and different types of flexible manufacturing systems.

For periods t=2,...,T, the choice a_t is supposed to describe the way the production process is run. In principle, a_t can be seen as a choice of input- and output-vectors, but it should be pointed out clearly that these vectors are to be regarded as rather high-dimensional. For instance, it is important to distinguish outputs according to quality so that minor design changes give rise to different outputs. On the input side, one should for instance distinguish according to the quality of raw materials that are used and the routes that components have to pass.

As objective of the firm, take maximization of the present value of profits. The profit term for period 1 should reflect the costs of investment. The terms for subsequent periods stand for the discounted profits of running the process in a certain way. They will depend on the state of the world, which may account for consumer tastes, the condition of the manufacturing system (which parts of the system are functioning properly, which are out of order?), the quality of inputs used, etc.

The firm will not be completely sure about the state of the world, but it can expect to learn more about it in the future. For instance, the development of prices in periods 1,2,...,t will presumably have an effect on its beliefs about prices in periods t+1,...,T. The message that a machine has broken down will tell the firm that this may remain so for some period of time (because it takes time to repair); the firm receives signals that may induce it to change its behaviour.

Such a change in behaviour may not necessarily be possible. If preferences shift from one product variant to another one, manufacturers using transfer lines will, in general, have to build up a new manufacturing system which may take considerable time. Similar considerations hold for changes in output quantities.

Also, if a firm uses a transfer line it will be unable to react in a flexible manner to the information that one machine tool in the system is defect. There is no way to reroute machining sequences, so that it will simply have to repair the machine, while production has to stop.

In other words, transfer lines can be seen as highly irreversible first period choices: if a transfer line is chosen, only very few options in terms of possible production patterns remain open, so that the arrival of new information will in general have little impact on the behaviour of the firm.

With job shop production and flexible manufacturing systems, things are different. Such systems leave open more options as to the quantity and quality of the products produced, the routes that workpieces have to follow, etc. Information, for example on consumer preferences or breakdown of machines is therefore likely to induce the firm to switch between different options.

If the choice set is to reflect this situation, it will have to contain several different choices, some of which leave many options open, while others restrict future choices.

It remains to be shown what kind of decision criterion the agent should use. Simple maximization of expected profits is inadequate, because this procedure does not pay tribute to the fact that the informational position of the agent changes over time. A criterion that is better suited for our purpose is Bayesian backward recursion. With this procedure, it is possible to model the behaviour of agents who consider the ability to react to future information as an important aspect of their decisions (cf. section 2.2).

We now summarize how the ideas of this chapter can be used in our general model.

1.3 Conclusions

In section 1.1, we saw how the appropriate modelling of the irreversibility or the rigidity of certain choices can affect the outcome.

In section 1.2, we showed how the expectation to receive additional information in the future can influence the optimal choices of agents, provided there are some choices that allow for an adequate reaction to new information and others that do not.

These observations give us some ideas as to the adequate procedure in the formulation of an abstract model of intertemporal choice that is general enough to incorporate the above examples (and some others, cf. chapter 2.1.2).

Firstly, we should define more precisely what we mean by "flexible" and "irreversible" choices, and, more generally, what we mean when we say that one choice is "more flexible than another". Our examples from investment theory suggest that there are two ways of doing that.

For instance, in the section on irreversible investment in the narrow sense (1.1.3), the idea of irreversibility is that, given a choice of the capital stock in one period, certain choices of future capital stocks become completely inaccessible (those involving $I(t) \leq 0$ for some t). Hence, in this example, the irreversibility is merely a property of the choice set (cf.chapter 2.1).

This is not true for the irreversibility that arrives from adjustment costs, because with adjustment costs present choices do not restrict the set of feasible choices tomorrow as such. However, they restrict the set of choices that can be reached, given a certain price of switching that one is willing to pay. This kind of irreversibility, which is reflected in both the structure of the set of available choices and the objective function, will be discussed in chapter 2.3.

Finally, the information that is received in the course of the decision process has to be modelled adequately.

In the investment theory model of section 1.1, information (about the occurrence of the demand shift) is taken into account ex post, but not ex ante. Once the decision maker receives information, he reacts to it. But there is no way in which the decision maker prepares for the fact that he will receive information in the future, i.e. there are no flexibility considerations.

The importance of such considerations was seen in section 1.2. Hence, what is needed in our model, is a general way of modelling agents who take information into account ex ante and ex post. This will be provided in chapters 2.2 and 2.3. We then have the tools we need to answer the questions posed in the introduction.

Chapter 2

THE ROLE OF IRREVERSIBILITY AND LEARNING IN SEQUENTIAL DECISION PROBLEMS - BASIC CONCEPTS

Having outlined the importance of irreversibility and learning by means of familiar economic examples, we are now ready for a more formal treatment of these issues. In this chapter, we shall introduce an abstract choice-theoretical framework. To begin with, we restrict ourselves to two periods. This is conceptually easier than the more general case of finitely many periods (cf. chapter 4), but it already allows us to deal with many of the issues that will crop up in the more general context.

In the model we shall present in the following, irreversibility is reflected in the structure of the choice set. Uncertainty is modelled by assuming that the agent's payoff depends on a state of the world which he does not know. He only has a subjective probability distribution on the set of possible states of the world. This probability distribution changes as time goes by, because messages are observed.

To keep complications at a minimal level, we start with a model without uncertainty in section 2.1. In section 2.2, we shall introduce uncertainty and learning. Finally, in section 2.3, we shall refine the structure of the problem by letting the irreversibility of actions depend on the price one is willing to pay to make these actions undone.

2.1 The Two-Period Model without Uncertainty

In this section, we introduce the simplest version of the basic formal model we shall use. In particular, we shall clarify in 2.1.1 what we mean by irreversibility and flexibility. As to those definitions, we do not claim that they are in any sense the only conceivable definitions. However, we shall show in 2.1.2 that in many economic examples they coincide with economic intuition. In

2.1.3, we shall prove a few simple results for our model and in 2.1.4, intertemporal opportunity costs are discussed.

2.1.1 The Elements of the Model

Consider the following choice problem. Let A_1, A_2 be arbitrary sets. In each of the periods t = 1,2 the decision maker selects an element $\mathbf{a_t} \varepsilon A_t$. This element can be a capital stock, an investment project, a consumption level, a measure of environmental pollution, etc. (cf. section 2.1.2 for more details). In general, choice of $\mathbf{a}$:= (a_1, a_2) will be restricted to some proper subset G of $A_1 x A_2$, which will be called **the set of feasible paths** (or the **choice set**). We shall assume that all elements of A_1 are possible first-period choices. However, we shall often consider the situation that for some first-period choices $a_1 \varepsilon A_1$ not all the elements of A_2 are possible second-period choices given a_1, i.e.

$$\mathbf{G(a_1)} := \{a_2 \varepsilon A_2 \mid (a_1, a_2) \text{ is feasible}\} \qquad (2.1.1)$$

is a proper subset of A_2, i.e. $G(a_1) \subsetneq A_2$.

The most extreme case is that $G(a_1)$ is a one-element set, i.e. that first-period choice completely determines second-period choice. Then we shall say that a_1 is **totally irreversible**. The opposite extreme is that $G(a_1)=A_2$. Then we shall say that a_1 is **perfectly flexible** or, alternatively, **totally reversible**.

To make this last definition meaningful, we assume that each element of A_2 is feasible for some initial choice a_1; i.e.

$$\bigcup_{a_1 \varepsilon A_1} G(a_1) = A_2; \qquad (2.1.2)$$

in other words, we define the set A_2 in such a manner that no second-period choice is impossible a priori, i.e. before a_1 is chosen. Without this assumption, the addition of irrelevant elements to A_2 could turn an action that is perfectly flexible into one that is not.

In the special case that all the a_1 are perfectly flexible, i.e. $G(a_1)=A_2$ for every $a_1 \varepsilon A_1$, we shall say that we are considering a **totally reversible** decision problem. If all the a_1 are irreversible, we shall say that the problem is **totally irreversible**. Though these two cases are not very interesting in themselves, they will be useful as cases of reference for the investigation of other models. When problems are neither totally reversible nor totally irreversible, we shall say that there is **partial irreversibility**.

If a problem is either totally irreversible or partially irreversible, we shall say that it is **irreversible**. When the problem is totally reversible, the first-period choice is definitely irrelevant to second-period choice possibilities. On the other hand, when the problem is partially irreversible, first-period choice affects second-period choice possibilities because there is at least one element of A_1 for which $G(a_1)$ is a proper subset of A_2. For this element, the elements of $A_2 \backslash G(a_1)$ are not feasible first-period choices, but according to (2.1.2) there must be choices of a_1 for which they are feasible. Hence, the set $G(a_1)$ of second-period choices does actually depend on a_1.

Intuition suggests that not only the extreme cases that a_1 is either totally irreversible or perfectly flexible should be comparable with respect to flexibility. One would want to call a decision more flexible than another if it leaves more future options open.

In accordance with this intuition, we call a_1 **at least as flexible** as a_1', $a_1 \geq_F a_1'$ if $G(a_1) \supset G(a_1')$, i.e. if the choice of a_1 leaves the decision maker with all the options that would have been open had his first-period choice been a_1' (cf. MARSCHAK/NELSON 1962).

Before going into economic examples, we shall illustrate the definitions by means of a simple numerical example.

<u>**Example 1**</u>

Let $A_1 = A_2 = \{1,2,3,4\}$,

$G = \{(1,1); (1,2); (1,3); (1,4); (2,2); (2,3); (2,4);$
$(3,3); (3,4); (4,4)\} \subset A_1 \times A_2$.

This set is represented in figure 2.1 (a line starting at i and ending at j stands for the element $(i,j) \varepsilon A_1 \times A_2$).

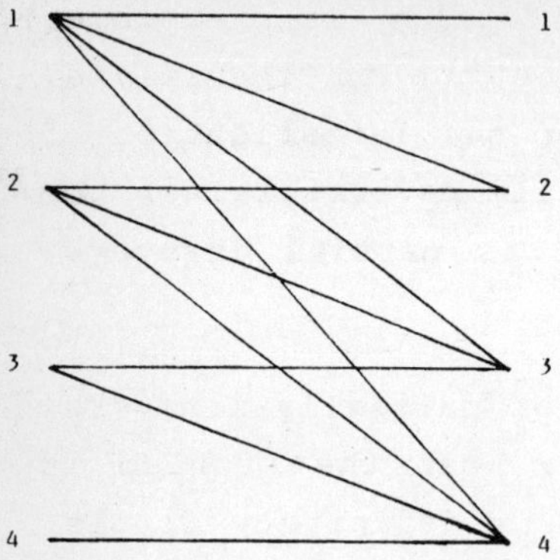

Figure 2.1: Example 1

Hence, we have G(1)={1,2,3,4}, G(2)={2,3,4}, G(3)={3,4}, G(4)={4}.

1 is perfectly flexible, 4 is irreversible. The set A_1 can be completely ordered with respect to flexibility: $1 \geq_F 2 \geq_F 3 \geq_F 4$.

In general, however, flexibility does not give a complete ordering on A_1, as can be seen from the following example.

Example 2

Take A_1 as before, but suppose the set of feasible paths is now given as
G = {(1,1);(1,2);(2,2);(2,3);(3,3);(3,4);(4,4)}; cf. figure 2.2.

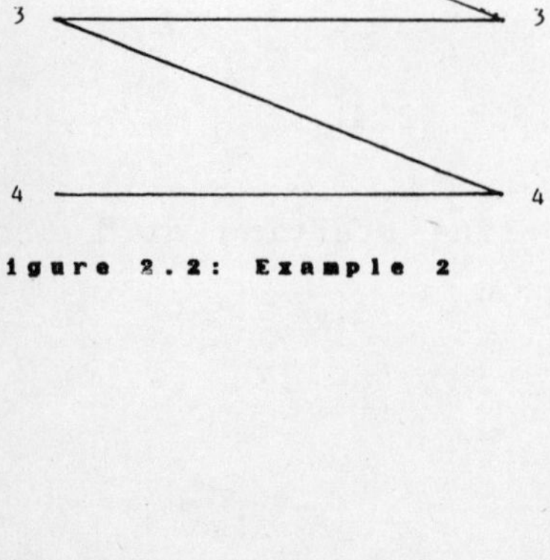

Figure 2.2: Example 2

Then, for instance 2 and 3 are not comparable with respect to flexibility, because G(2)={2,3}, G(3)={3,4}, so that neither $G(2) \supset G(3)$ nor $G(3) \supset G(2)$.

2.1.2 Economic Examples

Next, we shall formulate some familiar economic examples in our terminology. A more detailed discussion of these models will be presented in later sections.

Irreversible Investment I:

Suppose the decision maker is a firm that chooses its capital stock K_t in each of the periods t=1,2. As long as it can borrow and sell any quantity it likes, one can take $A_1 = A_2 = [0,\infty]$ and $G = A_1 \times A_2$. If, however, it is assumed that the sale of used capital goods is impossible because of the absence of the relevant markets (cf. ARROW (1968), NICKELL (1978), STEPHAN (1988) and chapter 1.1.3 of this thesis), the capital stock of the firm can only be reduced through deterioration. Hence, $G(K_1) = [(1-c)K_1,\infty)$ and $G = \{(K_1,K_2) \mid K_2 \geq (1-c)K_1\}$, where c is the rate of depreciation.

Irreversible Investment II:

Suppose a firm chooses an investment project from a given menu A = {1,...,n-1,f} of possibilities, where 1,...,n-1 are irreversible in the sense that, if one of them has been chosen in period 1, it will have to be chosen again in period 2. f is the flexible alternative of postponing investment, the merits of which are discussed in the option value literature (cf. WEISBROD 1964, ARROW/FISHER 1974, HENRY 1974, BERNANKE 1983, HANEMANN 1989 and section 2.2.1 of this thesis). Here we have $A_1 = A_2 = A = \{1,...,n-1,f\}$, G(1)={1}, ...,G(n-1)={n-1}, G(f)=A.

Intertemporal Consumption Choice

It is important to note that irreversibility may still be an issue when spot markets are complete. For instance, in reasonably specified models of intertemporal consumption choice, future consumption possibilities depend on today's consumption and savings decisions.

Formally, suppose an agent lives for two periods. Suppose there are no future markets, but the agent can transfer wealth from period 1 to period 2 by holding an asset "money". Suppose he is equipped with vectors e_1, e_2 of the consumption good and with an initial stock m_1 of money. Let c_t, p_t (t=1,2) denote the corresponding consumption and price vectors.

Then $a_1=(c_1,m_2)$ has to be chosen from the budget set $A_1=\{(c_1,m_2)\varepsilon R^2{}_+ \mid p_1c_1+m_2=p_1e_1+m_1\}$, while a_2 is chosen from $G(c_1,m_2)=\{c_2 \mid p_2c_2\leq p_2e_2+m_2\}$. Hence, $G(c_1,m_2)=G(c_1',m_2')$ if and only if $m_2=m_2'$, $G(c_1,m_2)\supset G(c_1',m_2')$ if and only if $m_2\geq m_2'$.

In other words, saving is the means of staying flexible.

Non-renewable resources:

Non-renewable resources provide another example to which our framework is applicable. Suppose a society extracts a_t units of the resource in period t. Suppose M is the exogenously given stock of the resource. Then a_t has to be chosen from $A_1=A_2=[0,M]$. The non-renewability of the resource is expressed by the fact that any unit of the resource that has been extracted in period 1 cannot be extracted in period 2. Hence $G(a_1)=[0,M-a_1]$, so that $G(a_1)=A_2$ if and only if $a_1=0$, hence $a_1=0$ is perfectly flexible, while all the other decisions are not. Moreover, $a_1\geq a_1'$ => $a_1'\geq_F a_1$, i.e. the lower first-period resource extraction, the more flexible is the choice.

The opportunity costs arising from the irreversibility of the extraction of resources figure prominently in the relevant literature (cf. DASGUPTA/HEAL 1979 and, in a slightly different spirit, FABER/NIEMES/STEPHAN 1987). They will be discussed later in section 2.1.4.

Renewable Resources

Even the use of renewable resources may give rise to irreversibility. Typically, if a stock of a natural resource (which may be an actual stock of animals or plants, but may also be an appropriate measure of the environmental quality of a given area[1])

---

[1] cf. DASGUPTA 1982, p.7, for this interpretation.

drops below a certain threshold level TL, it will never reach that level again.[2]

Let M>TL denote the maximum stock of the resource that is feasible a priori. Suppose that this is the same in both periods. Then, a reasonable way to model threshold effects is the following: take $A_1 = A_2 = [0, M]$. Then, if a_t denotes the stock of a natural resource, $G(a_1) \subset [0, TL]$ for $a_1 < TL$. In particular, a_1 is not perfectly flexible for $a_1 < TL$.

2.1.3 Some Basic Results

The consequences of irreversibility can only be fully understood when uncertainty is introduced into the model. Some important points, however, do not hinge upon uncertainty.

To see this, we introduce an objective function for the decision maker.[3] Suppose his goal is to maximize the utility function $U(a_1, a_2)$ which is defined on $A_1 x A_2$. Of course his choice has to satisfy the condition $(a_1, a_2) \varepsilon G$. The path thus obtained is called **(intertemporally) optimal**.

Suppose for a given decision problem with choice set $G \subset A_1 x A_2$ the **associated reversible problem** is defined as the problem with identical payoff function but with $G(R) = A_1 x A_2$ as set of feasible paths. For any given problem, the associated reversible problem is the reference point to which it should be compared in order to investigate the effects of irreversibility.

Proposition 2.1: (a) For a given decision problem, the associated reversible problem never leads to a lower payoff.
(b) The associated reversible problem may lead to a higher payoff, but this need not be the case.

---

[2] As a description of real-world threshold phenomena, this is oversimplified, but it brings out some essential aspects.

[3] The expressions objective function, utility function and payoff function will be used interchangeably.

Proof: (a) The set G(R) of feasible paths for the associated reversible problem is $A_1 x A_2$, hence it contains the set of paths G for the original partially irreversible problem, so that

$$\max_{a \varepsilon G} U(a) \leq \max_{a \varepsilon G(R)} U(a).$$

(b) This is shown by way of example. Let $A_1 = A_2 = \{0,1\}$, $G = \{(0,0), (0,1), (1,1)\}$, $r_1(0)=1$, $r_1(1)=3$, $r_2(0)=4$, $r_2(1)=0$.
Then U(0,0)=5, U(0,1)=1, U(1,0)=7, U(1,1)=3. Hence, the optimal path for the associated reversible problem, (1,0), is not feasible for the original partially irreversible problem. Instead of a payoff of 7 for (1,0) one has to make do with a payoff of 5 for (0,0).
If, on the other hand, in the above example $r_2(1)=5$ instead of 0, then it is easy to show that with or without irreversibility (1,1) is optimal with a payoff of 8.

This very simple proposition points out clearly that the fact that some decisions are irreversible is not in itself undesirable. As long as the choices that are rendered impossible by this irreversibility are known to be suboptimal under any circumstances, as (1,0) in the second example in the proof of proposition 2.1(b), this is not a problem (for a discussion of related aspects cf. DASGUPTA/HEAL 1979,p.148-151).

Moving on to slightly more complicated matters, let us define **myopic paths** (m_1, m_2). Suppose that U is of the additively separable form $U(a_1, a_2) = r_1(a_1)+r_2(a_2)$ with real-valued functions r_1 and r_2. Paths are myopic if they result from "short-sighted" optimization; i.e. m_1 maximizes r_1 over A_1 and m_2 maximizes r_2 over $G(m_1)$. Normally, one cannot expect myopic optimization to be intertemporally optimal. However, we shall now show that for totally reversible problems, there is no difference between myopic and intertemporal optimization.

Proposition 2.2: (a) For any totally reversible problem, a path is myopic if and only if it is intertemporally optimal.
(b) A myopic path of an irreversible problem need not be optimal.

<u>Proof</u>: (a) Suppose (m_1, m_2) is myopic. If it were not optimal, there would have to exist a path $(a_1, a_2) \varepsilon A_1 x A_2$ such that

(1) $r_1(a_1) > r_1(m_1)$ or
(2) $r_2(a_2) > r_2(m_2)$.

(1) is impossible because m_1 maximizes r_1 over A_1.
(2) is impossible because m_2 maximizes r_2 over $G(m_1)$ by definition of a myopic path and $G(m_1) = A_2$ because of the reversibility of the problem.
Hence, any myopic path is optimal.
Now suppose (b_1, b_2) is optimal. If (b_1, b_2) were not myopic, either

(3) $r_1(b_1) < r_1(m_1)$
or
(4) $r_2(b_2) < \max_{a_2 \varepsilon G(b_1)} r_2(a_2)$.

The optimality of (b_1, b_2) implies that b_2 maximizes r_2 over $G(b_1)$ so that (4) is impossible. But because the problem is totally reversible, (m_1, b_2) is feasible and (3) implies $r_1(m_1)+r_2(b_2) > r_1(b_1)+r_2(b_2)$, contradicting the optimality of (b_1, b_2).
Hence, (b_1, b_2) is myopic.
(b) Recall the first example that was used in the proof of proposition 1. The myopic path for the original irreversible problem is (1,1), which gives the suboptimal payoff 3.

Note that proposition 2.2 is well-known (cf. for instance JONES/OSTROY 1984, proposition 1). It is reminiscent of the familiar fact from neoclassical investment theory that the present value maximizing firm in the basic neoclassical model without adjustment costs, delivery lags and irreversibility of investment (cf. chapter 1.1.1) follows the myopic rule "maximize short-term profits". This result is usually proved for a continuous time, infinite horizon model, but it is possible to show that the concepts introduced so far, including proposition 2.2, can be translated to the above-mentioned framework.

2.1.4 Intertemporal Opportunity Costs

In the preceding section, we showed that a necessary condition for myopic and intertemporal optimization to lead to different choices is that the problem is partially irreversible. However, the condition is by no means sufficient. In this section, we refine it by an alternative necessary condition, which is closer to a sufficient condition.

In environmental economics and the theory of natural resources, one often encounters **intertemporal opportunity costs**. By this we mean that present day decisions affect the payoff that can be obtained in future periods. When natural resources are considered, intertemporal opportunity costs usually refer to the fact that today's economic activities affect future consumption possibilities and/or environmental quality.

In our model, this is best expressed by saying that a_1 **causes intertemporal opportunity costs** if

$$\max_{a_2 \varepsilon G(a_1)} r_2(a_2) < \max_{a_2 \varepsilon A_2} r_2(a_2). \tag{2.1.3}$$

The interpretation is straightforward: by choosing a_1, the best possible second-period result is foregone. This does by no means imply that a_1 is a bad choice: $r_1(a_1)$ may be so high that the gain in first-period pay-off makes up for future losses.

The following simple proposition shows how intertemporal opportunity costs relate to earlier concepts.

Proposition 2.3: (a) A decision a_1 can only cause intertemporal opportunity costs if it is not perfectly flexible.
(b) A decision that is not perfectly flexible does not necessarily cause intertemporal opportunity costs.

Proof: (a) From the perfect flexibility of a_1, it follows that $G(a_1)=A_2$, so that

$$\max_{a_2 \varepsilon G(a_1)} r_2(a_2) = \max_{a_2 \varepsilon A_2} r_2(a_2) .$$

(b) Suppose $A=\{0,1\}$, $G=\{(0,0),(0,1),(1,1)\}$, $r_1(0)=1$, $r_1(1)=3$, $r_2(0)=4$, $r_2(1)=5$: 1 is irreversible, but, as $r_2(1) > r_2(0)$, it does not cause intertemporal opportunity costs.

Finally, we note that proposition 2.2 can be generalized as follows.

Proposition 2.4: Suppose for a two-period choice problem no initial choice causes intertemporal opportunity costs. Then a path is myopic if and only if it is intertemporally optimal.

We do not give the proof, because it is similar to the proof of proposition 2.2. However, the result is intuitively plausible. If the only possible effect of present day decision making on the future is that undesirable second-period options are given up in the first-period, there is nothing wrong with myopic decision making. In other words, only when there are intertemporal opportunity costs does a decision problem really deserve to be called intertemporal.

The definitions and most of the propositions of this section are summarized in figure 2.3.

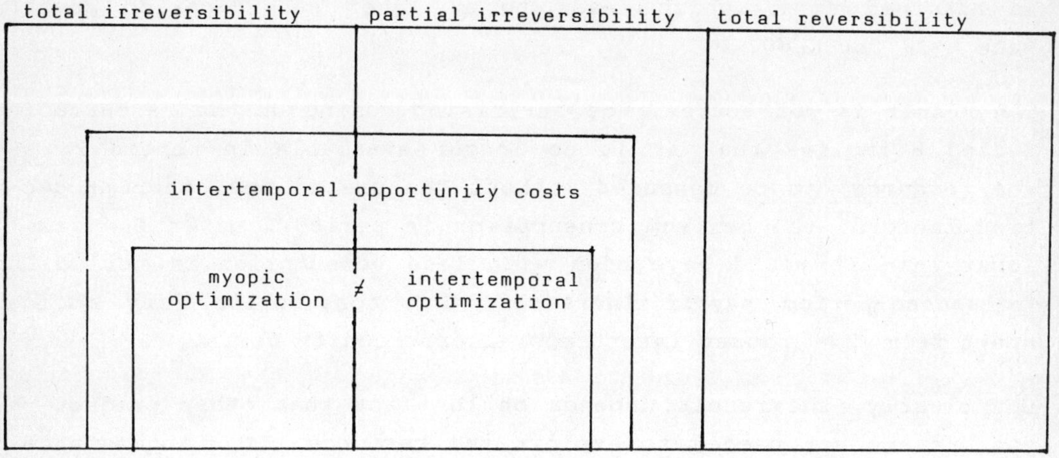

Figure 2.3: Types of Decision Problems

From this figure, we can see that there can only be intertemporal opportunity costs when there is irreversibility (though there is no need for them to occur). As long as there are no intertemporal opportunity costs (in particular, if the problem is totally reversible), optimal decisions are myopic.

As examples of intertemporal opportunity costs, we consider two resource models. The first one, known as the cake-eating model (cf. DASGUPTA/HEAL 1979, p.95ff.), is the simplest possible model of the use of non-renewable resources.

Suppose a society is given a quantity $M>0$ of an exhaustible resource, which is assumed to be consumable without costs. Let consumption (resource extraction) in period $t=1,2$ be denoted by C_t. Let $W(C_1,C_2)= r_1(C_1)+r_2(C_2)$ be a social welfare function that is strictly increasing in both variables. To find the optimal consumption path, $W(C_1,C_2)$ has to be maximized subject to $C_1+C_2 \leq M$. In order to use our general notation, we set $A_1=A_2=[0,M]$, $G=\{(C_1,C_2)\varepsilon R^2_+ \,|\, C_1 \varepsilon A_1, C_2 \leq M-C_1\}$.

Clearly, no first-period choice except $C_1=0$ is perfectly flexible, because $G(C_1) = [0,M-C_1]$, which equals A_2 only if $C_1=0$. But we have the stronger result that any choice except $C_1=0$ causes intertemporal opportunity costs: Because r_2 is monotonic, the maximum of r_2 over $G(C_1)$ is attained at $M-C_1$ and the maximum of r_2 over A_2 is attained at M, which leads to a higher second-period payoff than $M-C_1$ for $C_1\neq 0$.

The result is, of course, not surprising. Using up the resource in period 1 implies that it is no longer available in period 2; as the resource can be consumed without the use of any other production factors, the maximum consumption in period 2 given $C_1\neq 0$ is lower than it would have been with less consumption in period 1. As second-period payoff increases with consumption, any choice apart from $C_1=0$ causes intertemporal opportunity costs.

But clearly, the result depends on the fact that other production factors are not needed to exploit the resource. If, for instance, one unit of labour was needed to turn one unit of the resource into one unit of the consumption good and if the labour supply in each period was sufficiently low compared to the resource stock, no intertemporal opportunity costs would occur, because, with labour being the limiting factor of production, a higher resource stock in period 2 would not increase second-period payoff. Of course, with a sufficiently long time horizon, this reasoning will break down, so that long term intertemporal opportunity costs are to be expected (cf. chapter 4). But in the context of a two-period model, the boundedness of the resource stock and the irreversibility of extraction will not matter.

There are, however, reasons to believe that in many cases the exploitation of natural resources does in fact cause intertemporal opportunity costs even when there is no desire to fully exploit the stock in the last period. This idea can be expressed by means of a simple version of a model by FABER/NIEMES/STEPHAN (1987). These authors argue on the basis of the entropy law that a decrease in resource concentration leads to an increase in extraction effort (measured in labour units per units of resource extracted). Furthermore, they claim (in accordance with empirical evidence - cf. FABER/WAGENHALS 1988) that resource concentration in any given period is a declining function of total resource extraction in earlier periods. Given the assumption that only a limited amount of labour is available in each period, it is plausible that intertemporal opportunity costs are present, because more consumption in early periods means more extraction effort and hence less consumption in later periods.

To express this formally, we use a highly simplified version of the FABER/NIEMES/STEPHAN-model, which brings out the essential points only as far as intertemporal opportunity costs are concerned. We modify the cake-eating model in the following manner.

Again, society can dispose over a resource stock M, but we now distinguish between consumption C_t and resource extraction R_t. We suppose that $C_t=f(R_t)$ with a strictly increasing function f.

Suppose first-period consumption is bounded by $M_1>0$ (it is understood that the existence of this boundary is due to a bounded labour supply). Suppose second-period consumption is bounded by $M_2(C_1)>0$ with a strictly decreasing function M_2. This is to be understood as follows: higher first-period consumption implies higher first-period resource extraction, implying lower second-period concentration and hence higher labour effort to obtain any given level of consumption and, in particular, a lower maximal consumption. Therefore, $A_1 = A_2 = [0, M_1]$ and $G = \{(C_1, C_2) \in A_1 x A_2 \mid C_2 \leq M_2(C_1)\}$. Clearly, for $C_1 > 0$, the monotonicity of M_2 and the monotonicity of the payoff function imply that C_1 causes intertemporal opportunity costs.

In a multiperiod model, the preceding argument gives the result that resource extraction does not only lead to long-term opportunity costs due to the exhaustion of the resource stock, but also to short-term opportunity costs due to the lowering of resource concentration.

2.2 The Two-Period Model with Uncertainty

The full effect of irreversibility can only be felt when the future is not entirely known. Then, the decision maker has to form expectations or beliefs about the future. In general, this will change the optimal actions of the agent.

In accordance with most of the literature, we represent the agent's uncertainty by assuming that the payoff depends on a set S of future states of the world. The agent knows this set while he does not know which of the states will occur and has to form expectations as to which state is true, these expectations taking the form of a subjective probability distribution on S. Hence, we shall not deal with "true uncertainty" in the sense of KNIGHT (1921). We shall, however, add a further element of reality by assuming that the subjective probability distribution of the agent may change over time due to the fact that new information is received. In other words, we shall include the possibility of learning.

2.2.1 The Elements of the Model

From now on, we suppose that the utility function U does not only depend on the actions a_1 and a_2 but also on the state of the world s, an element of a set S. For simplicity, we shall assume S to be finite. The state of the world will not be revealed until the end of the second period. We do, however, assume that the agent knows the set S and has a subjective probability distribution Π on S.

To simplify, we assume that the set of feasible paths is independent of the state of the world. Hence, as before, the agent chooses a path $(a_1, a_2) \varepsilon G$. His utility is now given by a function

$$U: A_1 x A_2 x S \to R; \; U(a_1, a_2, s) = r_1(a_1, s) + r_2(a_2, s). \qquad (2.2.1)$$

For the moment, we shall simply assume that agents maximize expected utility,

$$\mathbf{E_S}[\mathbf{r_1}(\mathbf{a_1}, \mathbf{s}) + \mathbf{r_2}(\mathbf{a_2}, \mathbf{s})] := \sum_{s \varepsilon S} \Pi(s)(r_1(a_1, s) + r_2(a_2, s)). \qquad (2.2.2)$$

In many respects, the problem just stated hardly differs from the case of perfect knowledge. In particular, with or without risk, decisions can be made once and for all at the beginning of period 1, because we have not allowed for the possibility of improved knowledge at the beginning of period 2. Besides, all the propositions of chapter 2 can easily be generalized to this case.

An important fact about real world decisions, however, is that, as time goes by, the decision maker receives additional information about the state of the world that he may deem relevant to his decision. In some cases, this will lead the agent to change his prior beliefs about the state - a learning process takes place. To model this formally, we shall assume that the additional information is received at the end of period 1. With probability q_y, the agent receives a message $y \varepsilon Y$, where Y is a set, which, for simplicity, is assumed to be finite. Such a message induces a conditional (posterior) probability distribution $\Pi(s|y)$ on S. The expectation of receiving a message y that may change the prior distribution Π on S will, in general, change the agent's first-period choice.

To see how the agent behaves, it is best to work via backward induction. In each period, the agent maximizes his expected payoff given his information, which includes the message y in period 2 and his probability distribution q_y on Y in period 1. He receives a signal y before he takes his second-period choice but after having chosen a_1. Then he will maximize the expected value of second-period payoff,

$$\mathbf{E}_{s|y}[\mathbf{r}_2(\mathbf{a}_2,\mathbf{s})] := \sum_{s \varepsilon S} \Pi(s|y) r_2(a_2,s), \text{ subject to } a_2 \varepsilon G(a_1).$$

Hence, given a_1, the expected value of second-period payoff under maximizing behaviour is

$$\mathbf{V}(\mathbf{a}_1) = \mathbf{V}(\mathbf{a}_1;\Pi,\mathbf{q}) := E_Y \max_{a_2 \varepsilon G(a_1)} E_{s|y}[r_2(a_2,s)] =$$

$$\sum_{y \varepsilon Y} q_y \left[\max_{a_2 \varepsilon G(a_1)} \sum_{s \varepsilon S} \Pi(s|y) r_2(a_2,s)\right]. \qquad (2.2.3)$$

Noting that the expected first-period payoff for a_1 is

$$\mathbf{E}_s[\mathbf{r}_1(\mathbf{a}_1,\mathbf{s})] := \sum_{s \varepsilon S} \Pi(s) r_1(a_1,s), \qquad (2.2.4)$$

we find that for (b_1,b_2) to maximize expected total payoff, it is necessary that

$$b_1 \text{ maximizes } E_s[r_1(a_1,s)] + E_y\{\max_{a_2 \varepsilon G(a_1)} E_{s|y}[r_2(a_2,s)]\} \qquad (2.2.5)$$

or, in shorthand notation,

$$b_1 \text{ maximizes } E_s[r_1(a_1,s)] + V(a_1) \text{ over } A_1. \qquad (2.2.6)$$

We use a simple example to illustrate the model with uncertainty.

Example 1[4]

Suppose a society has to choose how to use a given natural resource, say an area of land, in two successive periods. Suppose that there are two ways of using it. The first option, "agricultural" usage (0), does not destroy the natural resource, while the second option, "industrial" usage (1), is irreversible in the sense that if it is chosen in period 1 the area will have to be used in the same fashion in the next period. A typical example would be the flooding of an agricultural area for the purpose of generating hydroelectric power.

Then we can represent the choice set for the society in the following way.

[4] Essentially, this example goes back to HENRY (1974).

We take $A_1 = A_2 = \{0,1\}$, $G = \{(0,0);(0,1);(1,1)\}$ so that 0 is perfectly flexible, 1 is totally irreversible.

The relation to the above example is clear. If 0 is chosen today, both 0 and 1 ("agricultural" or "industrial" usage) can be chosen in period 2, but if option 1 is chosen in period 1, option 0 cannot be chosen in period 2.

Furthermore, suppose the net benefits of the different choices are not known ex ante, but depend on a state of the world, which is revealed after the first choice has been made.

More precisely, suppose $S=\{s^1,s^2\}$ and $Y=\{y^1,y^2\}$ are two-element sets and the information structure is given by
$\Pi(s^1)=\Pi(s^2)=1/2$; $q_{y1}=q_{y2}=1/2$; $\Pi(s^1|y^1)=\Pi(s^2|y^2)=1$;
$\Pi(s^2|y^1)=\Pi(s^1|y^2)=0$,
so that the message y^i conveys perfect information about the state of the world. When y^i obtains, the agent is sure that the state of the world is s^i $(i=1,2)$.

Now assume that the payoffs are given by

$$E_s[r_1(0,s)]=2;\; r_2(0,s^1)=3;\; r_2(0,s^2)=4 \qquad (2.2.7)$$
$$E_s[r_1(1,s)]=3;\; r_2(1,s^1)=5;\; r_2(1,s^2)=1. \qquad (2.2.8)$$

The expected second-period payoffs $V(a_1)$ are therefore given as

$$V(0) =$$
$$q_{y1} \max_{a_2 \varepsilon G(0)} [\Pi(s^1|y^1)r_2(a_2,s^1)+\Pi(s^2|y^1)r_2(a_2,s^2)] +$$
$$q_{y2} \max_{a_2 \varepsilon G(0)} [\Pi(s^1|y^2)r_2(a_2,s^1)+\Pi(s^2|y^2)r_2(a_2,s^2)] =$$

$$1/2\; r_2(1,s^1) + 1/2\; r_2(0,s^2) = 4{,}5;$$

$$V(1) =$$
$$q_{y1} \max_{a_2 \varepsilon G(1)} [\Pi(s^1|y^1)r_2(a_2,s^1)+\Pi(s^2|y^1)r_2(a_2,s^2)] +$$
$$q_{y2} \max_{a_2 \varepsilon G(1)} [\Pi(s^1|y^2)r_2(a_2,s^1)+\Pi(s^2|y^2)r_2(a_2,s^2)] =$$
$$1/2\; r_2(1,s^1) + 1/2\; r_2(1,s^2) = 3.$$

Hence,

$E_s[r_1(0,s)] + V(0) = 6,5;\; E_s[r_1(1,s)] + V(1) = 6,$

so that the flexible choice 0 is optimal; i.e. when information is taken into account, society should abstain from the destruction of the natural resource. In other words, it should be prepared to pay a "liquidity premium" in terms of foregone first-period payoff in order to be able to make use of future information.

To understand more about the choice problem with uncertainty and learning, we shall start by looking at special cases and investigating the influence of different degrees of irreversibility and different learning possibilities on the choice of the optimal path.

2.2.2 Special Cases

As a starting point, we consider the special case that the decision maker does not expect the message that is received at the beginning of the second-period to change his prior probability distribution of the state of the world, i.e. $\Pi(s|y)=\Pi(s)$ for each $y \varepsilon Y$, so that (2.2.5) reduces to:

b_1 maximizes

$$[\sum_{s \varepsilon S} \Pi(s) r_1(a_1,s) + \sum_{y \varepsilon Y} q_y \max_{a_2 \varepsilon G(a_1)} (\sum_{s \varepsilon S} \Pi(s) r_2(a_2,s))] =$$
$$[\sum_{s \varepsilon S} \Pi(s) r_1(a_1,s) + \max_{a_2 \varepsilon G(a_1)} (\sum_{s \varepsilon S} \Pi(s) r_2(a_2,s))]$$

and hence

$$(b_1,b_2) \text{ maximizes } E_s[r_1(a_1,s)+r_2(a_2,s)], \qquad (2.2.9)$$

which is not surprising: as future information is not expected to be of any significance, the agent maximizes expected payoff as if he was not expecting any future information.

When learning is permitted, it is, in general, not optimal to behave according to rule (2.2.9). This can be seen by considering the example in section 2.2.1.

We have seen above that for this example, the optimal first-period choice is the flexible position 0. However, as

$E_s[r_1(0,s)+r_2(0,s)] = 5,5;$
$E_s[r_1(0,s)+r_2(1,s)] = 5$ and
$E_s[r_1(1,s)+r_2(1,s)] = 6,$

the optimal first-period choice is the irreversible position 1 when the possibility of learning is ignored.

This observation is the simplest possible formalization of the idea that "flexibility considerations" should make a difference in optimal behaviour. With flexibility considerations 0 is optimal, otherwise 1 is optimal.

For the special case at hand (i.e. the case of one totally irreversible and one perfectly flexible position), it has been shown by HENRY (1974) that ignoring the learning possibility leads to a systematic bias towards the irreversible position: while it may happen that learning does not change the optimal first-period choice at all in some examples, if there is a difference between the cases with and without learning, the optimal choice with learning is the flexible one.[5]

Henry argued that these findings are relevant to the application of cost-benefit-analysis to environmental problems. As cost-benefit-analysis is generally conducted in terms of expected utility maximization along the lines of (2.2.9)[6], it leads to a systematic bias towards irreversible decisions and hence to environmental destruction.

Similar statements can be extracted from the finance literature where the net present value rule "Invest when the value of a unit of capital is at least as large as the purchase and installation cost of the unit" has been criticized on the grounds that it ignores flexibility considerations (cf. PINDYCK 1988 and, similarly, BALDWIN 1982, MC DONALD/SIEGEL 1986).

---

[5] A similar result for a slightly different decision problem has been proved by ARROW/FISHER (1974).
[6] This is the net present value method (cf. e.g. IRVIN 1978).

While for more complex problems it is still true that informational considerations can have a significant impact on the optimal choice, a systematic bias towards irreversibility does not exist in general. However, JONES/OSTROY (1984) give sufficient conditions for an irreversibility bias to occur. These conditions can be used to show that there exist at least some examples of an irreversibility bias beside the aforementioned.

Having said that information generally has a significant effect on first-period choice, it is worthwhile to point out two simple cases where it does not make a difference whether information is taken into account or not.

Example 1: The Totally Reversible Case

In proposition 2.2, we showed that for the totally reversible problem without learning, the optimal decision was myopic. The prospect of further information does not change this: there is no reason to take the possibility of learning into account in the first period, because the set of possible future options is independent of first-period choice, $G(a_1)=A_2$ for all $a_1 \varepsilon A_1$. Hence $V(a_1)$ is the same whatever a_1 is, so that in this case (2.2.5) reduces to:

b_1 maximizes $E_s[r_1(a_1,s)]$ over A_1,

which is the myopic rule for the model with risk.

The following result is an immediate consequence.

<u>Proposition 2.5:</u> In the totally reversible case, the possibility of learning does not change the optimal first-period decision: with or without learning, it is optimal to maximize $E_s[r_1(a_1,s)]$.

Example 2: The Totally Irreversible Case

According to section 2.1.1, we speak of a totally irreversible problem if every $a_1 \varepsilon A_1$ is totally irreversible, i.e. for every $a_1 \varepsilon A_1$ there exists an element $g(a_1) \varepsilon A_2$ such that $G(a_1)=\{g(a_1)\}$.

From $G(a_1)=\{g(a_1)\}$ it follows that

$$\max_{a_2 \varepsilon G(a_1)} E_{s|y}[r_2(a_2,s)] = \sum_{s \varepsilon S} \Pi(s|y) r_2(g(a_1),s),$$

so that (2.2.5) reads

$$b_1 \text{ maximizes } E_s[r_1(a_1,s)] + \sum_{y \varepsilon Y} q_y [\sum_{s \varepsilon S} \Pi(s|y) r_2(g(a_1),s)] =$$

$$E_s[r_1(a_1,s)] + \sum_{s \varepsilon S} (\sum_{y \varepsilon Y} q_y \Pi(s|y)) r_2(g(a_1),s)] =^7$$

$$E_s[r_1(a_1,s)] + \sum_{s \varepsilon S} \Pi(s) r_2(g(a_1),s).$$

By the assumption of total irreversibility, all feasible paths (a_1,a_2) are of the form $(a_1,g(a_1))$. Therefore, the last equality implies that

(b_1,b_2) maximizes $E_s[r_1(a_1,s)+r_2(a_2,s)]$ over G

as in the case without learning; cf. (2.2.9).

Intuitively, this is clear: learning in period 2 is useless when second-period behaviour is completely determined by the action in period 1; hence, there is no need to care about learning possibilities when the first decision is taken. This is the same result as in the totally reversible case; when choice is totally reversible, there is no need to consider future learning possibilities in period 1, but for different reasons: because the set of feasible second-period actions is completely independent of first-period actions.

The most important example of a totally irreversible decision problem is the choice problem of an agent in an Arrow-Debreu model. With a complete set of future markets that do not reopen, the only "action" the consumer can take in period 2 is to consume what he decided to purchase in period 1. This is why learning considerations only become relevant in a world of incomplete future markets.

---

7 This equality holds because $\sum_{y \varepsilon Y} q_y \Pi(s|y) = \sum_{y \varepsilon Y} q_y pr(s \cap y)/q_y = \Pi(s)$, where $pr(s \cap y)$ is the joint probability that the signal y is received and the state of the world is s.

2.2.3 Flexibility and the Value of Information

To understand more about the influence of irreversibility, flexibility, etc. on the optimal path, it is useful to introduce the "value of information". Intuitively, it is clear that the value of the additional information received in period two depends on the initial choice. We saw that, when first-period choice is totally irreversible, the additional information is useless because the agent's choice is predetermined before the information arises. When the first-period choice is not totally irreversible, one would expect information to be potentially useful, because second-period choice is not determined before the information arrives. One would expect the value of second-period information to be greater for more flexible first-period choices. To investigate this idea, we introduce the concept of "value of information" formally (cf. MARSCHAK/MIYASAWA 1968, HIRSHLEIFER/ RILEY 1979 and, from a slightly different point of view, MENGES/HUSCHENS 1984).

Once the first-period decision a_1 has been made, the decision problem has the structure of a lottery on $G(a_1)$. For such lotteries, the **value of the message** y that induces a change from a prior distribution $\Pi(s)$ to a posterior distribution $\Pi(s|y)$ has been defined as the difference between the expected payoff (given the message) of the optimal choice based on the posterior distribution and the expected payoff (given the message) of the optimal choice that is based on the prior distribution (cf. for instance, HIRSHLEIFER/RILEY 1979, p.1395).

Formally, suppose the maximum of $E_s[r_2(a_2,s)]$ is attained at a_2^+. Then the value of a message y, given a_1, is defined as

$$\mathbf{VM(y;a_1)} = \max_{a_2 \varepsilon G(a_1)} [E_{s|y}[r_2(a_2,s)]] - E_{s|y}[r_2(a_2^+,s)]. \qquad (2.2.10)$$

The value of a message is non-negative and measures "the expected gain from revision of past action, estimated in terms of revised probabilities" (HIRSHLEIFER/RILEY 1979, p.1395). It is obviously an ex post concept which cannot be calculated without knowing the message.

To assess the **value of information** (i.e. of receiving <u>some</u> message) before the message is known, one needs to consider the expected value of $VM(y;a_1)$. Thus, the value of information conditional upon a first-period choice of a_1 is defined as

$$\mathbf{VI(a_1)} = E_Y\{ \max_{a_2 \varepsilon G(a_1)} [E_{S|y}[r_2(a_2,s)]] - E_{S|y}[r_2(a_2^+,s)]\}. \quad (2.2.11)$$

The following observations are straightforward:

(a) The value of information $VI(a_1)$ is a function of initial choice.
(b) $V(a_1)=0$ if the initial choice is totally irreversible.

Furthermore, there is a close relation between the flexibility of an initial position a_1 and the value $VI(a_1)$ of information.

To understand this, we start by considering example 1 from section 2.2.1. Because in this example a_2^+ was seen to be 0, we get

$$VI(0) = E_Y\{ \max_{a_2 \varepsilon G(0)} [E_{S|Y}[r_2(a_2,s)]] - E_{S|y}[r_2(0,s)]\} =$$

$$1/2[r_2(1,s^1)-r_2(0,s^1)] + 1/2[r_2(0,s^2)-r_2(0,s^2)] = 1/2(5-3) = 1,$$

while VI(1) is 0, because 1 is irreversible. Hence, in this example the value of information is greater the more flexible the initial choice.

This is not necessarily the case for more complex decision problems. In fact, we shall show in chapter 3.3 that the following two questions are equivalent:

- Does additional information always lead to a more flexible first-period choice?

- Is the value of information greater for more flexible first-period choices?

In example 1 in section 2.2.1, we saw that

$$E_S[r_1(0,s)]+V(0;\Pi,q) = 6,5,$$
$$E_S[r_1(1,s)]+V(1;\Pi,q) = 6,$$

while

$$E_s[r_1(0,s)] + \max_{a_2 \varepsilon G(a_1)} E_s[r_2(a_2,s)] = 5,5;$$

$$E_s[r_1(1,s)] + \max_{a_2 \varepsilon G(a_1)} E_s[r_2(a_2,s)] = 6.$$

Hence, the difference between the value of the first-period choice a_1 with and without learning is precisely the value of (perfect) information conditional on a_1. This will seen to be true in general (cf. proposition 3.4). The difference is never negative and can be positive. It expresses the value of the flexible choice that is due to the better adaptation to second-period information. It has therefore been termed the **option value** (cf. HANEMANN 1989).

Though the option value was originally defined for problems with one irreversible and one perfectly flexible choice (cf. example 1 in section 2.2.1), it is conveniently generalized to arbitrary decision problems by simply defining the option value of any initial position a_1 as the value of information conditional upon the first-period choice a_1.

2.2.4 An Example: Waiting to Invest

We now turn to an extension of the example in section 2.2.1. Suppose given a firm that can choose among different irreversible investment projects 1,...,n-1 and the possibility of deferring investment to period 2 (cf. section 2.1.2). Suppose further that the payoff for each project depends on a state of the world s and that the firm has a prior probability distribution $\Pi(s)$ on states of the world. Before the second choice is made, a signal $y \varepsilon Y$ is received (Y is a finite set). This leads to a revision of the prior probability distribution; the posterior distribution is $\Pi(s|y)$.

It has been shown (cf. BERNANKE 1983) that for an investment project i to be chosen, it is not enough that it leads to a positive expected payoff that is at least as high as the payoff of all the alternative projects, as would be true in the case where no future information is received. The reason is that it may be better to postpone investment, given the fact that postponing is the only position that is not totally irreversible, i.e. the only position that allows the use of future information. For a project to be chosen, the expected first-period payoff has to be at least as high as the expected loss because of the impossibility to give up the respective project in favour of another one. Though the flexible position gives no first-period payoff and, if repeated, no second-period payoff, choosing it in period 1 has the advantage of allowing the consideration of information which the competing alternatives have not.

Therefore the investment rule "invest into project i if the expected payoff is positive and at least as great as the expected payoff for all the alternative projects" has to be rewritten as follows (for a similar statement, cf. BERNANKE 1983).

<u>Proposition 2.6</u>: Let $A_1=A_2=A=\{1,...,n-1,f\}$, where $1,...,n-1$ are totally irreversible, f is perfectly flexible. Suppose $E_s[r_1(f,s)]=E_s[r_2(f,s)]=0$ and $r_t(a_1,s)>0$ for each $t\varepsilon\{1,2\}$, $a_1\varepsilon\{1,2,...,n-1\}, s\varepsilon S$.
Then $i\varepsilon\{1,...,n-1\}$ is an optimal choice, i.e it maximizes $E_s[r_1(a_1,s)] + V(a_1)$ over A_1, if and only if it maximizes $E_s[r_1(a_1,s)] + V(a_1)$ over $\{1,...,n-1\}$ and

$$E_s[r_1(i,s)] \geq Zi := E_Y\{\max_{a_2\varepsilon\{1,...,n-1\}} E_{s|y}[r_2(a_2,s)-r_2(i,s)]\}.$$

Before proving this proposition, note that Z_i stands for the expected value of the loss that is due to being committed to project i in period 1. Hence, though every investment project yields a positive payoff in both periods whatever the state of the world, it may be advisable to postpone investment to period 2.

<u>Proof:</u> We only need to show that

$$E_s[r_1(i,s)] + V(i) \geq E_s[r_1(f,s)] + V(f) \iff$$
$$E_s[r_1(i,s)] \geq Z_i.$$

Now

$$E_s[r_1(i,s)] + V(i) \geq E_s[r_1(f,s)] + V(f) \iff$$
$$E_s[r_1(i,s)] \geq E_s[r_1(f,s)] + V(f) - V(i) \iff$$
$$E_s[r_1(i,s)] \geq V(f) - V(i),$$

where the last equivalence holds because $E_s[r_1(f,s)]=0$.

By definition,

$$V(f)-V(i) = E_Y\{\max_{a_2 \varepsilon \{1,...,n-1,f\}} E_{S|y}[r_2(a_2,s)]\} - E_Y E_{S|y}[r_2(i,s)]\} =$$

$$V(f)-V(i) = E_Y\{\max_{a_2 \varepsilon \{1,...,n-1,f\}} E_{S|y}[r_2(a_2,s)-r_2(i,s)]\}.$$

But from $r_2(f,s)=0$ for each $s\varepsilon S$, $r_2(a_2,s)>0$ for each $s\varepsilon S$, $a_2\varepsilon\{1,...,n-1\}$, it follows that the last expression equals

$$V(f)-V(i) = E_Y\{\max_{a_2 \varepsilon \{1,...,n-1\}} E_{S|y}[r_2(a_2,s)-r_2(i,s)]\}.$$

Obviously, the assumptions of the above model are very restrictive. Hardly any decision problem can be reasonably described as the choice between a perfectly flexible action and a set of totally irreversible actions. In particular, in most investment problems, the decision not to invest also has an irreversible element, which is due to the fact that investment takes time because of delivery lags, gestation periods, adjustment costs, etc (cf. chapter 1.1.4, 4.1.2).

Nevertheless, two essential points remain unaffected by this critique. Firstly, the example shows that postponing an investment decision <u>may</u> be justified on grounds of ex ante flexibility considerations when it would not be justified otherwise. Secondly, the principle that in different economic decision problems there are some choices which benefit in a particularly strong manner from the expectation of future information is a very general one, as will be seen in the remainder of this study. To name only one such example, STOCK/WISE (1990) consider the situation of workers who have to decide whether or not to make use of early retirement schemes. Here the decision to retire has a highly irreversible character, while the decision to postpone retirement preserves the option to retire later.

2.3 Switching Costs

The way we modelled the effects of first-period choices on available second-period choices so far may be considered as somewhat crude: we do allow that choosing a_1 makes it completely impossible to choose a_2 in period 2, but if a_2 is feasible, the second-period payoff is totally unaffected by a_1. Now there are many examples where switching from a_1 to a_2 is possible but costly. For instance, if an agent decides to invest in an asset with low liquidity in period 1, it may be perfectly possible for him to switch to an alternative portfolio composition in period 2 but, in general, this will involve certain costs. Hence, we shall extend our model as to include such examples.

2.3.1 The Extended Model

If we are to model switching costs, our payoff function cannot possibly be of the form $U(a_1,a_2,s)= r_1(a_1,s)+r_2(a_2,s)$. Instead, we follow the approach of JONES/OSTROY (1984) and subtract a term $c(a_1,a_2,s)$ that reflects the costs of switching from a_1 to a_2, so that

$$U(a_1,a_2,s) = r_1(a_1,s)+r_2(a_2,s)-c(a_1,a_2,s). \qquad (2.3.1)$$

Furthermore, we assume that for each $a_1 \varepsilon A_1$ there is at least one feasible "status quo choice" $g(a_1)$ such that $c(a_1,g(a_1),s)=0$.

The function c will not be allowed to take negative values.

It is now appropriate to adapt our vocabulary to the new situation.

For $a_1 \varepsilon A_1$, $s \varepsilon S$, $\alpha \varepsilon R_+$, we define

$$G(a_1,s,\alpha) := \{a_2 \varepsilon A | c(a_1,a_2,s) \le \alpha\}. \qquad (2.3.2)$$

Hence, $G(a_1,s,\alpha)$ consists of those second-period actions that are available at costs that do not exceed α in state s.

Note that the set of positions that are feasible at finite costs, given a_1, will in general depend on the state of the world.

In particular, we can treat uncertainty about the irreversibility of first-period actions (cf. USATEGUI 1990) in the extended framework.

We shall say that a_1 is **at least as flexible** as a_1', $a_1 \geq_F a_1'$, if $G(a_1,s,\alpha) \supset G(a_1',s,\alpha)$ whenever $s \varepsilon S$ and α is a non-negative real number. Hence a_1 is at least as flexible as a_1' if the set of second-period options available at arbitrary costs α given a_1 contains the corresponding set for a_1', no matter what the state of the world is. This is compatible with our earlier definition of flexibility in the case without switching costs.

a_1 is called **perfectly flexible** (or **totally reversible**) if $G(a_1,s,0)=A_2$ for every $s \varepsilon S$, so that from a_1 all second-period positions can be reached without switching costs.

a_1 is called **totally irreversible** if for all $\alpha \geq 0$ and $s \varepsilon S$, $G(a_1,s,\alpha)$ is the one element set $\{g(a_1)\}$, so that switching is impossible at finite costs.

As a useful piece of notation, we sometimes write $G(a_1,s)$ for the set of second-period choices that are feasible at finite switching costs, given the state of the world s. If this set is independent of s, we write $G(a_1)$ as in sections 2.1 and 2.2.

In analogy to (2.2.5), we can find that the optimal behaviour in period 1 is to choose b_1 as to maximize

$$E_S[r_1(a_1,s)] + E_Y\{ \max_{a_2 \varepsilon G(a_1)} E_{S|Y}[r_2(a_2,s)-c(a_1,a_2,s)]\} \qquad (2.3.3)$$

over A_1. Generalizing (2.2.3) to

$$\mathbf{V(a_1) = V(a_1;\Pi,q)} := E_Y \max_{a_2 \varepsilon G(a_1)} E_{S|Y}[r_2(a_2,s)-c(a_1,a_2,s)], \qquad (2.3.4)$$

we obtain:

b_1 maximizes $[E_S r_1(a_1,s)+V(a_1)]$ over A_1; cf. (2.2.6).

We finish this section with a simple result that, in some cases, shows which of two initial choices is preferred: if one alternative dominates another in the sense of being at least as flexible as another and giving a greater short-term payoff, it is preferred.

Proposition 2.7: Suppose $a_1 \geq_F a_1'$, $E_s[r_1(a_1,s)] > E_s[r_1(a_1',s)]$. Then $E_s[r_1(a_1,s)] + V(a_1) > E_s[r_1(a_1',s)] + V(a_1')$.

Proof: From $a_1 \geq_F a_1'$, we get $V(a_1) \geq V(a_1')$. The result therefore follows immediately from $E_s[r_1(a_1,s)] > E_s[r_1(a_1',s)]$.

2.3.2 An Example: Money Demand as Demand for Flexibility

In chapter 5, we shall show that our general choice framework helps to understand the motives for the demand for money. As many authors, e.g. BERNHOLZ (1967), NIEHANS (1978, chapter 4), we interpret the demand for money as the outcome of an intertemporal choice problem.

In this section, we restrict ourselves to one aspect of this problem by means of an example that is due to JONES/OSTROY (1984). The authors claim that one reason for the demand for the non-interest bearing asset money (in the presence of interest-bearing assets) is its liquidity that allows to exchange it for other assets relatively easily. Their example is briefly summarized in the following; a more complex version will be presented in chapter 5.

Suppose that in periods t=1,2 an agent must choose between three non-diversified portfolios from $A_1 = A_2 = \{M,1,2\}$, where M is money, which is assumed to be perfectly flexible, while 1 and 2 are partially irreversible assets: Switching from 1 or 2 to any other involves "liquidation costs" of c.

The payoff on M in each period is zero with certainty. The first-period returns of both 1 and 2 are r>0 with certainty, while the second-period return of 1 and 2 depends on the state of nature, s, which is an element of a two-element-set $\{s^1, s^2\}$. Suppose $r_2(1,s^1)=1$, $r_2(1,s^2)=0$, $r_2(2,s^1)=0$, $r_2(2,s^2)=1$. Then, clearly, though 1 and 2 are not totally irreversible, M is more flexible than both of these assets[8]: For all $s \in S$, $a_1 \in A$, we get $G(a_1, s, \alpha) = A$ for $\alpha \geq c$, while for $0 \leq \alpha \leq c$, $G(M, s, \alpha) = A$, but $G(i, s, \alpha) = \{i\}$ for $i=1,2$.

These assumptions lead to the following two-period choices and (state-dependent) payoffs:

Choice of assets	payoff in state 1	payoff in state 2
(1,1)	r+1	r
(1,M)	r-c	r-c
(1,2)	r-c	r-c+1
(M,1)	1	0
(M,M)	0	0
(M,2)	0	1
(2,1)	r-c+1	r-c
(2,M)	r-c	r-c
(2,2)	r	r+1.

Finally, we suppose that the message that is received at the beginning of period 2 is an element of a two-element set $\{y^1, y^2\}$. Assume that the conditional probabilities are given by

$$\Pi(s^1|y^1) = \tau + ß(1-\tau),\ \Pi(s^1|y^2) = ß(1-\tau) \text{ and consequently}$$
$$\Pi(s^2|y^1) = 1-\tau-ß(1-\tau),\ \Pi(s^2|y^2) = 1-ß(1-\tau)$$

for some parameters $ß, \tau$ such that $0 \leq ß, \tau \leq 1$. It is always possible to write $\Pi(s^1|y^1)$ etc. in this form. To see this, one can take $ß = [\Pi(s^1|y^2)]/[1-\Pi(s^1|y^1)+\Pi(s^1|y^2)]$, $\tau = \Pi(s^1|y^1) - \Pi(s^1|y^2)$. This gives the desired parametrization except in the case $\Pi(s^1|y^1)=1$, $\Pi(s^1|y^2)=0$, where the denominator of α would be 0. In this case, $\tau=1$, $ß=0$ does the job.

Let $q_{y1} = ß$, $q_{y2} = 1-ß$. Then the parameters $ß$ and τ can be interpreted as follows.

$ß$: $\Pi(s^1) = q_{y1}\Pi(s^1|y^1) + q_{y2}\Pi(s^1|y^2) = ß(\tau+ß(1-\tau)) + (1-ß)(ß(1-\tau)) = ß$.

---

[8] This property depends strongly on the simple structure of the model, in general, choosing money is not necessarily more flexible than choosing other assets (cf. chapter 5.4).

τ: If $\tau=0$, y is not informative at all, because $\Pi(s^1|y^1)= \Pi(s^1)=\Pi(s^1|y^2)$.

If $\tau=1$, y reveals the state of the nature. The greater τ, the greater the difference between $\Pi(s^i)$ and $\Pi(s^i|y^j)$ $(i=1,2;j=1,2)$. Thus, in a sense that can be made precise, τ measures the additional information to be gained from second-period observations (cf. the concept of informativeness of information structures in chapter 3.1.2).

JONES/OSTROY (1984) show that increasing τ makes it more likely that the agent holds money: the more their informational position is expected to change, the more valuable is the perfectly flexible asset money. Similarly, the asset money benefits from an increase in liquidation costs and hence a decrease of flexibility.

2.4 Summary and Outlook

It was convenient to introduce some of the fundamental ideas about intertemporal decisions in a simple two-period model. We showed that (partial) irreversibility is needed to make intertemporal decision problems truly intertemporal. With total reversibility, myopic decision rules are certainly optimal, whereas irreversibility <u>may</u> change this: a necessary condition for myopic decisions to be suboptimal is that they give rise to intertemporal opportunity costs. Typical examples of intertemporal opportunity costs were provided. When uncertainty is added to the model, irreversibility has further consequences; the possibility of learning, which is irrelevant to first-period choices in the totally reversible case, will, in general, affect first-period behaviour when there is <u>partial</u> irreversibility. With <u>total</u> irreversibility, learning is useless because it cannot result in a change of second-period behaviour. The value of additional information, given a first-period choice, and the flexibility of that position are closely related. Finally, one can see how the advantage of flexibility can make certain "actions" like postponing investment and holding money (instead of return-bearing assets) more attractive.

Our approach will be extended in various directions in the following chapters. Some ideas can be discussed in the two-period framework of this chapter. For instance, in chapter 3 we shall investigate how the flexibility and the (appropriately defined) value of the initial choice depend on the structure of the problem (How "much" irreversibility is there? Which choice criterion does the agent use? How much does he expect to learn?). Other aspects, however, are more conveniently illustrated in a two-period-model. For instance, the implications of the fact that production takes time can only really be understood in a model with more than two periods. This fact is fundamental to Neo-Austrian capital theory (cf. BERNHOLZ/FABER 1973, FABER 1979, FABER/PROOPS 1990, STEPHAN 1989) and to some concepts of neoclassical investment theory (for instance the notion of delivery lags, cf. chapter 1). As another example, search-theoretical questions can be handled if more than two periods are allowed. Therefore, the framework of this chapter will be extended to $T \geq 2$ periods in chapter 4. This extension is also useful for other applications. For instance, the investigation of motives for money demand in chapter 5 will be carried out in a multiperiod framework.

Before moving on to the proposed extensions of the model, we touch upon an alternative approach to flexibility issues that goes back to KOOPMANS (1964)[9]. The idea is that in sequential choice problems, the first step is effectively the choice of a set of future options and the second step is the choice of an element of this set of options. In our language, one first chooses $G(a_1)$ and then $a_2 \in G(a_1)$. Instead of assuming that the agent chooses a_1 on the basis of an objective function that depends on (a_1, a_2), the agent is supposed to have a preference ordering on the set of future choice sets. A "preference for flexibility" can then be reflected in the nature of the preference ordering in various ways. For instance, one can say that preference for flexibility exists if for every pair (A,B) of sets such that B is a proper subset of A, A is strictly preferred to B. KREPS (1979,1988) has investigated the relationship between the approach of KOOPMANS (1964) and the approach that we described in this chapter.

---

[9] cf. MAIER (1984, p. 75-87) for more details.

Chapter 3

DETERMINANTS OF THE OPTIMAL CHOICE IN SEQUENTIAL DECISION PROBLEMS - THE TWO-PERIOD CASE

In chapter 2, we introduced a general two-period decision problem. We saw what kind of structure such a model must have to be able to handle irreversibility and learning. We proved several results for the model, but we have not yet given a systematic treatment. As a first step towards such a systematic treatment, it is important to note what kind of cases can be distinguished within the framework of the general model of chapter 2.

Firstly, the structure of the choice set is important. In particular, it is important to know whether the problem is totally reversible, partially irreversible or totally irreversible. More generally, it is important to know "how much irreversibility" there is.

Secondly, the "information structure" (cf. section 3.1.2) is important. Problems differ according to how much information the agent expects to receive between periods 1 and 2. The extreme cases are those of non-informative and perfectly informative information structures. In the first case, the agent knows that the message will be of no relevance to his future beliefs. In the second case, the signal reveals the true state of the world to the agent. More generally, information structures can be partially ordered according to informativeness.

Thirdly, it is important to know what kind of choice criterion the agent uses. For instance, we can distinguish Bayesians, intertemporal optimizers who ignore learning possibilities and myopic agents. Other aspects of the choice criterion, such as the attitude towards risk will not be discussed in this chapter though this would clearly make sense.

It will turn out in section 3.3 that the second and the third point are closely related. In section 3.1, we shall illustrate these three points in more detail. In sections 3.2-3.4, we shall show how the outcome of the choice problem depends on its structure, which is given by the choice set, the information structure and the choice criterion. By the outcome of the problem, we mean the flexibility of the first-period choice and its appropriately defined value. Finally, in section 3.5, our results are related to the questions raised in the introduction:

- How does an increase in uncertainty affect the optimal decision for an agent who takes flexibility considerations into account?
- How is the optimal choice of agents affected if flexibility considerations are ignored?

3.1 The Formulation of the Problem

Consider the following intertemporal decision problem.

Suppose an agent is given sets A_t $(t=1,2)$ and a subset G of $A_1 x A_2$. Suppose further that he has to choose a time path (a_1, a_2) from G.

His payoff is not completely determined by the choice of (a_1, a_2); it is given by a payoff function $U(a_1, a_2, s)$ that depends on a state of the world $s \varepsilon S$ (where S is a finite set) which is revealed after a_2 has been chosen.

The agent is supposed to have a subjective (prior) probability distribution Π on S.

Before he chooses a_2, he receives a message y, an element of some finite set Y, with probability q_y.

Observation of y induces the agent to revise his prior distribution $\Pi(s)$; his posterior distribution is $\Pi(s|y)$.

A **Bayesian decision maker** will choose a_2 such as to maximize his expected payoff given his initial choice a_1 and his observation y, i.e. he will maximize

$$\mathbf{E}_{s|y}[\mathbf{U}(\mathbf{a}_1,\mathbf{a}_2,\mathbf{s})] := \sum_{s \in S} \Pi(s|y)U(a_1,a_2,s)$$[1]

subject to $a_2 \in G(a_1)$, where $G(a_1)$ is the set of available second-period choices after an initial choice of a_1.

In period 1, he chooses a_1 from A_1 such as to maximize the expected value

$$\mathbf{BV}(\mathbf{a}_1) = \mathbf{BV}(\mathbf{a}_1;\Pi,\mathbf{q})^{2} = E_Y \max_{a_2 \in G(a_1)} E_{s|y}[U(a_1,a_2,s)] =$$

$$\sum_{y \in Y} q_y [\max_{a_2 \in G(a_1)} \sum_{s \in S} \Pi(s|y)U(a_1,a_2,s)] \qquad (3.1.1)$$

We shall often consider the special cases

(1) $U(a_1,a_2,s) = r_1(a_1,s) + r_2(a_2,s)$,

where r_1, r_2 are real-valued functions as in chapter 2.2. More generally, we shall consider

(2) $U(a_1,a_2,s) = r_1(a_1,s)+r_2(a_2,s)-c(a_1,a_2,s)$,

where c is a function with values in R_+ measuring the costs of switching from a_1 to a_2 given the state of the world s (cf. section 2.3.1 for details).

For decision problems of type (2) (and, in particular, of type (1)), (3.1.1) reads

$$BV(a_1) = E_Y \max_{a_2 \in G(a_1)} E_{s|y}[r_1(a_1,s)+r_2(a_2,s)-c(a_1,a_2,s)] =$$

$$E_Y E_{s|y}[r_1(a_1,s)] + E_Y \max_{a_2 \in G(a_1)} E_{s|y}[r_2(a_2,s)-c(a_1,a_2,s)] =$$

$$E_S[r_1(a_1,s)] + E_Y \max_{a_2 \in G(a_1)} E_{s|y}[r_2(a_2,s)-c(a_1,a_2,s)] =$$

$$E_S[r_1(a_1,s)] + V(a_1;\Pi,q).$$[3]

We shall, however, also consider agents who do not use the sophisticated Bayesian choice criterion. For instance, we shall discuss

---

[1] This is a slight generalization of the approach in chapter 2.3, where U was of the form $r_1(a_1,s)+r_2(a_2,s)-c(a_1,a_2,s)$.

[2] Though $BV(a_1;\Pi,q)$ depends s on Π,q as well as on a_1, we shall often write $BV(a_1)$ when there is no danger of misunderstanding.

[3] cf. (2.3.4) for this notation.

myopic optimizers who simply maximize expected first-period payoff $E_s[r_1(a_1,s)]$ and **expected payoff maximizers who ignore the learning possibility** when they choose a_1 and therefore maximize $E_s[r_1(a_1,s) + r_2(a_2,s)]$.

These choice criteria and others will be explained in more detail in section 1.1; for the time being, we do not specify them any further and simply suppose that, given the other parameters of the model, the agent has some way of choosing a_1 and a_2.

Summing up, we obtain the following formulation of the decision problem. A **two-period decision problem (DP)** is given by:

(1) sets A_1, A_2, $G \subset A_1 x A_2$,

(2) finite sets S, Y and probability distributions $\Pi(s), \Pi(s|y)$ on S, q_y on Y, the **information structure**. [Note that it is sufficient to specify $\Pi(s|y)$ and q_y; $\Pi(s)$ can be derived from $\Pi(s|y)$ and q_y as $\Pi(s) = \sum_{y \varepsilon Y} q_y \Pi(s|y)$. If $S=(s^1,...,s^m)$, $Y=(y^1,...,y^n)$, an information structure is therefore given by the (mxn)-matrix with typical entry $\Pi(s^i|y^j)$ and the vector $(q_{y1},...,q_{yn}) \varepsilon R^n$.]

(3) a way of choosing an optimal first-period choice from A_1 and an optimal second-period choice from $G(a_1)$, given a first-period choice a_1 and an observed message $y \varepsilon Y$.

The remainder of this chapter will be dedicated to the following question:

How does the outcome of the decision problem depend on the structure of the problem?

Here, the structure of the problem is given by

(a) the set G of feasible paths,
(b) the information structure,
(c) the choice criterion.

The "outcomes" can be distinguished according to

(d) the expected value of the initial choice and
(e) the flexibility of the initial choice.

3.1.1 Some Explanatory Remarks

We shall now explain (a)-(e).

(a) The Set of Feasible Paths

The main criterion we use to distinguish between different sets G is the degree of irreversibility. The extreme cases are the case of **total reversibility** ($G=A_1 x A_2$) and the case of **total irreversibility**, when $G(a_1)$ contains only one element for each $a_1 \varepsilon A_1$; cf. chapter 2.1.1.

More generally, one would like to call a problem DP at least as irreversible as another one (DP') if DP does not leave more options open for any first-period choice. To express this idea formally, we shall say that, for two decision problems DP and DP' with choice sets G and G', **G is at least as irreversible as G'** if $G(a_1) \subset G'(a_1)$ for all $a_1 \varepsilon A_1$, while the problems are otherwise identical.

A totally irreversible decision problem is at least as irreversible as any other problem to which it can be compared, while for totally reversible DP any other problem to which it can be compared is at least as irreversible as DP.
Note that our definition is satisfactory only for the case $U(a_1, a_2, s)=r_1(a_1, s)+r_2(a_2, s)$. When switching costs are admitted, it seems more reasonable to say that DP is at least as irreversible as DP' if $G(a_1, s, \alpha) \subset G'(a_1, s, \alpha)$ for each $a_1 \varepsilon A_1$, $\alpha \varepsilon R_+$, $s \varepsilon S$, where $G(a_1, s, \alpha)$ denotes the set of $a_2 \varepsilon A_2$ for which $c(a_1, a_2, s) \leq \alpha$ (and correspondingly for $G'(a_1, s, \alpha)$); i.e. DP is at least as irreversible as DP' if for arbitrarily given first-period choice a_1, state of the world s and switching costs α the set of second-period choices that can be achieved from a_1 at costs α, given the state s, for DP' contains the corresponding set for DP.

(b) The Information Structure

We are interested in the extent to which learning takes place before the agent chooses a_2. Again, we have two extreme cases. If, given a prior distribution Π, $\Pi(s|y) = \Pi(s)$ for all signals y that the agent receives with positive probability, we shall say that the information structure is **non-informative**. If, however, for each $y \varepsilon Y$ there exists an $s_y \varepsilon S$ such that $\Pi(s_y|y) = 1$, i.e. if no matter which message the agent receives, he knows exactly what the state of the world is, we shall say that the information structure **is perfectly informative**.

In fact, there is a partial ordering on the set of information structures for given A_1, A_2, G that is compatible with intuitive concepts of greater informativeness. As a satisfactory treatment of this partial ordering requires a fair amount of space, we devote section 3.1.2 to this topic and deal with (c)-(e) in the remainder of this section.

(c) The Choice Criterion

The rational decision criterion for an agent with payoff function U in our model is the Bayesian criterion (3.1.1). It has three main characteristics.

(i) When the agent makes his first-period decision, he takes the effect of his decision on second-period choice possibilities into account. In this sense, **he is an intertemporal optimizer**, in other words, he does not behave myopically.

(ii) The arrival of new information at the beginning of period 2 has an impact on his second-period decision, i.e. **he uses information ex post**.

(iii) Finally, when the agent takes his first-period decision, he already takes into account the fact that he will receive information later, i.e. **he uses information ex ante**.

None of the above characteristics is necessarily satisfied in the real world (or in economic models, for that matter). One can certainly imagine agents who, though interested in the effects of their choices on future periods, ignore these effects and use a myopic rule as a rule of thumb. It is also conceivable that an agent does not adjust his plans when new information arrives; instead he may want to stick to the path originally envisaged. It is even more easily conceivable that the agent does not take information into account <u>before</u> it arrives, in fact even in cost-benefit-analysis and most descriptive economic models, the possible arrival of information in the future is usually ignored (cf. the comments in HENRY 1974, VISCUSI 1988).

The chosen path will, in general, differ according to which of the three criteria are satisfied.

However, not all the combinations of (i) to (iii) are reasonable. For example, it does not make sense to consider agents who use information ex ante, but behave myopically. Likewise, one should expect an agent who uses information ex ante to also use it ex post: if, when the agent takes his first-period decision, he takes into account the fact that additional information will be available before he takes his second-period decision, it is somewhat unlikely that he will systematically ignore the new information once it has arrived.

The remaining combinations of (i) to (iii), however, are worth a discussion. The questions to be asked are:

Is the agent an intertemporal optimizer? (Yes/No)
Does he use information ex post? (Yes/No)
Does he use information ex ante? (Yes/No)

The following combinations are reasonable:

(YYY): the intertemporal optimizer who uses information ex post and ex ante (the Bayesian case). In period 1, he maximizes $E_Y \max_{a_2 \varepsilon G(a_1)} E_{S|y}[U(a_1, a_2, s)]$ over A_1 and in period 2 he maximizes $E_{S|y}[U(a_1, a_2, s)]$ over $G(a_1)$.

The optimal first-period choice will be called b_1. Note that b_1 need not be unique. However, we restrict ourselves to cases where b_1 is uniquely defined. The same restriction applies to e_1 and m_1 below.

(YYN): the intertemporal optimizer who uses information ex post, but not ex ante. He maximizes $E_s[U(a_1,a_2,s)]$ over A_1 in period 1 and $E_{s|y}[U(a_1,a_2,s)]$ over $G(a_1)$ in period 2.

(YNN): the intertemporal optimizer who does not use the information given by the message y at all. He maximizes $E_s[U(a_1,a_2,s)]$ over A_1 in period 1 and $E_s[U(a_1,a_2,s)]$ over $G(a_1)$ in period 2.[4] The optimal choice for (YYN) and (YNN) will be called e_1.

(NYN): the myopic optimizer who uses information ex post (but of course not ex ante). This makes sense only if the payoff function is given as in (1) or (2). Then the agent maximizes $E_s[r_1(a_1,s)]$ in period 1 over A_1 and $E_{s|y}[r_2(a_2,s)-c(a_1,a_2,s)]$ over $G(a_1)$ in period 2.

(NNN): the myopic optimizer who does not use the information given by the message y at all. Again, we suppose that the payoff function is given as in (1) or (2). Then the agent maximizes $E_s[r_1(a_1,s)]$ in period 1 and $E_s[r_2(a_2,s)-c(a_1,a_2,s)]$ over $G(a_1)$ in period 2. The optimal choice for (NYN) and (NNN) will be called m_1.

We now turn to a discussion of the criteria according to which we distinguish outcomes.

(d) The Value of the Initial Choice

To measure the value of the initial choice, we use the value that the "rational" Bayesian decision maker would assign to it ex ante, i.e. the value of a_1 is

---

[4] In the terminology of stochastic control theory, YNN is an open-loop control and YYN an open-loop feedback control (cf. HANEMANN 1989, p.27, where YNN and YYN are discussed).

$$BV(a_1) = E_Y \max_{a_2 \varepsilon G(a_1)} E_{S|y}[U(a_1, a_2, s)].$$

In most cases, we shall restrict ourselves to payoff functions of type (1), so that

$$BV(a_1) = E_Y \max_{a_2 \varepsilon G(a_1)} E_{S|y}[r_1(a_1,s)+r_2(a_2,s)] =$$

$$E_S[r_1(a_1,s)] + E_Y \max_{a_2 \varepsilon G(a_1)} E_{S|y}[r_2(a_2,s)]. \qquad (3.1.2)$$

It also makes sense to speak of the Bayesian value BV of any of the five above strategies. By this we mean the value that a Bayesian decision maker would assign to the optimal path for the respective strategy ex ante.

(YYY), (YYN) and (NYN) are strategies that use information ex post, i.e. they maximize $E_{S|y}$ $[U(a_1, a_2, s)]$ in the second period, where a_1 is their initial choice. Hence the respective values are

$$E_S[r_1(a_1,s)] + E_Y \max_{a_2 \varepsilon G(a_1)} E_{S|y}[r_2(a_2,s)],$$

where $a_1 = b_1$ for (YYY), $a_1 = e_1$ for (YYN), $a_1 = m_1$ for (NYN).

(YNN) and (NNN) do not use information at all; they maximize $E_S[U(a_1, a_2, s)]$ over $G(a_1)$ in period 2, so that their respective values are

$$E_S[r_1(a_1,s)] + \max_{a_2 \varepsilon G(a_1)} E_S[r_2(a_2,s)],$$

where $a_1 = e_1$ for YNN, $a_1 = m_1$ for NNN.

(e) Flexibility

In chapter 2.3.1, we introduced the following flexibility relation. We said that a_1 is **at least as flexible** as a_1', $a_1 \geq_F a_1'$, if

$$G(a_1, s, \alpha) \supset G(a_1', s, \alpha) \text{ for each } s \varepsilon S, \alpha \varepsilon R_+ . \qquad (3.1.3)$$

When the set of second-period choices is independent of α and s, this relation reduces to $a_1 \geq_F a_1'$ if

$G(a_1) \supset G(a_1')$. (3.1.4)

In most cases, we shall restrict ourselves to this case. Then we shall say that a_1 is **more flexible** than a_1' if $G(a_1) \supsetneq G(a_1')$ and **less flexible** if $G(a_1) \subsetneq G(a_1')$.

This appears to be a natural definition of flexibility, at least if switching costs are not admitted, and it fits in very well with examples in the literature (ARROW/FISHER 1974, HENRY 1974, EPSTEIN 1980, BERNANKE 1983).

However, there is at least one important objection against a flexibility criterion like (3.1.3). In many cases, it only gives a partial ordering of choices according to flexibility. The requirement that $G(a_1) \supset G(a_1')$ is often not fulfilled even when intuition would suggest to call one option more flexible than another one. For instance, though money is generally seen as more "flexible" than most interest-bearing assets, holding money will not be more flexible than holding interest-bearing assets in any reasonably specified model of consumption and portfolio choice, because the interest payments on those assets give certain options that holding money does not.

As another example that is frequently referred to (cf. STIGLER 1939, FUSS/MC FADDEN 1978, MILLS/SCHUMANN 1985, UNGERN-STERNBERG 1990) consider a firm that chooses between one production technology that allows it to do very well in some states of the world but badly in others and another one that allows it to do reasonably well whatever the state of the world is. It seems natural to call the second technology more flexible, but it does not necessarily leave more options open than the other technology.

In these cases, one is tempted to call some actions more flexible than others because they have certain advantages in the way they allow the agent to react to future information. As we shall see repeatedly in the following, this does not necessarily mean that they leave more options open than other choices.

Despite the limitations of the flexibility relation (3.1.4), it will be useful in many cases.

We now move to a more detailed treatment of information structures.

3.1.2 On the Comparison of Information Structures

We saw in chapter 2.2 that the optimal choice in our two-period problem will depend on whether or not additional information is expected.

More generally, one would like to see how it affects the initial choice whether "more" or "less" information is expected.

The purpose of this section is to clarify what "more" or "less" information could mean. We shall start with a few special cases where this is rather obvious and then introduce a partial ordering on the set of information structures that is compatible with the orderings in the special cases.[5]

To begin with, we shall restrict our attention to so-called **noiseless information structures**.

These are characterized by the condition that for every state of the world there exists only one message that is compatible with this message, i.e. for every $s \varepsilon S$, there exists an $h(s) \varepsilon Y$ such that $p(h(s)|s) = 1$, where $p(h(s))$ stands for the probability that the signal $h(s)$ is observed if the state of the world is s.

Therefore, for every message y, there exists a subset $h^{-1}(y)$ of states of the world that are only possible if this message is received.

In other words, the information structure defines a partition of S, as illustrated in figure 3.1.[6]

---

[5] The material in this section is well-known and is included only for the reader's convenience. More detailed accounts can be found in LAFFONT (1989, ch.4) and in MARSCHAK/MIYASAWA (1968).

[6] A partition O_i of a set S is a set of disjoint subsets P_i ($i \varepsilon I$, where I is some index set), the union of which is S, i.e. (i) $P_i \cap P_j = \{\}$ except when i=j, (ii) $\bigcup_{i \varepsilon I} P_i = S$.

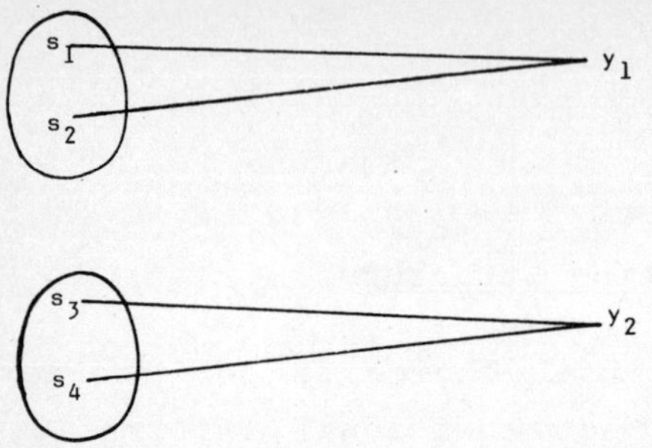

Figure 3.1: A Noiseless Information Structure

In general, of course, the mapping h is not one-to-one. If it is, i.e. if for every $y \varepsilon Y$ there exists only one $s \varepsilon S$ such that s is possible after y has been observed, this is the case of **a perfectly informative information structure**. In this case, the partition of S is a partition into singletons (cf. figure 3.2).

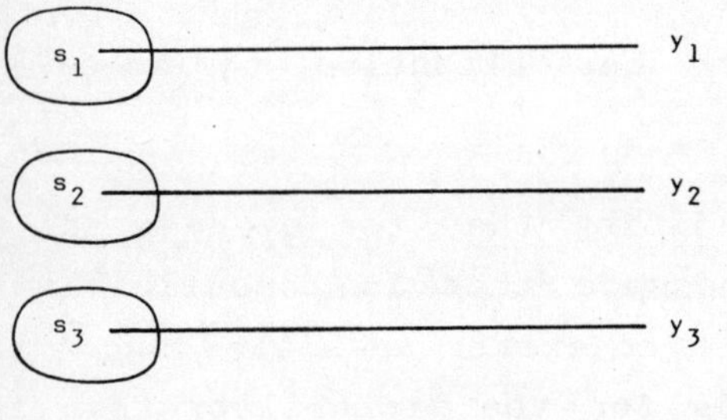

Figure 3.2: Perfect Information

The opposite case is that there exists a $y \varepsilon Y$ such that $h^{-1}(y) = S$. In this case, we have a **non-informative information structure** and the partition of S consists of the single set S (cf. figure 3.3).

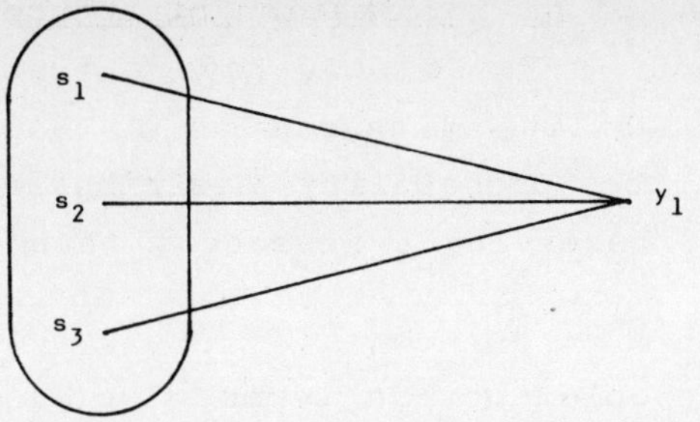

Figure 3.3: Non-informative Information Structure

Now suppose two noiseless information structures (Π,q), (Π',q') are given. It is intuitively convincing to say that one noiseless information structure is more informative than another one if the partition into sets $h^{-1}(y)$ induced by the first information structure is finer[7] than the corresponding partition for the second one.

In figure 3.4, the information structure given by the first partition is more informative than the information structure given by the second partition.

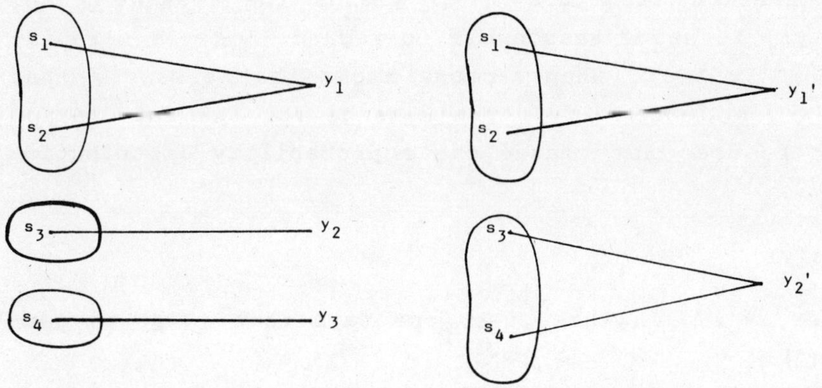

Figure 3.4: Comparison of Noiseless Information Structures

---

[7] Given two partitions O_i and O_i' of any set S, O_i is said to be finer than O_i' if every element P_i of O_i is a subset of an element P_i' of O_i'.

We now consider the more general case of <u>an information structures with noise</u>: instead of a function $h: S \to Y$, we only have a function from S into the space of probability measures on Y. This function assigns to each state s the probability distribution $p(y|s)$ that gives the probability of receiving a message y when s is the state of the world.[8]

As we have formulated our decision problem not in terms of $p(y|s)$ but in terms of the conditional probability $\Pi(s|y)$ that a state of the world s occurs given that a message y is received, it is appropriate to see what the relation between the two concepts is. Simple calculations show that

$$\Pi(s|y) = \frac{\Pi(s \cap y)}{q_y} = \frac{p(y|s)\Pi(s)}{q_y} .$$

For information structures with noise, the concept of "garbling" provides a first idea of what greater informativeness could mean. This concept is explained as follows.

Suppose given two information structures (Π,q), (Π',q') on S. Define $\Pi(s|y,y')$ as the probability of the state of the world s given that information structure (Π,q) yields the message y and (Π',q') yields y'. It seems reasonable to regard (Π,q) as more informative than (Π',q') if, whenever one knows the message y that (Π,q) gives, the knowledge of y', the message for the information structure (Π',q'), does not change one's probability distribution on S, i.e. if

$$\Pi(s|y,y') = \Pi(s|y)$$

for all $s \in S$, $y \in Y$, $y' \in Y$. In this case, one says that (Π,q) is **garbled** into (Π',q').[9]

A special case of garbling is given by noiseless information structures (Π,q), (Π',q') such that (Π,q) induces a finer partition of S than (Π',q'). To see this, consider figure 3.4: if one

---

[8] Of course, a noiseless information structure is a special case of an information structure with a Dirac distribution $p(y|h(y)) = 1$, $p(y|s) = 0$ otherwise.

[9] Alternative but equivalent definitions of garbling can be found in MARSCHAK/MIYASAWA (1968, p. 149).

has received an arbitrary message y from the information structure (Π,q), it is clear which message y' one will get from the information structure (Π',q'). Hence, $\Pi(s|y,y') = \Pi(s|y)$.

Any reasonable ordering of informativeness should be compatible with the above examples. By this we mean that, for noiseless information structures, (Π,q) should be more informative than (Π',q') if it gives a finer partition of S, whereas for non-informative information structures, that (Π,q) should be called more informative than (Π',q') if (Π,q) is garbled into (Π',q'). It has been shown (cf. MARSCHAK/MIYASAWA 1968) that an ordering which satisfies this requirement is the following.

Define $(\Pi,q) \geq (\Pi',q')$ (**(Π,q) is more informative than (Π',q')**) if and only if

$$E_Y \max_{a_2 \varepsilon G(a_1)} E_{S|y} [U(a_1,a_2,s)] \geq E_{Y'} \max_{a_2 \varepsilon G(a_1)} E_{S'|y} [U(a_1,a_2,s)] :=$$

$$\sum_{y \varepsilon Y} q_y' \max_{a_2 \varepsilon G(a_1)} \sum_{s \varepsilon S} \Pi'(s|y) U(a_1,a_2,s) \qquad (3.1.5)$$

for all $a_1 \varepsilon A_1$ and U for which the expressions in (3.1.5) exist.[10]

The meaning of this relation is that any agent with payoff function U is better off with an information structure (Π,q) than with an information structure (Π',q'), no matter what his first-period choice was.

In order to use this concept of informativeness, it is often useful to apply the following result (cf. MARSCHAK/MIYASAWA 1968, p. 164 for a proof):

Let m denote the cardinality of the set S, and let Π_y denote the vector of probabilities $(\Pi(s^1|y),\dots,\Pi(s^m|y))$. This an element of Σ^{m-1}, the unit simplex in Σ^{m-1}, because the probabilities sum up to one.

---

[10] The relationship between the concepts "greater informativeness" and "greater risk" has been investigated by EICHHORN/VOGT (1990).

<u>Theorem 3.1:</u> (Π, q) is more informative than (Π', q') if and only if

$$\sum_{y \varepsilon Y} q_y \, k(\Pi_y) \geq \sum_{y \varepsilon Y} q_y' k(\Pi_y')$$

for any convex function k on Σ^{m-1}, the unit simplex in R^m, where m is the cardinality of S.

To avoid misunderstandings, a few cautionary remarks on the interpretation of the informativeness relation are called for. Greater informativeness is sometimes interpreted as greater uncertainty about the agent's environment. This should not be confused with greater risk in the sense of ROTHSCHILD/STIGLITZ (1970) because, by assumption, we only compare information structures such that the prior probability distributions $\Pi(s)$ and $\Pi'(s)$ are identical so that there is no difference with respect to risk. It is only the "difference between present and expected future knowledge" that is considered. For a more informative information structure, "more" uncertainty is resolved before the second period. Hence, if greater informativeness is identified with greater uncertainty, this can only be the uncertainty in period 1 <u>relative</u> to the uncertainty in period 2.

This concludes our presentation of the concepts from information theory that we shall use in the following and, more generally, the description of the criteria according to which we distinguish between different decision problems and different outcomes. We now set out to answer the question how the outcomes depend on the structure of the problem.

We start with the impact of the choice set in section 3.2; section 3.3 will deal with the impact of the choice criterion and section 3.4 with the impact of the information structure.

3.2 The Influence of the Choice Set

In this section, we state two simple results about the influence of the structure of the choice set, more specifically the degree of irreversibility, on the outcome.

According to the definition in section 3.1.1, we say that a problem DP is at least as irreversible as another problem DP' if for the choice sets $G(a_1)$ for DP and $G'(a_1)$ for DP', $G(a_1) \subset G'(a_1)$ for every $a_1 \varepsilon A_1$, but apart from that the problems are identical. With this terminology, we can generalize proposition 2.1.

Proposition 3.1: (a) If DP is at least at irreversible as DP', the value $BV(b_1')$ of the optimal initial choice for DP' is never smaller than the corresponding value $BV(b_1)$ for DP.
(b) $BV(b_1')$ may, but need not be greater than $BV(b_1)$.

Proof: (a) By definition,

$$BV(b_1) = \max_{a_1 \varepsilon A_1} E_Y \max_{a_2 \varepsilon G(a_1)} E_{S|y} [U(a_1, a_2, s)],$$

$$BV(b_1') = \max_{a_1 \varepsilon A_1} E_Y \max_{a_2 \varepsilon G'(a_1)} E_{S|y} [U(a_1, a_2, s)].$$

As $G(a_1) \subset G'(a_1)$ for all a_1, we have

$$\max_{a_2 \varepsilon G(a_1)} E_{S|y} [U(a_1, a_2, s)] \leq \max_{a_2 \varepsilon G'(a_1)} E_{S|y} [U(a_1, a_2, s)]$$

for all $y \varepsilon Y$, $a_1 \varepsilon A_1$ and hence

$$BV(b_1) = \max_{a_1 \varepsilon A_1} E_Y \max_{a_2 \varepsilon G(a_1)} E_{S|y} [U(a_1, a_2, s)] \leq$$

$$\max_{a_1 \varepsilon A_1} E_Y \max_{a_2 \varepsilon G'(a_1)} E_{S|y} [U(a_1, a_2, s)] = BV(b_1').$$

(b) cf. proposition 2.1(b).

Apart from a tendency to increase the value of the optimal path, the effect of decreasing the irreversibility of the problem is that it no longer matters whether the agent is a Bayesian, an expected utility maximizer or a myopic agent. This is expressed formally in the following generalization of proposition 2.2.

<u>Proposition 3.2:</u> If $U(a_1, a_2, s) = r_1(a_1, s)+[r_2(a_2, s)-c(a_1, a_2, s)]$ and the problem is totally reversible, it follows that $b_1=e_1=m_1$.

<u>Proof:</u> With total reversibility, $V(a_1;\Pi,q)=V(a_1';\Pi,q)$ for arbitrary $a_1, a_1' \varepsilon A_1$. This statement holds because total reversibility implies $G(a_1)=A_2=G(a_1')$ and hence

$$V(a_1;\Pi,q) = E_Y \max_{a_2 \varepsilon G(a_1)} E_{S|Y}[r_2(a_2, s)-c(a_1, a_2, s)] =$$

$$E_Y \max_{a_2 \varepsilon G(a_1')} E_{S|Y}[r_2(a_2, s)-c(a_1, a_2, s)] = V(a_1';\Pi,q).$$

Hence, $BV(a_1) = E_S[r_1(a_1, s)]+V(a_1;\Pi,q)$ is maximal if and only if $E_S[r_1(a_1, s)]$ is maximal, i.e. a_1 is myopic. This shows $b_1=m_1$. Specializing to the non-informative case $(\Pi,q)=(\Pi_*, q_*)$ gives $e_1=m_1$.

In other words, if the decision problem is perfectly flexible, the decision criterion has <u>no</u> impact on the optimal first-period choice. For irreversible decision problems, this is not true. We now set out to investigate in greater generality the impact of alternative choice criteria.

3.3 The Impact of the Decision Criterion

Recall from section 3.1.1 that we distinguish the five strategies YYY, YYN, YNN, NYN, NNN.

In this section, we compare the five strategies with respect to their values and the properties of the initial choice.

As the initial choices are m_1 for NNN and NYN, e_1 for YYN and YNN, and b_1 for YYY (cf. 3.1.1), there are only three different initial choices to compare. As the value of a path also depends on the second-period choice, however, we have to consider all five strategies when we want to compare these values.

3.3.1 Comparison of Bayesian Values

We start by recalling the values of the strategies that were given in section 3.1.1. Here and in the following, we shall only consider decision problems of type (1). Also, we shall restrict our attention to problems where the second-period choice set is independent of the state of the world, i.e. it can be written as $G(a_1)$ instead of $G(a_1,s)$. We get the following values:

$$BV(YYY) = E_s[r_1(b_1,s)] + E_Y \max_{a_2 \varepsilon G(b_1)} E_{s|y}[r_2(a_2,s)],$$

$$BV(YYN) = E_s[r_1(e_1,s)] + E_Y \max_{a_2 \varepsilon G(e_1)} E_{s|y}[r_2(a_2,s)],$$

$$BV(YNN) = E_s[r_1(e_1,s)] + \max_{a_2 \varepsilon G(e_1)} E_s[r_2(a_2,s)],$$

$$BV(NYN) = E_s[r_1(m_1,s)] + E_Y \max_{a_2 \varepsilon G(m_1)} E_{s|y}[r_2(a_2,s)],$$

$$BV(NNN) = E_s[r_1(m_1,s)] + \max_{a_2 \varepsilon G(m_1)} E_s[r_2(a_2,s)].$$

The values of the optimal paths for the three strategies where the agent uses information ex post are identical to the values of the three different optimal initial choices:

$$BV(YYY) = BV(b_1),\ BV(YYN)=BV(e_1),\ BV(NYN)=BV(m_1).$$

We shall show that the five values can be ordered as follows.

Proposition 3.3: (a) $BV(YYN) \geq BV(YNN)$; (b) $BV(NYN) \geq BV(NNN)$; (c) $BV(YYY) \geq BV(YYN)$; (d) $BV(YYY) \geq BV(NYN)$; (e) $BV(YNN) \geq BV(NNN)$.

This proposition is summarized in figure 3.5.

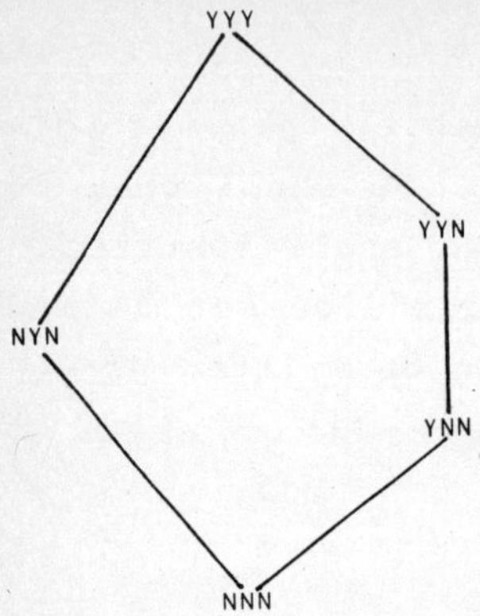

Figure 3.5: Comparison of the Values of Different Strategies

In parts (a) and (b) of the proof, we shall use a simple identity.

Suppose, as in chapter 2, that the maximum of $E_S[r_2(a_2,s)]$ over $G(a_1)$ is attained for a_2^+.

<u>Lemma:</u> $E_Y E_{S|y}[r_2(a_2^+,s)] = \max_{a_2 \varepsilon G(a_1)} E_S[r_2(a_2,s)]$ for each $a_1 \varepsilon A_1$.

<u>Proof:</u> By definition,

$$E_Y E_{S|y}[r_2(a_2^+,s)] = \sum_{y \varepsilon Y} q_y \left[\sum_{s \varepsilon S} \Pi(s|y) r_2(a_2^+,s)\right] =$$

$$\sum_{s \varepsilon S} r_2(a_2^+,s)\left[\sum_{y \varepsilon Y} q_y \Pi(s|y)\right].$$

Because $\Pi(s) = \sum_{y \varepsilon Y} q_y \Pi(s|y)$, the last expression is equal to

$$\sum_{s \varepsilon S} r_2(a_2^+,s)\Pi(s) = \max_{a_2 \varepsilon G(a_1)} E_S[r_2(a_2,s)].$$

We can now prove proposition 3.3.

<u>Proof of proposition 3.3:</u>

By the lemma,

$$BV(YNN) = E_S[r_1(e_1,s)] + E_Y E_{S|y}[r_2(e_2^+,s)],$$

where e_2^+ is the value where the maximum of $E_S[r_2(a_2,s)]$ over $G(e_1)$ is attained. As

$$BV(YYN) = E_S[r_1(e_1,s)] + E_Y \max_{a_2 \varepsilon G(e_1)} E_{S|y}[r_2(a_2,s)],$$

(a) follows because

$$\max_{a_2 \varepsilon G(a_1)} E_{S|y} [r_2(a_2,s)] \geq E_{S|y}[r_2(a_2',s)] \qquad (3.3.1)$$

for each $a_1 \varepsilon A_1$, $a_2' \varepsilon A_2$.

Applying the lemma once again, we see that

$$BV(NNN) = E_S[r_1(m_1,s)] + E_Y E_{S|y}[r_2(m_2^+,s)],$$

where m_2^+ is the value where the maximum of $E_S[r_2(a_2,s)]$ over $G(m_1)$ is attained. Because

$$BV(NYN) = E_S[r_1(m_1,s)] + E_Y \max_{a_2 \varepsilon G(m_1)} E_{S|y}[r_2(a_2,s)],$$

we obtain (b) from (3.3.1).

(c) and (d) follow immediately from the fact that b_1 maximizes

$$\{E_S[r_1(a_1,s)] + E_Y \max_{a_2 \varepsilon G(a_1)} E_{S|y} [r_2(a_2,s)]\} \text{ over } A_1.$$

Finally, (e) follows from

$$BV(YNN) = E_S[r_1(e_1,s)] + \max_{a_2 \varepsilon G(e_1)} E_S[r_2(a_2,s)] =$$

$$\max_{a_1 \varepsilon A_1} [E_S[r_1(a_1,s)] + \max_{a_2 \varepsilon G(a_1)} E_S[r_2(a_2,s)]] \geq$$

$$E_S[r_1(m_1,s)] + \max_{a_2 \varepsilon G(m_1)} E_S[r_2(a_2,s)] = BV(NNN).$$

The proposition does not contain any general relation between BV(NYN) and BV(YYN) or between BV(NYN) and BV(YNN). In fact, one can show that no such relation exists. From the vantage point of the Bayesian decision maker, the intertemporal criteria YYN and

YNN are not necessarily preferable to the myopic criterion NYN (and vice versa).

At first sight, this may be surprising: one may expect an inter-temporal optimizer who uses information ex post, but not ex ante, to be better off than a myopic agent who uses information ex post, but not ex ante. After all, unlike the myopic agent the inter-temporal optimizer considers the effects of his decisions on the second period, which appears to be better than ignoring them completely. However, he does this in an inadequate manner because he ignores the possibility of receiving information in the future. Of course, the myopic agent ignores this possibility as well, so that there is no reason that NYN should <u>systematically</u> lead to a higher payoff than YYN. To see in what kind of situations it is possible that BV(YYN) < BV(NYN), we use the above lemma to prove another proposition which will be valuable in the sequel.

It shows that the difference between the Value a Bayesian and a non-Bayesian decision maker would assign to an initial choice is equal to the expected value of information conditional upon a_1, which, according to (2.2.11), is defined as

$$VI(a_1) = E_Y\{\max_{a_2 \varepsilon G(a_1)} [E_{S|y}[r_2(a_2,s)]] - E_{S|y}[r_2(a_2^+,s)]\} .$$

<u>Proposition 3.4:</u> $BV(a_1;\Pi,q) = E_S[r_1(a_1,s)]+V(a_1,\Pi_*,q_*)+VI(a_1)$, where $V(a_1;\Pi_*,q_*) = \max_{a_2 \varepsilon G(a_1)} E_S[r_2(a_2,s)]$ stands for the expected second-period value of a_1 when future information is not taken into consideration.

<u>Proof:</u> By definition,

$$BV(a_1;\Pi,q) = E_S[r_1(a_1,s)]+E_Y \max_{a_2 \varepsilon G(a_1)} E_{S|y}[r_2(a_2,s)].$$

Therefore, we have to show that

$$E_Y \max_{a_2 \varepsilon G(a_1)} E_{S|y}[r_2(a_2,s)] = \max_{a_2 \varepsilon G(a_1)} E_S[r_2(a_2,s)]+VI(a_1). \qquad (3.3.2)$$

By definition,

$$VI(a_1) = E_Y\{\max_{a_2 \varepsilon G(a_1)} [E_{S|y}[r_2(a_2,s)]] - E_{S|y}[r_2(a_2^+,s)]\} =$$

$$E_Y\{\max_{a_2 \varepsilon G(a_1)} E_{S|y}[r_2(a_2,s)]\} - E_Y E_{S|y}[r_2(a_2^+,s)].$$

Applying the lemma to the last term, we find that

$$VI(a_1) = E_Y \max_{a_2 \varepsilon G(a_1)} [E_{S|y}[r_2(a_2,s)]] - \max_{a_2 \varepsilon G(a_1)} E_S[r_2(a_2,s)],$$

as required for (3.3.2) to hold.

From the proposition and the fact that the YNN-agent maximizes $E_S[r_1(a_1,s)]+V(a_1;\Pi_*,q_*)$, it is clear in what kind of situations $BV(NYN)=BV(m_1)$ can be greater than $BV(YYN)=BV(e_1)$. $VI(m_1)$ has to be significantly greater than $VI(e_1)$ in order to offset the difference between $E_S[r_1(e_1,s)] + V(e_1;\Pi_*,q_*)$ and $E_S[r_1(m_1,s)] + V(m_1;\Pi_*,q_*)$. Such an example can easily be provided.

<u>Example 1</u>

Suppose $A_1=\{0,1,2\}$, $A_2=\{0,1,2\}$ and $G=\{(0,0),(0,1),(1,2),(2,2)\}$; cf. figure 3.6.

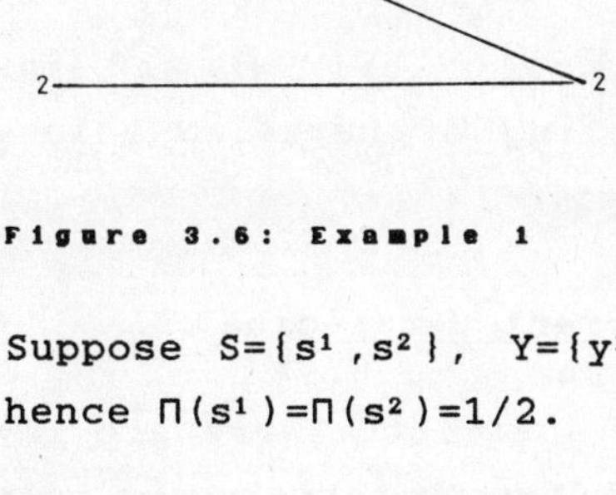

Figure 3.6: Example 1

Suppose $S=\{s^1,s^2\}$, $Y=\{y^1,y^2\}$, $\Pi(s^1|y^1)=\Pi(s^2|y^2)=1$, $q_{y1}=q_{y2}=1/2$ and hence $\Pi(s^1)=\Pi(s^2)=1/2$.

Suppose the payoffs are given by

$E_s[r_1(0,s)]=5$, $r_2(0,s^1)=10$, $r_2(0,s^2)=0$,
$E_s[r_1(1,s)]=3$, $r_2(1,s^1)=0$, $r_2(1,s^2)=10$,
$E_s[r_1(2,s)]=1$, $r_2(2,s^1)=20$, $r_2(2,s^2)=0$.

Then

$E_s[r_1(0,s)]+V(0;\Pi_*,q_*)=10$,
$E_s[r_1(1,s)]+V(1;\Pi_*,q_*)=13$,
$E_s[r_1(2,s)]+V(2;\Pi_*,q_*)=11$,

while $BV(0;\Pi,q)=15$, $BV(1;\Pi,q)=13$, $BV(2;\Pi,q)=11$.

Hence, choosing myopically ($m_1=0$) leads to a higher value than choosing the intertemporally optimal action without learning ($e_1=1$). The reason is, as argued before, the fact that the value of information, given 0, is considerably higher than the corresponding value for 1. For 1, the value of information is zero, because 1 is irreversible. By proposition 3.4, however, the value of information for the initial choice 0 is $BV(0;\Pi,q)-E_s[r_1(0,s)]-V(0;\Pi_*,q_*) = 5$.

Having shown that BV(NYN) may be greater than BV(YYN), it follows immediately from BV(YYN) ≥ BV(YNN) (proposition 3.3(a)) that in this example BV(NYN) > BV(YNN).

On the other hand, in proposition 2.2(b) we saw that the myopic path need not be intertemporally optimal in the case of perfect certainty. Hence, BV(NYN)>BV(YYN). By proposition 3.3(a), BV(YNN) ≤ BV(YYN) and hence, in this example, BV(NYN) < BV(YYN).

Summing up, we have examples for BV(NYN) >(<) BY(YYN) and for BV(NYN) >(<) BV(YNN). Therefore, the ordering of Bayesian values given in figure 3.5 cannot be refined.

3.3.2 Conditions for the Equality of Different Strategies

None of the inequalities of proposition 3 is strict. There are important examples where the values of different strategies are identical, i.e. where there is no difference between myopic and intertemporal optimization with or without taking information into account. We shall confine ourselves to comparing the values of b_1 and e_1 (which are equal to BV(YYY) and BV(YYN), respectively).

By proposition 3.4,

$BV(b_1) = E_s[r_1(b_1,s)] + V(b_1;\Pi_*,q_*) + VI(b_1)$,
$BV(e_1) = E_s[r_1(e_1,s)] + V(e_1;\Pi_*,q_*) + VI(e_1)$.

Therefore,

$$BV(b_1)-BV(e_1) = E_s[r_1(b_1,s)]+V(b_1;\Pi_*,q_*)-E_s[r_1(e_1,s)]- V(e_1;\Pi_*,q_*)+VI(b_1)-VI(e_1). \quad (3.3.3)$$

By definition of e_1 as the maximum $E_s[r_1(a_1,s)]+V(a_1;\Pi_*,q_*)$, we get

$$E_s[r_1(b_1,s)]-E_s[r_1(e_1,s)]+V(b_1;\Pi_*,q_*)-V(e_1;\Pi_*,q_*)\leq 0. \quad (3.3.4)$$

From $BV(b_1)-BV(e_1)\geq 0$, (3.3.3) and (3.3.4), it follows that $VI(b_1)-VI(e_1)\geq 0$.

When $BV(e_1)$ and $BV(b_1)$ are not identical, b_1 maximizes BV while e_1 does not, so that

$$BV(b_1)-BV(e_1) = E_s[r_1(b_1,s)]-E_s[r_1(e_1,s)]+V(b_1;\Pi_*,q_*)-V(e_1;\Pi_*,q_*)+ VI(b_1)-VI(e_1) > 0. \quad (3.3.5)$$

When $VI(b_1)=VI(e_1)$, (3.3.5) can be rewritten as

$$E_s[r_1(b_1,s)]-E_s[r_1(e_1,s)]+V(b_1;\Pi_*,q_*)-V(e_1,\Pi_*,q_*) > 0,$$

contradicting (3.3.4). It follows that $VI(b_1)-VI(e_1)=0$ is a sufficient condition for $BV(e_1)$ and $BV(b_1)$ to be identical. From $VI(b_1)-VI(e_1)\geq 0$ and $VI(e_1)\geq 0$, it therefore follows that $BV(b_1) = BV(e_1)$ if $VI(b_1)=0$.

As

$$VI(b_1)=E_Y\{\max_{a_2\in G(b_1)} E_{s|y}[r_2(a_2,s)]-E_{s|y}[r_2(a_2^+,s)]\},$$

$VI(b_1)=0$ certainly holds if for all $y \varepsilon Y$ with $q_y \geq 0$,

$$\max_{a_2 \varepsilon G(b_1)} E_{s|y}[r_2(a_2,s)] = E_{s|y}[r_2(a_2^+,s)],$$

i.e. if the maximum of $E_s[r_2(a_2,s)]$ and $E_{s|y}[r_2(a_2,s)]$ are attained at the same value.

This is certainly true if one of the following two conditions holds.

(a) the problem is totally irreversible, i.e. $G(a_1)$ contains only one element,

(b) the information service is non-informative, i.e. $\Pi(s|y) = \Pi(s)$ for every $y \varepsilon Y$.

In these two extreme cases, the value of the optimal initial decision is therefore independent of the choice criterion that is used.

Before proceeding, we note that from (3.3.5) we can derive an upper bound for $BV(b_1)-BV(e_1)$, namely the value of information conditional on b_1, $VI(b_1)$. This is so because the sum of the first four terms on the right hand side of (3.3.5) is non-positive and $VI(e_1)$ is non-negative.

3.3.3 Comparison of the Flexibility of Initial Choices

We now compare different strategies with respect to the extent to which they give rise to irreversible first-period decisions. As we are only concerned with first-period choices, we need only compare b_1, e_1 and m_1. The seminal articles in this area were ARROW/FISHER (1974) and HENRY (1974), cf. section 2.2.1. In these papers, it was shown that for special decision problems, b_1 is always at least as flexible as e_1 and, in many cases, more flexible. To recall, they considered the following special cases.

HENRY (1974) took $A_1=A_2=\{0,1\}$, $G=\{(0,0),(0,1),(1,1)\}$. In this case, 0 is perfectly flexible and 1 is totally irreversible. He showed that if b_1 is irreversible, so is e_1. He also provided examples where b_1 is perfectly flexible while e_1 is not.

ARROW/FISHER (1974) took $A_1=A_2=A=[0,1]$ and $G(a_1)=\{a_2 \varepsilon A | a_2 \geq a_1\}$; it is understood that a_t stands for the proportion of a stock of a natural resource that has been depleted in periods up to and including t. Unlike HENRY, they had to restrict their attention to linear payoff functions to obtain the result that b_1 is at least as flexible as e_1.

One may ask to which extent these results depend on the special models investigated by ARROW/FISHER (1974) and HENRY (1974), in other words: If b_1 and e_1 are comparable with respect to flexibility, is it always true that b_1 is at least as flexible as e_1?

The answer is not as obvious as it may seem at first sight. For the time being, we only note that the question is a special case of one of the other problems on our list, namely the comparison of the first-period choices with respect to different information structures.

To see this, note that, for a given information structure (Π,q), e_1, though not the solution of

$$\max_{a_1 \varepsilon A_1} [E_s[r_1(a_1,s)]+V(a_1,\Pi,q)],$$

is the solution of

$$\max_{a_1 \varepsilon A_1} [E_s[r_1(a_1,s)]+V(a_1;\Pi_*,q_*)],$$ where (Π_*,q_*) stands for the

non-informative information structure given by $\Pi_*(s|y)=\Pi(s)$, $q_{y*}=q_y$, for $s \varepsilon S, y \varepsilon Y$.

As (Π,q) is more informative than (Π_*,q_*), the question whether b_1 is more flexible than e_1 is therefore a special case of the question whether a more informative information structure will necessarily lead to a more flexible first-period choice for the Bayesian decision maker. This more general question will be treated in section 3.4.

We now turn to a simpler issue, namely to the comparison of the flexibility of initial choices for myopic and non-myopic decision rules. Intuitively, one would expect myopic decision rules to favour irreversible developments: if one does not care about the future, there is no reason to refrain from irreversible actions.

This turns out to be unambiguously true, as the following proposition shows.

<u>Proposition 3.5:</u> Suppose that the elements b_1 and m_1 (e_1 and m_1) of A_1 are comparable with respect to flexibility.
(a) Then b_1 (e_1) is at least as flexible as m_1.
(b) b_1 (e_1) may be more flexible than m_1.

<u>Proof</u>: (a) <u>b_1 is at least as flexible as m_1</u>

By definition of b_1,

$$E_s[r_1(b_1,s)]+V(b_1;\Pi,q) \geq E_s[r_1(m_1,s)]+V(m_1;\Pi,q). \tag{3.3.6}$$

Suppose m_1 is at least as flexible as b_1, so that

$$V(m_1;\Pi,q) = E_Y \max_{a_2 \varepsilon G(m_1)} E_{s|y}[r_2(a_2,s)] \geq$$

$$E_Y \max_{a_2 \varepsilon G(b_1)} E_{s|y}[r_2(a_2,s)] = V(b_1;\Pi,q). \tag{3.3.7}$$

(3.3.6) and (3.3.7) imply

$$E_s[r_1(b_1,s)] \geq E_s[r_1(m_1,s)]. \tag{3.3.8}$$

Without loss of generality we may assume that the optimal and the myopic choice do not coincide, because if they do the result is trivially true.

Hence, from the definition of m_1, $E_s[r_1(m_1,s)] > E_s[r_1(b_1,s)]$, contradicting (3.3.8).

<u>e_1 is at least as flexible as b_1:</u>

This is proved by substituting $V(b_1,\Pi_*,q_*)$ for $V(b_1;\Pi,q)$ and $V(m_1;\Pi_*,q_*)$ for $V(m_1;\Pi,q)$ in the above argument.

(b) We provide an example for the case of certainty, where of course $e_1=b_1$. In this example m_1 is irreversible, but b_1 is not.

Suppose that $A_1=A_2=\{0,1\}$, $G=\{(0,0);(0,1);(1,1)\}$ and that payoffs are given by

$r_1(0)=0,\quad r_2(0)=3,$
$r_1(1)=2,\quad r_2(1)=0.$

Clearly, $b_1=e_1=0$, while $m_1=1$, which is irreversible. This finishes the proof.

There is a class of problems for which the "comparability" condition for $b_1(e_1)$ and m_1 is always fulfilled, namely those problems for which $\geq_F$ defines a complete relation on A_1, i.e. for two <u>arbitrary</u> elements a_i, a_j of A_1, either $a_i \geq_F a_j$ or $a_j \geq_F a_i$. Hence, we obtain the following corollary.

<u>Corollary:</u> Suppose $\geq_F$ defines a complete relation on A_1. Then the intertemporally optimal choice b_1 is at least as flexible as the myopic choice m_1.

<u>3.4 The Impact of the Information Structure</u>

In section 3.3.3, we asked how e_1 differs from b_1, i.e. how the expectation of some future information as opposed to none changes the optimal first-period decision and the value of the optimal choice.

In this section, we want to shed more light on this problem by asking more generally:

How does an increase in the informativeness of the information structure influence the outcome of the decision problem?

The difference in values between any choice a_1 with learning and without learning is precisely the conditional value of information, $VI(a_1)$, cf. proposition 3.4. As this quantity is not negative, <u>every</u> first-period choice benefits from the arrival of information (or does not lose, to be precise). In particular, the value $BV(b_1)$ of the optimal position with information (ex ante and ex post) is always at least as high as the value of the optimal position without information. Even though we recognized an overall increase in the value of each position from the arrival of information, we said nothing about the relative increases for different positions. We shall see that such relative effects have to be investigated to find an answer to the central question that had to remain open in section 3.3: will a decision that takes into account the fact that more information will be available tomorrow necessarily be at least as flexible as a decision that ignores future information? We pointed out that this issue can be approached more generally, namely by asking whether or not a more informative information structure necessarily leads to a more flexible first-period choice.

Answers to this more general question were provided by EPSTEIN (1980) and JONES/OSTROY (1984). Essentially, their results say that the impact of a more informative information structure is ambiguous, but they give conditions under which more information benefits the more flexible first-period choice. In the following section, we shall provide a relatively simple presentation of their results, relate them to earlier findings in the literature and discuss their significance.

Most of the time, we shall follow the line of argument of JONES/OSTROY (1984). However, we remind the reader that their definition of flexibility is slightly different from ours (cf. section 2.3.1). Also, sections 3.4.1 and 3.4.5 are not taken from JONES/OSTROY (1984) or any other source: 3.4.1 adds examples that help to understand the problem, and 3.4.5 contains a critical evaluation of the statement that greater uncertainty implies greater flexibility, including an alternative version of this statement.

3.4.1 A Counterexample

We have noted in section 3.3.3 that for many simple models, a more informative information structure will always lead to the choice of more flexible positions (cf. also ARROW/FISHER 1974, HENRY 1974, BERNANKE 1983 and some of the examples by EPSTEIN 1980). This might seem to be a plausible result even in more general situations: if an agent expects more information, this would appear to make a more flexible choice more likely. After all, more flexible positions allow for a better exploitation of the incoming information.

When there are only perfectly flexible and totally irreversible choices as in model by HENRY (1974) and, essentially, also in the ARROW/FISHER-model[11], this argument is correct. The Bayesian value of the irreversible element is unaffected by the arrival of additional information (as there is no way to react to it), while the value of the perfectly flexible element cannot fall and, in many cases, will actually rise. Hence the tendency towards greater flexibility when there is additional information.

When, however, the agent can choose between many different non-irreversible elements, one has to argue more carefully. It is perfectly possible that two such elements, where one is more flexible than the other, both benefit from the additional information. In fact, it is even possible that the less flexible element benefits more than the more flexible element. In particular, it may happen that the optimal choice in the case of the more informative information structure is less flexible than in the less informative case.

We now proceed to construct such an example.

---

[11] ARROW/FISHER (1974) take $A = [0,1]$, where 0 is perfectly flexible, 1 is totally irreversible and $a \geq_F a' \iff a \leq a'$. As they use a linear objective function, the optimal choice is either 0 or 1, so that, effectively, choice is between a totally irreversible element (1) and a perfectly flexible element (0).

Example 1

Suppose $A_1 = \{0,1,2\}$, $A_2 = \{0,1,2\}$ and G is given as in figure 3.7; i.e. $G=\{(0,0),(1,0),(1,1),(2,0),(2,1),(2,2)\}$.

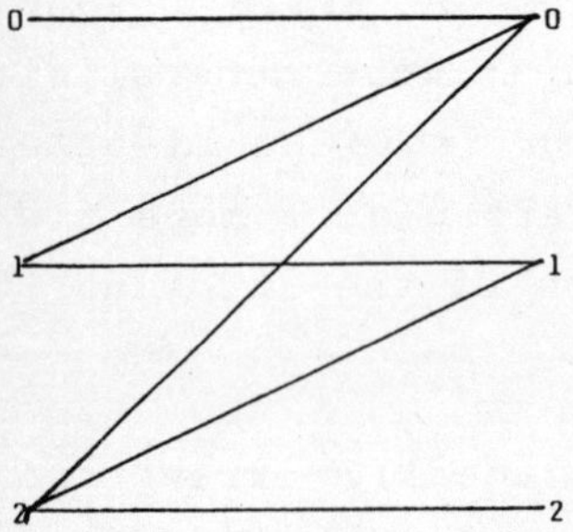

Figure 3.7: A Counterexample

Let $S = \{s^1, s^2\}$, $Y = \{y^1, y^2\}$.

Suppose two information structures (Π, q) and (Π_*, q_*) are given by

(i) $\Pi(s^1) = \Pi(s^2) = 1/2;\ q_{y1} = q_{y2} = 1/2$

$\Pi(s^1|y^1) = \Pi(s^2|y^2) = 1;\ \Pi(s^2|y^1) = \Pi(s^1|y^2) = 0.$

(ii) $\Pi_*(s^1) = \Pi_*(s^2) = 1/2;\ q_{y1*} = q_{y2*} = 1/2$

$\Pi_*(s^1|y^1) = \Pi_*(s^1|y^2) = \Pi_*(s^2|y^1) = \Pi_*(s^2|y^2) = 1/2.$

The second information structure is non-informative, whereas the first conveys perfect information.

Suppose the payoffs are given by

$E_s[r_1(0,s)] = 2 \quad r_2(0,s^1) = 0 \quad r_2(0,s^2) = 10$

$E_s[r_1(1,s)] = 2 \quad r_2(1,s^1) = 8 \quad r_2(1,s^2) = 3$

$E_s[r_1(2,s)] = 1 \quad r_2(2,s^1) = 4 \quad r_2(2,s^2) = 10.$

Then

$BV(0;\Pi_*,q_*) = E_s[r_1(0,s)] + V(0;\Pi_*,q_*) = 2+5 = 7$

$BV(1;\Pi_*,q_*) = E_s[r_1(1,s)] + V(1;\Pi_*,q_*) = 2+5,5 = 7,5$

$BV(2;\Pi_*,q_*) = E_s[r_1(2,s)] + V(2;\Pi_*,q_*) = 1+7 = 8.$

On the other hand,

On the other hand,

$BV(0;\Pi,q) = E_s[r_1(0,s)]+V(0,\Pi,q) = 2+5 =7$

$BV(1;\Pi,q) = E_s[r_1(1,s)]+V(1,\Pi,q) = 2+9 = 11$

$BV(2;\Pi,q) = E_s[r_1(2,s)]+V(2,\Pi,q) = 1+9 = 10,$

so that 1 is the optimal choice for the more informative information structure even though it is less flexible than 2, the choice for the non-informative case.

In other words, the result that increased uncertainty implies increased demand for flexibility is not unambiguously true in the framework of our model.

The essential point in the example is that the two positions that are not totally irreversible both benefit from the increase in informativeness, and 1 does so to a greater extent than the perfectly flexible position 2: While

$BV(2;\Pi,q) - BV(2;\Pi_*,q_*) = 10-8 =2,$

$BV(1;\Pi,q) - BV(1;\Pi_*,q_*) = 11-7,5 = 3,5;$ hence,

$$BV(2,\Pi,q) - BV(2;\Pi_*,q_*) < BV(1,\Pi,q) - BV(1;\Pi_*,q_*). \qquad (3.4.1)$$

The validity of inequalities of the type of (3.4.1) is crucial for the question whether a more flexible position is chosen when information is taken into account.

3.4.2 Relative Gains from Information for Different Positions

More generally, suppose given two decision problems DP and DP' that differ only in information structures (Π,q), (Π',q'). Suppose that $(\Pi,q) \geq (\Pi',q')$, $a_1 \varepsilon A_1$.

If we can show that $a_1 \geq_F a_1'$ implies

$$BV(a_1;\Pi,q) - BV(a_1;\Pi',q') \geq BV(a_1';\Pi,q) - BV(a_1';\Pi',q'), \qquad (3.4.2)$$

this will prove that the increase in informativeness never leads to a less flexible position.

As we have seen in section 3.4.1 above, however, there are examples where inequality (3.4.2) does not hold for arbitrary $a_1 \geq_F a_1'$,

$(\Pi,q) \geq_F (\Pi',q')$. In example 1 in section 3.4.1, the optimal choice 2 for the problem with no additional second-period information (information structure Π_*, q_*) was more flexible than the choice 1 for the problem with perfect second-period information. This was only possible because

$$BV(1;\Pi,q) - BV(1;\Pi_*,q_*) = 3,5 > 2 = BV(2;\Pi,q) - BV(2;\Pi_*,q_*),$$

i.e. the gains from the additional information were greater for 2 than for 1. Having seen that the desired relation between information structure and flexibility of first-period choice is not generally valid, one may ask whether reasonable conditions can be found for such a relation to hold.

3.4.3 The JONES/OSTROY-Theorem

First of all, we give the desired relation a name (cf. JONES/ OSTROY 1984, p.19).

We say that **$\geq$ induces an order-preserving relation on $\geq_F$** whenever the following statement holds.

Suppose given information structures (Π,q), (Π',q') such that, whenever two elements a_1, a_1' of A_1 can be compared with respect to flexibility, (3.4.3) and (3.4.4) imply (3.4.5) :

a_1 is optimal for (Π,q) and a_1' is optimal for (Π',q'); (3.4.3)

a_1 is not optimal for (Π',q') or a_1' is not optimal for (Π,q). (3.4.4)

If $(\Pi,q) \geq (\Pi',q')$, then $a_1 \geq_F a_1'$. (3.4.5)

In other words, if the optimal choices for a more informative and a less informative information structure can be compared with respect to flexibility and neither of the two is optimal in both cases, the optimal choice for the more informative structure will be the more flexible one.

A sufficient condition for such a relation to hold is given by the following lemma, which is proved in the appendix (it is similar to proposition 0 in JONES/OSTROY 1984).

Lemma: If for each $a_1, a_1' \varepsilon A_1$ such that $a_1 \geq_F a_1'$, $v(a_1,\Pi)-v(a_1',\Pi) =$

$$\max_{a_2 \varepsilon G(a_1)} \sum_{s \varepsilon S} \Pi(s) r_2(a_2,s) - \max_{a_2 \varepsilon G(a_1')} \sum_{s \varepsilon S} \Pi(s) r_2(a_2,s)$$

is convex on Σ^{m-1}, the unit simplex in R^m, as a function of Π, $\geq$ induces an order-preserving relation on $\geq_F$.

Proof: cf. appendix.

To apply this lemma, we shall give a sufficient condition to guarantee the convexity of $v(a_1,\Pi) - v(a_1',\Pi)$.

Assumption 3.1: For every $(a_1^*, a_2^*) \varepsilon A_1 x A_2$ either

$$\max_{a_2 \varepsilon G(a_1^*)} \sum_{s \varepsilon S} \Pi(s) r_2(a_2,s) \geq \sum_{s \varepsilon S} \Pi(s) r_2(a_2^*,s), \qquad \text{(i)}$$

or there exists a $c_2 \varepsilon G(a_1^*)$, which is independent of Π, such that

$$\max_{a_2 \varepsilon G(a_1^*)} \sum_{s \varepsilon S} \Pi(s) r_2(a_2,s) = \sum_{s \varepsilon S} \Pi(s) r_2(c_2,s). \qquad \text{(ii)}$$

In other words, if (a_1^*, a_2^*) is preferred to (a_1^*, a_2^+) for more than one set of prior beliefs Π, the optimal choice of a_2 in $G(a_1^*)$ is independent of Π.

Theorem (JONES/OSTROY 1984): If assumption 1 holds, $\geq$ induces an order preserving relation on $\geq_F$.

Proof: cf. Appendix.

In section 3.4.4, we shall give examples for which assumption 1 is satisfied.

3.4.4 Examples and Modifications

We now give applications of the JONES/OSTROY-theorem.[12]

(a) As one should expect, the theorem is applicable whenever there is only an irreversible choice and a perfectly flexible choice.

[12] cf. JONES/OSTROY (1984).

With $A_1=A_2=\{0,1\}$ and $G=\{(0,0),(0,1),(1,1)\}$, assumption (1) is satisfied because for the perfectly flexible element $a_1^*=0$ and $a_2^*\varepsilon A_2=G(a_1^*)$

$$\max_{a_2\varepsilon G(a_1^*)} \sum_{s\varepsilon S} \Pi(s)r_2(a_2,s) \geq \sum_{s\varepsilon S} \Pi(s)r_2(a_2^*,s)$$

and for the irreversible element $a_1^*=1$

$$\max_{a_2\varepsilon G(a_1^*)} \sum_{s\varepsilon S} \Pi(s)r_2(a_2,s) = \sum_{s\varepsilon S} \Pi(s)r_2(1,s),$$

independent of Π (because 1 is the only element in $G(a_1^*)$), so that assumption (1) is satisfied with $c_2=1$.

(b) More interestingly, suppose A_1 is an arbitrary set and A_2 is a subset of the real numbers.
Suppose that $G(a_1)$ is given by a set $\{a_2\varepsilon R|a_2\leq z(a_1)$ for some function z on $R\}$, so that $a_1\geq_F a_1' \Leftrightarrow z(a_1)\geq z(a_1')$. Assume that $r_2(a_2,s)$ is concave in a_2 for each s. Then, for arbitrary $(a_1^*,a_2^*)\varepsilon A_1 x A_2$, $\Pi\varepsilon\Sigma^{m-1}$

$$\max_{a_2\varepsilon G(a_1^*)} \sum_{s\varepsilon S} \Pi(s)r_2(a_2,s) \geq \sum_{s\varepsilon S} \Pi(s)r_2(a_2^*,s) \quad \text{(i)}$$

or

$$\max_{a_2\varepsilon G(a_1^*)} \sum_{s\varepsilon S} \Pi(s)r_2(a_2,s) = \sum_{s\varepsilon S} \Pi(s)r_2(z(a_1^*),s) \quad \text{(ii)}$$

independent of Π, i.e. assumption (1) holds with $c_2=z(a_1^*)$.
To see this, suppose both (i) and (ii) are violated, so that

$$\sum_{s\varepsilon S} \Pi(s)r_2(a_2^*,s) > \max_{a_2\varepsilon G(a_1^*)} \sum_{s\varepsilon S} \Pi(s)r_2(a_2,s)$$

and there exists $a_2'' < z(a_1^*)$ such that

$$\sum_{s\varepsilon S} \Pi(s)r_2(a_2'',s) > \sum_{s\varepsilon S} \Pi(s)r_2(z(a_1^*),s) \text{ for some } \Pi \varepsilon \Sigma^{m-1}.$$

Hence, we have

$$\sum_{s\varepsilon S} \Pi(s)r_2(a_2^*,s) > \sum_{s\varepsilon S} \Pi(s)r_2(z(a_1^*),s) < \sum_{s\varepsilon S} \Pi(s)r_2(a_2'',s),$$

so that $\sum_{s\varepsilon S} \Pi(s)r_2(a,s)$ cannot be concave in a_2 (cf. figure 3.8).

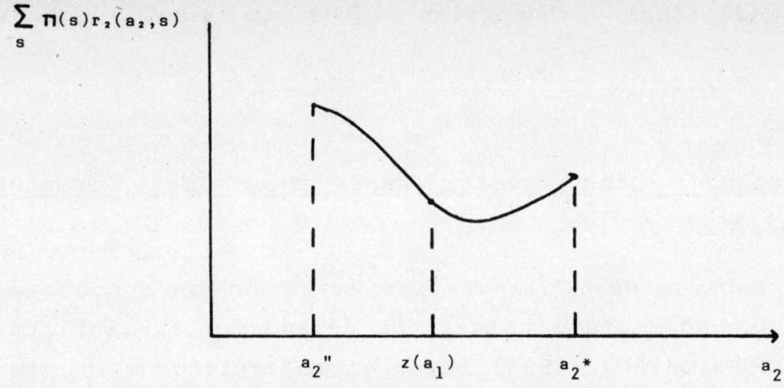

Figure 3.8: Example (b)

As concavity is preserved by addition and scalar multiplication, this contradicts the concavity of $r_2(a_2,s)$.
As an economic example take the "cake-eating model", the simplest conceivable model of resource use (cf. section 2.1.4). Here $a_t = C_t$ denotes the quantity of exhaustible resources extracted and consumed by a society from a given stock M in period t. Clearly, a_2 is bounded by $z(a_1) = M - a_1$. Suppose that a welfare function $r_1(a_1,s)+r_2(a_2,s)$ is maximized, where r_2 is concave in a_2. Then we are in case (b), so that greater uncertainty will lead to less resource extraction, because less resource extraction means greater flexibility.[13]

An important precursor of the paper by JONES/OSTROY (1984) was an article by EPSTEIN (1980). His analysis, however, was restricted to the case that choice is made from subsets of the real line or from two-element sets. He also made convexity assumptions on G and differentiability assumptions on U (which is not restricted to be of type (2)) to obtain a result similar to the lemma in 3.4.3.

Using this result, he discussed the effect of irreversibility in different economic contexts, including savings decisions and the timing of orders for capital. In the light of our counterexample in section 3.4.1 it is not surprising that he also found plausible

---

[13] The flexibility given by saving resources is discussed by MAIER (1984, p.262-284).

examples where additional information leads to less flexible choices.

3.4.5 Interpretation: Does Greater Uncertainty Imply Greater Demand for Flexibility?

The goal of this section was to investigate the common sense statement that greater uncertainty raises the demand for flexibility. The analysis of JONES/OSTROY (1984) has been interpreted as a confirmation of this statement, both by the authors and other writers such as MAKOWSKI (1989). What do we make of such a statement in the light of the preceding analysis?

If greater uncertainty is identified with a more informative information structure or, in the terminology of JONES/OSTROY (1984), with greater variability of beliefs, i.e. roughly speaking with a "greater difference between present and expected future knowledge", then the above analysis shows that there are several examples where the statement "greater uncertainty leads to a desire for flexibility" is correct, while there are also non-pathological examples where it is not (cf. section 3.4.1). If a general positive relation between uncertainty and the desire for flexibility is to be supported, additional arguments are therefore necessary.

One possible line of approach would be to go through all the counterexamples and hope to find that they are economically irrelevant. It is, however, highly unlikely that such an approach would prove to be successful. After all, many examples, for instance those by EPSTEIN (1980), are perfectly reasonable from an economic point of view.

The more promising strategy is to check whether the mathematical expressions for "greater uncertainty" and "greater flexibility" are really in line with economic intuition.

We concentrate on the definition of flexibility. In section 3.1, we have already argued that it is not entirely satisfactory from an economic point of view. We now add a further aspect to our earlier discussion.

This will show why it is not always true that for $a_1 \geq_F a_1'$

$$V(a_1;\Pi,q)-V(a_1;\Pi_*,q_*) \geq V(a_1';\Pi,q)-V(a_1';\Pi_*,q_*) , \qquad (3.4.5)$$

which would at least have to hold for more uncertainty to induce more flexible behaviour.

The advantage of flexibility, as it is commonly understood, is seen in the improved opportunity to use future information. The key to the understanding of the ambiguity of the above results lies in the observation that greater flexibility of an initial position gives it two advantages.

One of the two advantages is relevant even when no future information is expected. It is simply the fact that one has more options to choose from in period 2. Therefore, even if future information is ignored, a_1 yields an expected payoff in period 2 that is higher (or at least as high) as the payoff for a_1', i.e.

$$V(a_1;\Pi_*,q_*) \geq V(a_1';\Pi_*,q_*) \qquad (3.4.6)$$

and possibly even

$$V(a_1;\Pi_*,q_*) > V(a_1';\Pi_*,q_*) \qquad (3.4.7)$$

as in the example in section 3.4.1 for $a_1=2, a_1'=1$: There $2 \geq_F 1$ and $V(2;\Pi_*,q_*) = 7 > 5,5 = V(1_*;\Pi_*,q_*)$.

The effect that is closer to the intuitive meaning of flexibility is that, whatever the signal that is received, the expected payoff for an agent who has chosen a_1 (given that signal) is at least as great as the corresponding payoff for a_1', i.e for each $y \varepsilon Y$, $v(a_1,\Pi(y)) \geq v(a_1',\Pi(y))$ and consequently

$$V(a_1,\Pi,q) = \sum_{y \varepsilon Y} q_y v(a_1,\Pi(y)) \geq$$

$$\sum_{y \varepsilon Y} q_y v(a_1',\Pi(y)) = V(a_1';\Pi,q). \qquad (3.4.8)$$

But of course this second effect is not enough to assure that (3.4.5) holds, because the effect of (3.4.7) also has to be taken into account.

Therefore, what one really has to investigate is whether (3.4.7) holds. When (3.4.7) is not true, i.e. when

$V(a_1,\Pi_*,q_*) = V(a_1';\Pi_*,q_*)$,

then clearly (3.4.8) implies (3.4.5), so that the following proposition holds.

Proposition 3.7: Suppose a_1 is more flexible than a_1'. Furthermore, suppose $V(a_1;\Pi_*,q_*) = V(a_1';\Pi_*,q_*)$.
Then a_1 benefits relatively more from information than a_1'.

Compared to the theorem of JONES/OSTROY (1984), this result is very simple. But it does improve the understanding of the counterintuitive result that greater uncertainty does not always lead to a more flexible initial position. The reason is simply that flexible positions have an advantage that is completely independent of information. If this effect were absent or at least comparatively weak, it would always be true that greater uncertainty leads to more flexible choices.

3.5 The Two-Period Model - Final Thoughts

In this chapter, we gave a systematic treatment of a general choice-theoretic model. We investigated how the value and the flexibility of the optimal choice in sequential decision problems depend on the structure of the problem, which is given by the choice set, the choice criterion and the information structure of the problem.

The central results of sections 3.2-3.4 can be interpreted in two ways.

The first interpretation concentrates on the comparative statics of uncertainty. Suppose that agents are modelled as Bayesians. Then the informativeness of the information structure is an exogenous parameter that can be taken as a measure of the uncertainty or, more precisely, the resolvable uncertainty of the decision-maker's environment. The greater the expected value of the information that the agent will receive, the greater the uncertainty.

The analysis of this chapter can then be used to answer the question how an agent's behaviour is influenced by the uncertainty of his environment. The intuitive result that "flexible" choices such as postponing investment are more likely to be made in a more uncertain environment can only be supported in some situations, e.g. when choice is between two alternatives, one of which is perfectly flexible and one is totally irreversible. In more general decision situations, one has to argue more carefully.

The result that agents will choose more flexible positions in an uncertain world is only true if it is clear that the more flexible choice does not have advantages that are independent of the expected arrival of new information.

As an illustration, consider the following example that is due to BERNANKE (1983). He argued that a partial explanation for investment crises as consequences of oil price rises is the following.

When investors have to choose new projects after an unanticipated rise in the price of oil, they have to decide whether to use energy-intensive capital or energy-saving capital. These decisions have strong irreversible elements, while the decision not to invest allows for an exploitation of future information on the stability of the new prices. Therefore, in periods when investors are not sure about the stability of prices but expect to receive more information in the not too distant future, they will tend to refrain from investment.

Here, we are in the situation described in proposition 3.7. If one of the options "invest in energy-using capital" or "invest in energy-saving capital" promises a positive expected payoff that is higher than the payoff from the other project, abstaining from investment does not have an advantage over the two investment projects for a decision-maker that expects no future information. Therefore, by proposition 3.7, the option "postpone investment" will benefit from additional uncertainty.

The second interpretation starts from the observation that, despite the fact that flexibility considerations appear to be important in reality, they are ignored in many economic models. This is usually justified on grounds of simplicity, but of course it must be expected to lead to results that differ from the case where flexibility considerations are taken into account.

So even if one prefers to work with models which do not deal with flexibility issues, one might want to know how this simplification affects the results. The preceding analysis gives answers to this question.

Firstly, as long as the problem is totally reversible, the simplification does not matter (cf. proposition 3.2): the agent will in general make the same choices in both cases. Secondly, as soon as the problem is partially irreversible, choices will in general differ according to whether flexibility considerations are taken into account or not. For a certain class of simple examples, those satisfying the conditions of the theorems by EPSTEIN (1980) and JONES/OSTROY (1984) or of proposition 3.7, ignoring flexibility considerations leads to an irreversibility bias, i.e. to a tendency to choose positions that are less flexible than they should be. This result is not necessarily true when general choice problems are considered. Then less flexible positions may, at first glance paradoxically, benefit more than others from the inclusion of flexibility considerations. This is so because part of the advantage of a more flexible position is relevant even when no future information is expected.

In the same spirit, one may ask how a more drastic simplification, namely the assumption of myopic optimization, performs relative to intertemporal optimization procedures. It turns out that here a general irreversibility bias can be found (proposition 3.5). Furthermore, though myopic optimization is clearly inferior to Bayesian optimization, it may, in some cases be superior to ordinary expected utility maximization (cf. the example in section 3.3.1).

There are several limitations of the result that ignoring flexibility considerations leads to an irreversibility bias.

Firstly, many interesting decision problems cannot reasonably be modelled in a manner that allows different first-period choices to be compared with respect to flexibility (cf. the discussion about the flexibility of different types of assets in section 3.1.1).

Secondly, of course, even if they can be modelled in such a way, it is, in general, not evident whether the assumptions of the JONES/OSTROY-theorem or similar results hold.

There are several other limitations. They go further, in the sense that they do not merely affect the applicability of the JONES/OSTROY-theorem, but the entire structure of the model.

For many learning processes, it appears to be true that the degree of learning depends on the action that is chosen, which is contrary to the assumptions of the model, where learning is completely exogenous.[14] In particular, it may happen that the agent will only learn if he is willing to make an irreversible commitment (like R&D-investment). Then, the more flexible choice may benefit from ignoring future information (cf. MILLER/LAD 1984). This is also true in two other different but related types of problems.

The first problem relates to so-called consistency issues. If an agent plans over several periods, in our case over two periods, with an intertemporal utility function, he usually has to choose on the basis of judgements about future preferences. For instance, his optimal consumption, seen from his present point of view, may involve very low second-period consumption of chocolate or cigarettes in future periods. Nearer to the time, he may however find himself unable to resist temptation and consume more than he originally wanted to. Anticipating this, he may want to commit himself to a strategy that limits his flexibility to choose between more or less consumption of the addictive goods, e.g. by keeping

[14] This is called the case of "dependent learning" by FISHER/HANEMANN (1987).

low stocks of these goods at home. For a formal discussion and a critique of these arguments, cf. HAMMOND 1975, but the subject goes back to STROTZ 1955/6.[15]

Finally, it is clear that in a game-theoretical setting pre-commitment may be advantageous, for instance because it may make threats more credible (cf. RASMUSEN 1989,p. 85-87) or because it may be interpreted as a signal of product quality.

No matter how certain results will be affected when the framework is modified, it will in general remain true that results are modified when the expectation of receiving information during the course of the decision process is taken into account. In most relevant decision problems, choices that are unattractive from the point of view of an ordinary expected utility maximizer may be optimal for the agent who cares about his ability to react to new information. However, these optimal choices need not be strictly speaking more flexible. They may simply be incomparable with respect to flexible or, in some cases, they may even be less flexible. Therefore, though the principle that greater uncertainty leads to more flexible choices (in the narrow sense of section 3.1.1) is not generally valid, the more fundamental principle that a change in the degree of uncertainty will somehow change the optimal behaviour of the agent remains unaffected.

---

[15] Consistency issues have also received attention in the "rules versus discretion"-debate in modern macroeconomics (cf. KYDLAND/PRESCOTT 1977, PERSSON/PERSSON/SVENSSON 1987, HOOVER 1990, p.80/81).

APPENDIX

1. Proof of the lemma in 3.4.3

Suppose the statement is not true. By definition of an order-preserving relation, this implies that for some $(\Pi,q) > (\Pi',q')$, $a_1, a_1' \varepsilon A_1$ such that (3.4.3)-(3.4.4) hold, it is true that $a_1' \geq_F a_1$. Because $(\Pi,q) \geq (\Pi',q')$, the convexity of $v(a_1',\Pi)-v(a_1,\Pi)$ implies

$$\sum_y q_y [v(a_1',\Pi(y))-v(a_1,\Pi(y))] \geq \sum_y q_y [v(a_1',\Pi'(y))-v(a_1,\Pi'(y))]$$

by the theorem in section 3.1.1(b).

By definition of V, we therefore get

$$V(a_1';\Pi,q) - V(a_1;\Pi,q) \geq V(a_1';\Pi',q') - V(a_1;\Pi',q'). \qquad (A.1)$$

We shall now show that (3.4.3) and (3.4.4) lead to a contradiction of (A.1).

By (3.4.3),

$$E_s[r_1(a_1,s)] + V(a_1;\Pi,q) \geq E_s[r_1(a_1',s)] + V(a_1';\Pi,q)$$

and

$$E_s[r_1(a_1',s)] + V(a_1';\Pi',q') \geq E_s[r_1(a_1,s)] + V(a_1;\Pi',q').$$

By (3.4.4), at least one of the two last inequalities is strict. Hence addition of the inequalities and rearrangement of terms gives

$$V(a_1';\Pi,q) - V(a_1;\Pi,q) < V(a_1';\Pi',q') - V(a_1;\Pi',q'),$$

the desired contradiction of (A.1).

2. Proof of the theorem 3.4.3:[16]

By the lemma in 3.4.3, it is only necessary to show that $v(a_1,\Pi)-v(a_1',\Pi)$ is convex if $a_1 \geq_F a_1'$.

---

[16] The proof is identical to that of JONES/OSTROY (1984), except for the fact that we use a slightly different definition of flexibility.

By definition, for all $\Pi \varepsilon \Sigma^{m-1}$, $v(a_1,\Pi) - v(a_1',\Pi) =$

$$\max_{a_2 \varepsilon G(a_1)} \sum_{s \varepsilon S} \Pi(s) r_2(a_2,s) - \max_{a_2 \varepsilon G(a_1')} \sum_{s \varepsilon S} \Pi(s) r_2(a_2,s)$$

Because of $G(a_1) \supset G(a_1')$, $G(a_1)$ can be written as $G(a_1') \cup \{b \varepsilon G(a_1) \backslash G(a_1')\}$.

If the maximum of $\sum_{s \varepsilon S} \Pi(s) r_2(a_2,s)$ over $G(a_1)$ lies in $G(a_1')$,

$$\max_{a_2 \varepsilon G(a_1)} \sum_{s \varepsilon S} \Pi(s) r_2(a_2,s) = \max_{a_2 \varepsilon G(a_1')} \sum_{s \varepsilon S} \Pi(s) r_2(a_2,s);$$ otherwise

$$\max_{a_2 \varepsilon G(a_1)} \sum_{s \varepsilon S} \Pi(s) r_2(a_2,s) = \max_{b \varepsilon G(a_1) \backslash G(a_1')} \sum_{s \varepsilon S} \Pi(s) r_2(b,s).$$

Therefore,

$$\max_{a_2 \varepsilon G(a_1)} \sum_{s \varepsilon S} \Pi(s) r_2(a_2,s) - \max_{a_2 \varepsilon G(a_1')} \sum_{s \varepsilon S} \Pi(s) r_2(a_2,s) =$$

$$\max \{0, \max_{b \varepsilon G(a_1) \backslash G(a_1')} [\sum_{s \varepsilon S} \Pi(s) r_2(b,s) - \max_{a_2 \varepsilon G(a_1')} \sum_{s \varepsilon S} \Pi(s) r_2(a_2,s)]\}.$$

Applying assumption 1 of the theorem to (a_1',b),

$$[\sum_{s \varepsilon S} \Pi(s) r_2(b,s) - \max_{a_2 \varepsilon G(a_1')} \sum_{s \varepsilon S} \Pi(s) r_2(a_2,s)]$$

is either non-positive or equal to

$$[\sum_{s \varepsilon S} \Pi(s) r_2(b,s) - \sum_{s \varepsilon S} \Pi(s) r_2(c_2,s)]$$

for some $c_2 \varepsilon G(a_1')$ which is independent of $\Pi(s)$.
Hence, we obtain

$$V(a_1,\Pi) - V(a_1',\Pi) =$$

$$\max \{0, \max_{b \varepsilon G(a_1) \backslash G(a_1')} [\sum_{s \varepsilon S} \Pi(s) r_2(b,s) - \sum_{s \varepsilon S} \Pi(s) r_2(c_2,s)]\}.$$

Now the functions $\sum_{s \varepsilon S} \Pi(s) r_2(b,s) - \sum_{s \varepsilon S} \Pi(s) r_2(c_2,s)$ are linear (and therefore convex) in Π for every given b. Hence, the inner maximum in the last equation is a maximum of convex functions and therefore it is a convex function of Π itself.
Similar reasoning applied to the outer maximum shows that $v(a_1;\Pi) - v(a_1';\Pi)$ is convex in Π, which, by the lemma, proves the proposition.

Chapter 4

A T-PERIOD MODEL OF INTERTEMPORAL CHOICE WITH IRREVERSIBILITY AND UNCERTAINTY

In chapters 2 and 3, we presented a model of sequential choice with uncertainty and learning. Our aim was to provide a framework for the simultaneous treatment of various economic phenomena that are consequences of the interplay of irreversibility and uncertainty. Here irreversibility was interpreted in a very broad sense meaning that today's choice influences tomorrow's choice possibilities (though sometimes we specialized to the case that there exist choices that <u>completely</u> determine tomorrow's choice).

First of all, we saw that irreversibility is a necessary condition for intertemporal decision problems to differ from static decision problems. Without irreversibility, the future can be ignored when decisions are made. This is no longer true with irreversibility. Irreversibility can lead to so-called intertemporal opportunity costs that make it advisable to consider the future when decisions are made. If choice has to be made under uncertainty, totally irreversible decisions have the disadvantage that they make it impossible to utilize future information. More generally, the flexibility (or reversibility) of a decision is closely related to the value of future information given that decision.

The general results were tentatively applied to more concrete economic examples. However, it was felt that the applicability of our concepts would benefit from a generalization to $T \geq 2$ periods, because in such a more general context additional features of intertemporal choice problems can be investigated. For instance, we are thinking of the idea that, in most cases, irreversibility is of a temporary nature or, more generally, that irreversibility is, in some sense, "weaker" in the long run. We also have in mind another relatively obvious statement, namely that there is, in general, more uncertainty about events in the distant future than about events in the near future.

The economic problems we are thinking of as fields for applications are capital and investment theory, where gestation periods and delivery lags in the production of capital goods play a fundamental role (cf. chapter 1). The concepts also pertain to the investigation of environmental problems; pollution often leads to a destruction of the environment that is irreversible in the short term. Later in this thesis (cf. chapter 5), we shall show how the concepts of this chapter can be applied to investigate consumption and savings decisions of households. Furthermore, applications to the theory of financial markets seem conceivable (cf. HUANG/ LITZENBERGER 1987, ch. 7/8).

We proceed as follows.

In section 4.1, we generalize our two-period model of choice to a T-period framework and state a few general results.

Section 4.2 provides a verbal discussion of possible strategies in intertemporal choice problems. In particular, we shall take up the question of the choice of the right time horizon. We do not claim that this chapter contains any new insights; it is merely a summary of the relevant literature.

Finally, in section 4.3, we turn to an alternative approach to sequential decision making under uncertainty, which we then apply to neoclassical growth models and Neo-Austrian capital theory models.

4.1 The General T-Period Model of Choice

In this section, we generalize the two-period model of choice presented in chapters 2 and 3 to T periods, where T is an arbitrary positive integer. Partly, this amounts to obvious restatements of familiar concepts, but in many cases new ideas are needed.

In section 4.1.1, fundamental concepts will be presented. These concepts will be related to familiar economic ideas in 4.1.2. In 4.1.3, the basic results of the two-period case will be extended to the T-period case. In 4.1.4, we shall introduce intertemporal opportunity costs. In 4.1.5, uncertainty and learning are added to the model.

The following treatment of the T-period case is new, except for the backward recursion model in section 4.1.5 which is standard dynamic programming.

4.1.1 The Structure of the Choice Set

In this section, we shall extend the concepts of section 2.1.1 to the T-period case. We shall explain them with a numerical example as we go along; economic examples will be provided in section 4.1.2.

As long as there is no uncertainty, the formulation of the problem is an obvious restatement of the two-period problem: we assume that an agent has to choose a variable a_t from an arbitrary set A_t in each of the periods $t=1,\dots,T$. His choice of $(a_1,\dots,a_T)$ is restricted to a subset G of $A_1 x\dots xA_T$.

As for the two period model, we assume without loss of generality that for every $t\varepsilon\{1,\dots,T\}$, A_t is chosen in such a way that it contains only elements that are feasible a priori, i.e. for every $a_t \varepsilon A_t$, there exists some feasible path $(a_1,\dots,a_t)$.

A path $(a_1,\dots,a_T)$ ε $A_1 x\dots xA_T$, which is an element of G, or any subsequence $(a_s,\dots,a_t)$ ε $A_s x\dots xA_t$, $1\le s\le t\le T$, of such a path, will be called a **feasible path**.

We illustrate our concepts with a simple numerical example.

Example 1

Suppose T=4. Suppose $A_1 = A_2 = A_4 = \{1,2,3\}$, $A_3 = \{1,2\}$. We assume that G is given by the graph in figure 4.1.

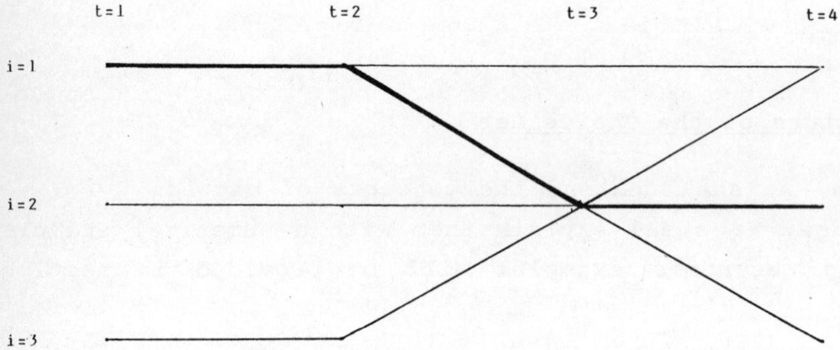

Figure 4.1: A Numerical Example

Every edge path from the left hand side of the graph to the right hand side stands for a member of G: if the point of the edge path in column t lies in row i, then $a_t = i$. For instance, the bold path represents $(a_1, \ldots, a_4) = (1,1,2,2)$.

Suppose G consists of all the paths representable by edge paths of the above graph in this manner.

Again, we introduce an abbreviation for the set of future choices which remain open for an agent after a sequence $a^t := (a_1, \ldots, a_t)$ of choices during the first t periods $(t \varepsilon 1, \ldots, T-1)$.

We define

$$G(a_1, \ldots, a_t) :=$$
$$\{(a_{t+1}, \ldots, a_T) \ \varepsilon \ A_{t+1} x \ldots x A_T \mid (a_1, \ldots, a_t, a_{t+1}, \ldots, a_T) \varepsilon G\}.$$

Before defining flexibility and irreversibility formally, we introduce a name for the set of paths that are feasible during periods t+1,...,t+k after an initial choice of $(a_1, \ldots, a_t)$. We define

$G_{t+1...t+k}(a_1,...,a_t) = \{(a_{t+1},...,a_{t+k}) \varepsilon A_{t+1} x...x A_{t+k} |$there exists an $(a_{t+k+1},...,a_T) \varepsilon A_{t+k+1} x...x A_T$ such that $(a_{t+1},...,a_{t+k},a_{t+k+1},...,a_T) \varepsilon G(a_1,...,a_t)\}$.

Similarly, we introduce a name for the set of all paths starting in period r and ending in period s that are feasible a priori, i.e. before any choice has been made. More formally, we define

$G_{r...s} = \{(a_r,...,a_s) \varepsilon A_r x...x A_s |$there exists an $(a_1,...,a_{r-1},a_{s+1},...,a_T) \varepsilon A_1 x...x A_{r-1} x A_{s+1} x...x A_T$ such that $(a_1,...,a_{r-1},a_r,...,a_s,a_{s+1},...,a_T) \varepsilon G\}$,

In example 1, for instance, $G_{12}=\{(1,1),(2,2),(3,3)\}$, $G_{23}= \{(1,1),(1,2),(2,2),(3,2)\}$.

The definition of perfectly flexible and irreversible actions generalizes immediately to the T-period case. For $t \varepsilon \{1,...,T-1\}$, we call $(a_1,...,a_t)$ **perfectly flexible** if $G(a_1,...,a_t) = G_{t+1,...T}$, i.e. if no path that is feasible a priori is excluded by choosing $(a_1,...,a_t)$. We call $(a_1,...,a_t)$ **totally irreversible** if $G(a_1,...,a_t)$ contains only one element. In others words, a path $(a_1,...,a_t)$ is called totally irreversible if it leaves no choice open in the future.

In the above example, $G(1,1,1) = \{1\}$, so that (1,1,1) is totally irreversible, $G(3,3,2)=A_4$, so that (3,3,2) is perfectly flexible.

In the special case that all feasible paths $(a_1,...,a_t)$ $(t=1,2,...,T-1)$ are perfectly flexible, we shall say that we are considering a **totally reversible** decision problem. In the case that all feasible paths are totally irreversible, we shall speak of a **totally irreversible** decision problem. As before, these cases are not interesting in themselves, they merely serve as reference points for the investigation of the remaining cases, in which we shall say that the problem is **partially irreversible**.

In a T-period context, it makes sense to speak of short-term irreversibility. Intuitively, one would consider a path $(a_1,...,a_t)$ as totally irreversible in the short term if it determines choice uniquely during the next few periods, but not necessarily in all future periods.

We shall say that $(a_1,\ldots,a_t)$ is **totally k-irreversible** if $G_{t+1\ldots t+k}(a_1,\ldots,a_t)$ contains only one element, i.e. if, given the initial choice $(a_1,\ldots,a_t)$, there is only one feasible choice for the path $(a_{t+1},\ldots,a_{t+k})$.

Obviously, a path that is k-irreversible is k'-irreversible for any k'<k.

A path will be called **totally irreversible in the short term**, if it is totally 1-irreversible i.e. if at least in period t+1 it leaves only one feasible choice.

A path $(a_1,\ldots,a_t)$ that is neither totally irreversible in the short term nor such that $G_{t+1}(a_1,\ldots,a_t) = A_{t+1}$ is called **partially irreversible in the short term**.

In example 1, $G_2(3)=\{3\}$, so that (3) is totally 1-irreversible (and hence totally irreversible in the short term).

There is a straightforward generalization of the flexibility relation that we used in the preceding chapters. We shall say that **a_T is at least as flexible as b_T**, $a^T \geq_F b^T$, if $G(a^T) \supset G(b^T)$.

In example 1, (1,1) is more flexible than (2,2).

For r=t+1,...,T we introduce a name for the set of elements which may occur as the r-th component of some feasible path, given the first t components $(a_1,\ldots,a_t)$. More formally, we define

$$\mathbf{G_r(a_1,\ldots,a_t)} = \{b \in A_r \mid \text{there exists } (a_{t+1},\ldots,a_T) \in G(a_1,\ldots,a_t) \text{ such that } a_r = b\}.$$

In example 1, for instance, $G_3(1)=A_3$, $G_3(2)=\{2\}$.

Finally, we note that we will sometimes consider choice problems that differ in some exogenous parameter ß. To distinguish between the sets $G(a_1,\ldots,a_t)$ etc. for different parameter values, we write

$G(a_1,\dots,a_t;\mathcal{B})$	for $G(a_1,\dots,a_t)$,
$G_{t+1\dots t+k}(a_1,\dots,a_t;\mathcal{B})$	for $G_{t+1\dots t+k}(a_1,\dots,a_t)$
$G_r(a_1,\dots,a_t;\mathcal{B})$	for $G_r(a_1,\dots,a_t)$
$G_{r\dots s}(\mathcal{B})$	for $G_{r\dots s}$
$G(\mathcal{B})$	for G.

4.1.2 Economic Examples

All the examples for the two-period case (cf. chapter 2.1.2) can easily be generalized to the T-period case. We concentrate on the discussion of issues that only make sense for $T>2$.

We start by taking the decision maker to be a firm that chooses its capital stock K_t in each of the periods $t=1,2,\dots,T$, given an initial stock K_0. To draw attention to the essential points, we abstract from other aspects of the firm's activity like the choice of labour inputs (cf. the neoclassical investment theory model in chapter 1.1.1). Including them would merely involve additional notation, not additional insights.

When investment is reversible, A_t should be taken as $[0,\infty)$ for $t=1,\dots,T$ and G should be taken as $A_1 x \dots x A_t$.

When investment is irreversible and capital can be reduced through depreciation only (with a constant factor c), $A_1=[(1-c)K_0,\infty)$, $A_2=[(1-c)^2K_0,\infty)$, etc. Similarly, $G_{t+1}(K_t) = [(1-c)K_t,\infty)$ for each $t\varepsilon\{1,2,\dots,T-1\}$. Therefore,
$G = \{(K_1,\dots,K_T)\varepsilon A_1 x \dots x A_T \mid K_{t+1}\geq(1-c)K_t \text{ for } t=1,\dots,T-1\}$.

We now take up the discussion in chapter 1.1 by adding a further element to the model. In general, the production and delivery of capital takes time, in some cases many years. Hence, it seems reasonable to distinguish between the time when a capital good is ordered and the time when it is delivered (cf. chapter 1.1.4). One way to capture this idea of a delivery lag is to consider not only the capital stock as the variable to be chosen but also the amount of capital J_t that is ordered in period t. Hence, in each period t, the agent chooses an element (K_t,J_t) from an appropriately defined set G of feasible paths.

To see how this set should be defined, suppose the time lag between ordering and delivery of the capital good is m periods. Then the capital stock in each period is the sum of the capital stock of the period before that (minus depreciation) and the amount of the capital good that was ordered m periods before, i.e.

$$K_{t+1} = (1-c)K_t + J_{t+1-m}.$$

Repeated application of this equation gives

$$K_{t+2} = (1-c)^2 K_t + (1-c)J_{t+1-m} + J_{t+2-m},$$
$$\ldots,$$
$$K_{t+m} = (1-c)^m K_t + (1-c)^{m-1} J_{t+1-m} + \ldots + J_t.$$

Hence, the capital stock in periods t+1,...,t+m is completely determined by decisions in periods up to and including t. It follows that the set of feasible capital stocks in periods 1,...,m is completely determined by the initial capital stock and orders that have been made in earlier periods that are not taken into account explicitly. More precisely, one has

$$A_1 = \{(1-c)K_0 + J_{1-m}\} \times [0,\infty),$$
$$A_2 = \{(1-c)^2 K_0 + (1-c)J_{1-m} + J_{2-m}\} \times [0,\infty),$$
$$\ldots,$$
$$A_m = \{(1-c)^m K_0 + (1-c)^{m-1} J_{1-m} + \ldots + J_0\} \times [0,\infty).$$

As J_1 can be chosen freely from $[0,\infty)$, the capital stock is not completely determined by choices in periods up to and including 0:

$$A_{m+1} = [(1-c)^{m+1} K_0 + (1-c)^m J_{1-m} + \ldots + (1-c)J_0, \infty) \times [0,\infty).$$

Similarly,

$$G_{t+1}[(K_1, J_1), \ldots, (K_t, J_t)] = \{(1-c)K_t + J_{t+1-m}\} \times [0,\infty),$$
$$\ldots,$$
$$G_{t+m}[(K_1, J_1), \ldots, (K_t, J_t)] =$$
$$\{(1-c)^m K_t + (1-c)^{m-1} J_{t+1-m} + \ldots + J_t\} \times [0,\infty).$$

The situation changes for G_{t+m+1}. As

$$K(t+m+1) = (1-c)^{m+1} K_t + (1-c)^m J_{t+1-m} + \ldots + (1-c)J_t + J_{t+1}$$

and J_{t+1} can be chosen freely from $[0,\infty)$, the capital stock in period t+m+1 is not completely determined by the choice of $((K_1,J_1),...,(K_t,J_t))$. The irreversibility of investment implies

$$K_{t+m+1} \geq (1-c)^{m+1}K_t + (1-c)^m J_{t+1-m} +... + (1-c)J_t,$$

but there is no upper bound to K_{t+m+1} because J_{t+1} can be chosen arbitrarily high, hence

$$G_{t+m+1}((K_1,J_1),...,(K_t,J_t)) =$$
$$[(1-c)^{m+1}K_t + ... + (1-c)J_t,\infty) \times [0,\infty).$$

With delivery lags and <u>reversible</u> investment, the last condition would read

$$G_{t+m+1}((K_1,J_1),...,(K_t,J_t)) = [0,\infty)\times[0,\infty) = A_{t+m+1},$$

whereas

$G_r((K_1,J_1),...,(K_t,J_t))$ is a proper subset of A_r for $r \in \{t+1,...,t+m\}$.

Hence, delivery lags introduce an additional element of irreversibility: $((K_1,J_1)),...,(K_t,J_t))$ is partially irreversible in the short term.

We only touch upon other examples of short-term irreversibility. In Neo-Austrian Capital Theory models, capital stocks usually take "time to build" (cf. FABER/NIEMES/STEPHAN 1987, STEPHAN 1988). It is easy to show that this fact can be reflected as short-term irreversibility in a general T-period choice model.

Short-term irreversibility also pertains to environmental problems. In many cases, pollutants are naturally degradable but the degradation process takes time. Hence, any non-zero emission path will have a temporarily irreversible impact on the concentration of pollutants in the environment.

Further examples will be provided after the introduction of the complete model in section 4.1.5.

4.1.3 Results

The results of 2.1.3 carry over to the T-period case without exception.

We suppose that the agent's goal is to maximize the utility function $U(a_1,...,a_T)$.

For every irreversible decision problem, we define the associated reversible problem as the problem with identical payoff function but with $G=A_1 x...xA_T$. We obtain the following generalization of proposition 2.1.

Proposition 4.1: (a) For a T-period decision problem, the associated reversible problem never leads to a lower payoff.
(b) It may lead to a higher payoff.

The proof is the same as for the two period case, so that we omit it.

Proposition 2.2 also generalizes to the T-period case. To formulate this result, we restrict ourselves to additively separable utility functions $U(a_1,...,a_T) = r_1(a_1)+...+r_T(a_T)$ with real-valued spot-utility functions $r_1,...,r_T$. For such functions, we define a path $(m_1,...,m_T)$ as **myopic** if

m_1 maximizes r_1 over A_1, m_2 maximizes r_2 over $G_2(m_1),...,$
m_T maximizes r_T over $G_T(m_1,...,m_{T-1})$.

In other words, in every period $t\varepsilon\{1,...,T\}$, the agent maximizes instantaneous payoff r_t under the restrictions given by his previous choices.

Using this terminology, we have the following result.

Proposition 4.1.2: (a) For a totally reversible problem, a path is myopic if and only if it is intertemporally optimal.
(b) A myopic path for an irreversible problem need not be intertemporally optimal.

Again, the proof is obtained by a straightforward generalization of the argument in the proof for the two-period case.

4.1.4 Intertemporal Opportunity Costs

The generalization of what we tentatively called intertemporal opportunity costs in 2.1.4 to the T-period case is not entirely unambiguous. Intuitively, one would want to say that a path $(a_1,\dots,a_t)$ causes intertemporal opportunity costs if an alternative feasible choice of the first t elements exists that gives a higher payoff in the future. But what exactly do we mean by a higher payoff in the future when there is more than one future period? Possible candidates are:

(1) higher payoff in the immediately following period,
(2) higher payoff in some future period,
(3) higher payoff in all future periods and
(4) higher total payoff.

All these concepts seem to be potentially useful and will therefore be defined formally and discussed briefly below.

A path $(a_1,\dots,a_t)$ causes **k-period opportunity costs** (for some $k \varepsilon \{1,\dots,T-t\}$) if

$$\max_{a_{t+k} \varepsilon G_{t+k}(a_1,\dots,a_t)} r_{t+k}(a_{t+k}) < \max_{a_{t+k} \varepsilon A_{t+k}} r_{t+k}(a_{t+k}) ,$$

i.e. if the maximum feasible payoff in period t+k after having chosen $(a_1,\dots,a_t)$ is lower than the maximum feasible payoff before a_1 has been chosen.

We say that a path $(a_1,\dots,a_t)$ causes

short-term opportunity costs, if it causes k-period opportunity costs for k=1 (corresponds to (1) above);

weak opportunity costs, if there exists a k≥1 such that it causes k-period opportunity costs (corresponds to (2) above);

strong opportunity costs, if it causes k-period opportunity costs for all future periods, i.e. for k=1,...,T-t (corresponds to (3) above);

long-term opportunity costs, if

$$\max \sum_{k=1}^{T-t} r_{t+k}(a_{t+k}) \quad (\text{subject to } (a_{t+1},\ldots, a_T)\varepsilon G(a_1,\ldots,a_t)) \quad <$$

$$\max \sum_{k=1}^{T-t} r_{t+k}(a_{t+k}) \quad (\text{subject to } (a_{t+1},\ldots,a_T)\varepsilon G_{t+1\ldots T})$$

(corresponds to (4) above).

It is obvious from the definitions that strong opportunity costs imply both short-term and long-term opportunity costs and that weak opportunity costs are implied by both short-term and long-term opportunity costs.

These ideas are summarized in figure 4.2.

strong opportunity costs	=>	long-term opportunity costs
$\Downarrow$		$\Downarrow$
short-term opportunity costs	=>	weak opportunity costs

Figure 4.2: Intertemporal Opportunity Costs

With these definitions, propositions 2.3 and 2.4 can be generalized.

<u>Proposition 4.3:</u> A decision can only lead to weak opportunity costs if it is not perfectly flexible.

<u>Proof</u>: By contradiction. Suppose the decision $(a_1,\ldots,a_t)$ were perfectly flexible. Then $G(a_1,\ldots,a_t) = A_{t+1}x\ldots xA_T$ and therefore $G_{t+k}(a_1,\ldots,a_t) = A_{t+k}$ for $k=1,\ldots,T-t$. Hence,

$$\max_{a_{t+k}\varepsilon G_{t+k}(a_1,\ldots,a_t)} r_{t+k}(a_{t+k}) = \max_{a_{t+k}\varepsilon A_{t+k}} r_{t+k}(a_{t+k}),$$

so that $(a_1,\ldots,a_t)$ does not cause k-period opportunity costs for any $k\varepsilon(1,\ldots,T-t)$; in other words: it does not cause weak opportunity costs.

The appropriate generalization of proposition 2.4 uses long-term opportunity costs.

Proposition 4.4: Suppose that no feasible $(a_1,\dots,a_t)$ gives rise to long-term opportunity costs. For simplicity, suppose there exists a unique optimal path and a unique myopic path. Then the myopic path and the optimal path are identical.

Proof: All we need to show is that the optimal path is myopic. Suppose the path $b=(b_1,\dots,b_T)$ is optimal but not myopic. Hence, there exists a path $m=(m_1,\dots,m_T)$ such that for some $t\varepsilon\{1,\dots,T\}$ the inequality $r_t(m_t)>r_t(b_t)$ holds. Choose $t=s$ minimal with that property.

We shall show that

$$\max \sum_{k=1}^{T-s} r_{s+k}(a_{s+k}) \text{ subj. to } (a_{s+1},\dots,a_T)\varepsilon G(m_1,\dots,m_s) \quad <$$

$$\max \sum_{k=1}^{T-s} r_{s+k}(a_{s+k}) \text{ subj. to } (a_{s+1},\dots,a_T)\varepsilon G(b_1,\dots,b_s) \qquad (4.1.1)$$

and hence that $(m_1,\dots,m_s)$ gives rise to long-term opportunity costs, contradicting the assumption that no feasible choice gives rise to long-term opportunity costs.

The proof of inequality (4.1.1) runs as follows.

By definition of s,

$$r_1(b_1)=r_1(m_1),\dots,r_{s-1}(b_{s-1})=r_{s-1}(m_{s-1}) \qquad (4.1.2)$$

and

$$r_s(m_s) > r_s(b_s). \qquad (4.1.3)$$

Now suppose inequality (4.1.1) does not hold. Then there exists a path $(n_{s+1},\dots,n_T)$ ε $G(m_1,\dots,m_s)$ such that

$$\sum_{t=s+1}^{T} r_t(n_t) \geq \sum_{t=s+1}^{T} r_t(b_t). \qquad (4.1.4)$$

(4.1.2), (4.1.3) and (4.1.4) imply

$$\sum_{t=1}^{S} r_t(m_t) + \sum_{t=S+1}^{T} r_t(n_t) > \sum_{t=1}^{T} r_t(b_t).$$

As $(m_1,\ldots,m_S,n_{S+1},\ldots,n_T)$ is feasible, this contradicts the optimality of b.

4.1.5 Uncertainty and Learning

As in the two-period case, uncertainty introduces qualitatively new features into the model if learning is permitted. The modelling of the decision procedure in the T-period case proceeds along the same lines as in the two-period case, but it is slightly more difficult.

We suppose that the payoff depends on a state of the world, an element s of a (finite) set S which is not revealed until the end of period T. We suppose that the payoff function is of the form

$$U(a_1,\ldots,a_T,s) = \sum_{t=1}^{T} r_t(a_t,s)$$

with t-period payoff functions $r_t : A_t x S \to R$.

To achieve further generality, we also allow the set of feasible actions to depend on the state of the world. Hence, $(a_1,\ldots,a_T)$ is chosen from a set $G(s) \subset A_1 x\ldots xA_T$ where $s \in S$.

Similarly, the sets $G(a_1,\ldots,a_t)$, $G_r(a_1,\ldots,a_t)$, etc. depend on s. According to our general convention in section 4.1.1, we shall therefore denote these sets as $G(a_1,\ldots,a_t;s)$, $G_r(a_1,\ldots,a_t;s)$, etc.

However, this only makes sense if, in each period $t \in \{1,\ldots,T\}$, the agent knows enough about the state of the world to tell which set $G_t(a_1,\ldots,a_{t-1};s)$ of choices is open to him in that period.

Before clarifying this point formally, we sketch an example that helps to understand the problem[1]. Suppose an agent wants to make consumption/portfolio-decisions for periods 1,...,T. His set of

[1] This example will be dealt with at length in chapter 5.

feasible paths depends on the prices in all of these periods. When he makes a decision for period t, he will, in general, not know prices for periods t+1,...,T. However, to determine his budget constraint in period t, it is enough for him to know prices in period t. Hence, while the state of the world can be described as the sequence of prices in periods 1,...,T, choice possibilities in period t depend only on the part of the sequence that is already known.

To make sure that this property also holds in our general model, we suppose that a state of the world is a history of events, one in each period $t \in \{1,...,T\}$. These events are chosen by nature from a finite set E. Then the following picture emerges (here E is a two-element set).

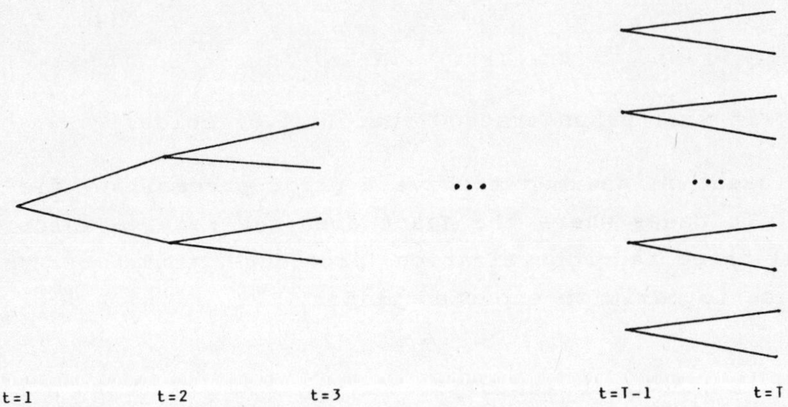

Figure 4.3: States of the World

A state of the world is then a path in the resulting tree starting at the left hand side of figure 4.3 and ending in one of the points at the right hand side.

If we assume that the new information y_{t-1} the agent acquires at the beginning of period t (t=2,...,T) is precisely the knowledge of the event that has occurred at the beginning of that period, we can identify E with Y. An event in period t can thus be identified with an element of Y; a state of the world can be identified with a sequence $(y_1,\dots,y_T)$ of elements of Y. Unlike $y_1,\dots,y_{T-1}$, the message y_T cannot be used in the decision process. It is merely the final message that reveals the state of the nature after the agent has taken all his decisions.

It is now easy to fit in the assumption that $G_t(a_1,\dots,a_{t-1};s)$, the set of feasible choices in period t, is known to the decision-maker at the beginning of period t. We only have to assume that $G_t(a_1,\dots,a_{t-1};s)$ does not depend on the entire sequence $s=(y_1,\dots,y_T)$, but only on those messages that have occurred in periods up to and including t, i.e. in periods 1,...,T the agent chooses from

$$\begin{aligned} &G_1(s) = A_1, \\ &G_2(a_1;s) = G_2(a_1;y_1), \\ &\dots, \\ &G_T(a_1,\dots,a_{T-1};s) = G_T(a_1,\dots,a_{T-1};y_1,\dots,y_{T-1}).^2 \end{aligned} \tag{4.1.5}$$

In the following, it will be understood that (4.1.5) holds.

Furthermore, the agent is assumed to have a prior probability distribution Π on S. In cases where the agent does not receive information, a widely accepted optimization procedure would be to choose $a_1,\dots,a_t$ as to maximize expected utility

$$E_s[\sum_{t=1}^{T} r_t(a_t,s)] := \sum_{s\varepsilon S}[\sum_{t=1}^{T}\Pi(s)r_t(a_t,s)];$$

i.e. to choose a_1 as to maximize

$$E_s[r_1(a_1,s)+ \max_{a_2\varepsilon G(a_1,s)}[E_s r_2(a_2,s)+ \max_{a_3\varepsilon G(a_1,a_2,s)}[E_s r_3(a_3,s)+\dots]]].$$

But as we suppose that the agent receives a message $y_{t-1}\varepsilon Y$ (Y is a finite set) at the beginning of period t, which changes his probability distribution on S into a conditional probability distribution $\Pi(s|y_1,\dots,y_{t-1})$, a different procedure is adequate.

---

[2] This is the "measurability property", cf. HUANG/LITZENBERGER 1987, ch.7.

As in the two-period case, the appropriate behaviour is obtained by backward recursion. Given $y_1,\ldots,y_{T-1}$ and $a_1,\ldots,a_{T-1}$, the optimal choice of a_T is given by the solution of

$$v(y_1,\ldots,y_{T-1};a_1,\ldots,a_{T-1};\Pi,q) =$$
$$\text{Max} \sum_{s\varepsilon S} \Pi(s|y_1,\ldots,y_{T-1})r_T(a_T,s) \quad \text{subject to } a_T \;\varepsilon\; G_T(a_1,\ldots,a_{T-1};s).$$

As in the two-period case, we usually suppress Π,q and write $v(y_1,\ldots,y_{T-1};a_1,\ldots,a_{T-1})$ when there is no danger of misunderstandings.

When the agent chooses a_{T-1}, he does not know y_{T-1}, but he knows $y_1,\ldots,y_{T-2}$. We assume that he has a probability distribution $q(y_{T-1}|y_1,\ldots,y_{T-2})$ on Y (in fact, we assume that he has a probability distribution $q(y_t|y_1,\ldots,y_{t-1})$ for each $t\varepsilon\{1,\ldots,T\}$). The expected payoff in period T if he chooses a_{T-1} in period T-1 and chooses a_T as to obtain $v(y_1,\ldots,y_{T-1};a_1,\ldots,a_{T-1})$ in period T is therefore

$$V(y_1,\ldots,y_{T-2};a_1,\ldots,a_{T-1};\Pi,q)^3 :=$$
$$\sum_{y_{T-1}\varepsilon Y} q(y_{T-1}|y_1,\ldots,y_{T-2})\, v(y_1,\ldots,y_{T-1};a_1,\ldots,a_{T-1}).$$

Given $y_1,\ldots,y_{T-2}$ and $(a_1,\ldots,a_{T-2})$, the agent will therefore choose $a_{T-1} \;\varepsilon\; G_{T-1}(a_1,\ldots,a_{T-2};s)$ so as to obtain

$$v(y_1,\ldots,y_{T-2};a_1,\ldots,a_{T-2};\Pi,q) =$$
$$\max\Big[\sum_{s\varepsilon S} \Pi(s|y_1,\ldots,y_{T-2})r_{T-1}(a_{T-1},s) + V(y_1,\ldots,y_{T-2};a_1,\ldots,a_{T-1})\Big]$$

subject to $a_{T-1} \;\varepsilon\; G(a_1,\ldots,a_{T-2};s)$.

Defining $v(y_1,\ldots,y_t;a_1,\ldots,a_t)$ recursively for $t=T-1,\ldots,1$ in this manner, we find that the optimal first-period choice is to choose $a_1 \varepsilon A_1$ so as to maximize

$$E_s[r_1(a_1,s)] + V(a_1) = \sum_{s\varepsilon S} \Pi(s)r_1(a_1,s) + \sum_{y_1\varepsilon Y} q(y_1)v(y_1;a_1). \quad (4.1.6)$$

The results presented in chapter 2.2 on the difference between various decision rules can be generalized to the T-period case.

---

[3] Again, Π,q will usually be suppressed in the following.

Hence, when learning is permitted, maximization of expected utility will in general lead to a suboptimal first-period choice. Exceptions are the polar cases that all first-period decisions are perfectly flexible or all first-period decisions are irreversible. In the first case, there is no need to think about the learning possibility in period 1, because possible choices in periods 2,3,... are not restricted by first-period choice; in the second case, there is no need to consider learning because when a new message arrives, it is too late to react.

One result, however, will be explicitly proved, because it will often be used in chapter 5. It is a generalization of proposition 2.7 that is often useful to show that one choice is preferred to another one.

<u>Proposition 4.5:</u> Suppose for some $t<T$ and $(a_1,\dots,a_{t-1},a_t)$, $(a_1,\dots,a_{t-1},a_t')\varepsilon G_{1,\dots,t}(s)$, $r_t(a_t,s)<r_t(a_t',s)$ and $G(a_1,\dots,a_{t-1},a_t,s)\subset G(a_1,\dots,a_{t-1},a_t',s)$ for each $s\varepsilon S$. Then a_t' is preferred to a_t given $a_1,\dots,a_{t-1}$, i.e.

$$\sum_{s\varepsilon S} \Pi(s|y_1,\dots,y_{t-1})r_t(a_t,s) + V(y_1,\dots,y_{t-1};a_1,\dots,a_{t-1},a_t) <$$

$$\sum_{s\varepsilon S} \Pi(s|y_1,\dots,y_{t-1})r_t(a_t',s) + V(y_1,\dots,y_{t-1};a_1,\dots,a_{t-1},a_t')$$

<u>Proof:</u> By definition of $v(y_1,\dots,y_t;a_1,\dots,a_t)$ as a maximum of a function on $G(a_1,\dots,a_{t-1},a_t,s)$, it is clear that

$G(a_1,\dots,a_{t-1},a_t,s)\subset G(a_1,\dots,a_{t-1},a_t',s)$ implies

$v(y_1,\dots,y_t;a_1,\dots,a_t) \le v(y_1,\dots,y_t;a_1,\dots,a_{t-1},a_t')$

for each $y_t\varepsilon Y$ and hence

$V(y_1,\dots,y_{t-1};a_1,\dots,a_t) \le V(y_1,\dots,y_{t-1};a_1,\dots,a_{t-1},a_t')$.

The result now follows because $r_t(a_t,s) < r_t(a_t',s)$ for each $s\varepsilon S$ implies

$$\sum_{s\varepsilon S} \Pi(s|y_1,\dots,y_{t-1})r_t(a_t,s) < \sum_{s\varepsilon S} \Pi(s|y_1,\dots,y_{t-1})r_t(a_t',s).$$

Our general treatment of intertemporal choice problems with learning has now been carried out in enough detail to allow for economic applications. In this chapter, we restrict ourselves to an example from consumer search theory.[4] Further applications can be found in chapter 5.

A standard problem of consumer search theory can be described as follows. Suppose that a consumer wishes to purchase one unit of some good which is known to be for sale in a large number of shops (infinitely many). The price p of the good is not known ex ante, but its probability density function f (with support $[\alpha,\beta]$, $\alpha\geq 0$ is. To find out the price that a particular shop is charging, the agent has to pay a search fee c, which is assumed to be the same for all shops.

The typical problem of search theory is to find out what number of shops the consumer should sample before purchasing the good. The approaches to the subject are distinguished according to whether the sample size has to be predetermined or whether the agent can adjust his plans to the early results of his search. In general, the last strategy can be regard as more reasonable: as an extreme case suppose that the agent observes the minimum price α in the first shop. Then, rationality would demand to react to this information by stopping the search and buying immediately. Under a predetermined strategy, the agent would not stop (except in the trivial case that he had decided to stop after one shop anyway).

It will be shown that all this can be regarded as a variation of our general theme. The consumer search problem can be formulated as a general choice problem of the type discussed in 4.1.5 (with $T=\infty$). The predetermined sample size strategy corresponds to expected utility maximization without flexibility considerations, the sequential strategy to the Bayesian strategy. To see this, take $A_1=\{0,1\}$, $A_t=\{0,1,2\}$ for $t=2,3,...$, where 0 stands for the choice "search", 1 stands for the choice "buy" and 2 stands for the choice "do nothing at all". Any feasible sequence $(a_1,a_2,...)$

---

[4] Our treatment is somewhat cursory, for a more detailed survey of consumer search theory, the reader is referred to HEY (1979; ch.11). After minor modifications, the following ideas also pertain to labour search theory, cf. HEY (1979, ch.14).

starts with a 0 (if the agent decides to search at least one shop) or a 1 (if he buys the good immediately). A feasible sequence can start with arbitrarily many zeros, the first non-zero element has to be a 1, the remaining elements have to be 2's. Formally,

$$G=\{(a_1,a_2,a_3,\dots)\varepsilon A_1 x A_2 x \dots \mid [a_t=1 \Rightarrow a_{t-1}=0;\ a_t\neq 0 \Rightarrow a_{t+1}=2]\}.$$

Hence, the elements of G are uniquely determined by the number of zeros, which is identical to the sample size. As to the information structure, $Y_1=Y_2=\dots=[\alpha,\beta]$, $S= Y_1 x Y_2 x \dots$. Because we are now considering a continuum of states, we have to modify the approach of section 4.1.5 by supposing that the prior distribution on Y is given by Prob $(p\leq y)=F(y)$, where F is the distribution function corresponding to f. Assuming that the search results are independent, this induces a prior distribution on $S=Y_1 x Y_2 x \dots$ and, by Bayes's theorem, a posterior distribution on S.

The payoff functions r_t are given by $r_t(0,s)=-c$, $r_t(1,s)= -\min(y_1,\dots,y_{t-1})$, $r_t(2,s)=0$. Here the formula for $r_t(1,s)$ reflects the so-called perfect recall assumption: an agent who decides against accepting a price when he is fist offered it, does not lose the opportunity to use it at a later time. With a predetermined sample size N, the goal is therefore to choose N as to maximize the expected value of

$$\sum_{t=1}^{\infty} r_t(a_t,s) = -Nc - \min(y_1,\dots,y_N);$$

i.e. to minimize expected total costs (search+purchase).

We do not give a full treatment of the results of the model. We restrict ourselves to one point: a simple adaptation of earlier arguments shows that the predetermined search strategy leads to a bias towards stopping search too early. At first sight, this may sound counterintuitive. Indeed, it is not true that the predetermined strategy never leads to a shorter search, as the above example readily shows. The point is slightly more subtle: an agent who uses a predetermined sample size strategy will never search any shop if he would not do so under a sequential strategy. This can be seen by using the arguments of chapter 3.4. We have to show that $V(0,\Pi,q) - V(0,\Pi_*) \geq V(1,\Pi,q) - V(1,\Pi_*,q_*)$.

This is trivially true, because 1 is totally irreversible, so that the second term is 0, while the first term is non-negative.

The remainder of this chapter is devoted to a slight deviation from the main course of argument. The model with learning that we discussed so far has many attractive characteristics. In particular, it allows to investigate flexibility considerations of agents as a response to uncertainty about future developments. One may, however, object that the kind of behaviour that is postulated in the model is too sophisticated to allow anything but misleading conclusions about real-world behaviour. We shall therefore discuss an alternative approach to sequential decision-making.

4.2 Some Generalities on Intertemporal Planning

In the preceding section, we have set up a specific model of intertemporal decision making. Decision problems were investigated where agents chose a certain variable, taking into account the effect of this decision on the present period and a number of future periods. The number of periods that the agent should consider was not explicitly taken as a matter of choice. Instead, we assumed that this number, the time horizon (planning horizon), was given exogenously. A question which appears to be worth pursuing both with respect to the last section (4.1) and the next section (4.3) is what kind of considerations should lie behind the choice of a time horizon in economic models. Specifically, in section 4.2.1, we shall raise the question whether rational economic agents should take all future periods into account when they make decisions and, more generally, which weight they should give to future periods. In section 4.2.2, we shall discuss a special planning procedure that is modelled upon real world planning procedures, and we shall relate it to the discussion in section 4.1.

4.2.1 Maximum Lifetime, Time Horizon and Time Preference[5]

Firstly, it is useful to distinguish between two different quantities, the lifetime and the planning horizon of the agent. The lifetime will, for simplicity, be considered as given exogenously. The fact that individuals, business firms and most probably even entire economies have finite lives may suggest that the relevant decision-makers should act with a finite planning horizon, i.e. should ignore the effect of their decisions on all periods after some period $T<\infty$ when taking their initial decision.

Though this argument bears some truth, it is not as convincing as it may seem at first sight. The crucial point is that the precise date at which the life of the decision-maker[6] ends is not known ex ante. As long as one considers individual consumers who do not care about the well-being of their offsprings, this kind of ignorance is not a serious argument against assuming a finite horizon: granted that no human being has ever reached the age of 200 (at least not since the Old Testament was written), there is obviously an upper bound to the set of possible lifetimes of consumers. Therefore, whenever the agent takes a decision, he may safely assume that his life is over when this bound is reached and he need not care about the effect of his decision on later periods.

The situation changes when the agent is a firm or a social planner. Though it is highly likely that any existing firm or national economy will cease to exist at some point, it is, in general, not possible to name an upper bound for the possible age of the firm or the economy. Even if the decision maker is sure that his life will be finite, if, for every $t<\infty$ there is a positive probability, however small, that he is still alive, he should take infinitely many periods into account. Therefore, the finiteness of life is not in itself an argument for ignoring any future period, though it may clearly justify giving little weight to distant periods. It

---

[5] Some of the material in this section is dealt with in the literature on economic planning (cf. HEAL 1973, p.265-268).

[6] If the decision maker is a social planner, by the "life of the decision maker" we obviously do not literally mean <u>his</u> life, but the "life" of the economy. The reader is asked to accept this somewhat sloppy terminology because of its convenience.

has been shown (cf. for instance HEAL 1973, p.265-268) that the finiteness of the agent's life should be reflected in the size of the discount-rate and not in the length of the planning horizon if for every $T<\infty$, there is a positive probability that the agent is still alive.

We find that figure 4.4 is a convenient way to summarize these findings.

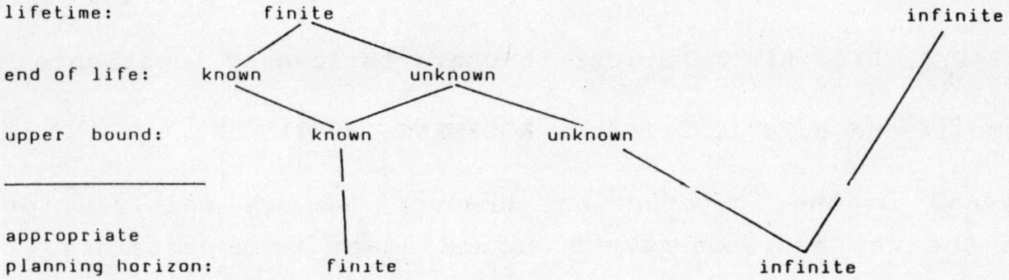

Figure 4.4: The Influence of Lifetime on the Decision Horizon

Of the four cases reflected in the figure, finite lifetime with known end and infinite lifetime are of little practical relevance. As long as the expected duration of the agent's life is the only factor that is considered in the determination of the length of the time horizon, the question whether or not lifetime expectations should lead to the choice of a finite horizon therefore boils down to the question whether or not an upper bound for the (finite) lifetime is known. Taking for granted that the decision maker expects to have a finite lifetime, but does not know the precise date of the end of his life, he should choose a finite planning horizon if he knows an upper bound for his lifetime and an infinite horizon if he does not.

Having gained clarity about this point, the agent will be able to name a number $M\leq\infty$ ("Maximum Lifetime") such that he will not care about the influence of his present action on periods after M because he is sure not to be around after that time. But even within the limits prescribed by M, there may be reasons to give little or no weight to some (in general, later) periods. To a great extent, but not entirely, this is due to uncertainty.

Even when uncertainty is ignored, there is still the possibility that a consumer prefers consumption in early periods to consumption in later periods. This phenomenon is usually referred to as **impatience to consume**. Several authors have given precise formal definitions of impatience (e.g. STACKELBERG 1939, KOOPMANS 1960, BROWN/LEWIS 1981 - for a survey cf. STEPHAN 1988a). We do not discuss impatience in any detail, but we remind the reader of the most familiar definition. If an agent evaluates a consumption stream $(C_1,\dots,C_T)$ with a utility function of the form

$\sum_{t=1}^{T} \delta^{t-1}U(C_t)$, $0<\delta$, his behaviour is characterized by impatience

to consume if and only if $\delta<1$ (cf. KOOPMANS 1960)[7].

As mentioned in the introduction, however, we are mainly interested in the way decision-makers should adapt to uncertainty. Of course, not any kind of uncertainty about the future is in itself a reason to neglect the future when decisions are made. As long as one has (or believes to have) the faintest idea about the effects of today's decisions on the distant future, these effects should be taken into consideration. For example, the uncertainty of the effects of nuclear waste deposits on human health in a few hundred years is not a justification for ignoring them altogether in policy decisions. If one believes that these effects are deleterious, then this should have some influence on cost-benefit analysis. The framework of 4.1 offers a method of approaching this kind of problem.

There is, however a different kind of uncertainty that is sometimes brought forward to justify the neglect of the distant future in decision-making.

A model as in section 4.1.5 is only a crude description of real-world decision situations. This is particularly true for the structure of the choice set. It may not be altogether misleading to assume that the agent has some idea about the effect of today's decisions on choice possibilities in the near future, but it certainly is a brute force abstraction to assume that he has a pre-

---

[7] A similar statement holds for the evaluation of infinite consumption streams, cf. the definition by BROWN/LEWIS 1981.

cise idea about this kind of effect on choice possibilities in the distant future. It is evident that for many relevant decision problems, the environment changes in such a rapid way that knowledge about the effects of today's decisions on choice possibilities in the distant future is highly limited. It has therefore been argued that despite the fact that economic agents may be interested is the long-term effects of their choices, their understanding of these effects is so limited that their behaviour can be reasonably modelled by assuming that they ignore the distant future altogether. Of course, even in an environment that changes rapidly, this kind of assumption can only be taken as an "as if"-approximization of human behaviour: many economic decisions can only be understood because of their positive effects in the very long run; a drastic example is provided by a young person that buys a retirement insurance. But of course, the agent is not completely ignorant about the distant future in this example: though the agent's environment changes in a rapid manner and the agent will be uncertain about many aspects of his life in his old age, he has enough confidence in the regularity of the world that he expects that investing into a retirement insurance will give him options he would not have if, for instance, he used the money for consumption today. Therefore, assuming that the agent completely ignores some periods of his life when he makes decisions would yield misleading conclusions concerning consumer behaviour.

In other decision situations, this assumption may not be entirely misleading. For instance, the long-term effects of many investment decisions on the position of the firm in industries that are subject to rapid change, such as the microelectronics industry, depends on a host of factors that are not subject to the firm's control and impossible to predict. Therefore, it does not lose a lot if it ignores the distant future completely.

Consequently, in situations where the firm knows very little about the structure of its long-term choice set, it may sometimes be reasonable modelling practice to cut off the planning horizon after some period $T<M$.[8] Generalizing the terminology of 4.1.1, we

---

[8] However, there is no straightforward way of deciding how to choose T.

shall say that the firm uses a T-myopic rule. The original term myopic would therefore be rephrased as 1-myopic[9].

Summarizing our discussion, we note that for an agent with a maximum lifetime M, it may well be reasonable not to give all periods 1,...,M equal weight and, what is more, it may even be reasonable to ignore some periods completely. In what follows, we shall concentrate on the effects of the second part of this statement and therefore assume that our agents are T-myopic for some period T<M.

4.2.2 Rolling Myopic Plans

If one accepts that it is worth a try to model economic agents that use myopic planning procedures, one has to add assumptions about the behaviour of the agent after the end of period T to get a complete description of the path the agent chooses in periods 1,...,M. We assume a planning procedure that resembles a planning strategy which is actually applied by real-world business firms. A well-known planning procedure of firms, which is sometimes called a rolling myopic plan, is the following: Plans are set up with a horizon of, say, T periods ($T<\infty$). After a certain number S of periods, which is in most cases smaller than T, new plans are made on the basis of new information with the time horizon being T as before. For instance, such a procedure is described by KOCH (1982, p.168). Such plans have also been used for economic modelling (FABER/PROOPS/RUTH/MICHAELIS 1990, FABER/PROOPS 1990).

This kind of behaviour is close to what we should expect from our theoretical discussion: in the light of the preceding argument, optimization with a horizon T which is shorter than maximum life-

---

9 It should be pointed out that the term "myopic", though always referring to some kind of shortsightedness, is not used in an entirely unambiguous manner in the literature. For instance, we have
(1) myopic = maximizing short-term payoff (e.g. ARROW 1968, NICKELL 1978, FABER/PROOPS/RUTH/MICHAELIS 1990)
(2) myopic = using a positive discount rate (e.g. STROTZ 1955/6 and, similarly, BROWN/LEWIS 1981).
Our usage of the term "myopic" is of course (1). (2) is closer in spirit to the notion of "impatience to consume".

time may be a good approximization of rational behaviour in a world where the effects of present decisions on the future are not well known. Recalling the arguments of 4.1.5, it is also to be expected that plans are reevaluated after S<T periods, if the initial choice is sufficiently flexible and the informational position has changed when period S is reached. However, it is not to be expected from our argumentation that T and S are constant over time. In our abstract framework, the choice of T should itself be a matter of optimization and should, among other things, depend on how well the agent believes to understand the future. This belief may change over time because

"... volatility tends to vary greatly over time, quiescent eras with little period-by-period fluctuations alternating with eras of rapid fluctuation". (ARROW 1988, p.278)

Therefore, one would also expect T to change over time. Similar considerations apply to the choice of S. Though certain planning decisions are reevaluated regularly, the frequency of this reevaluation will, in general, change according to the frequency and nature of the new information that is received and should not be determined a priori.

In the following, we shall nevertheless restrict ourselves to rolling myopic plans with fixed T and S. Given the above remarks, it is clear that this restriction is not justified on grounds of "realism". Instead, it is supposed to be a methodological simplification that allows to model sequential decision making in a particularly simple way. In section 4.3, we shall give a formal treatment of this planning procedure. To model rolling myopic plans, we shall assume that an agent with maximum lifetime M chooses a path $(a_1,...,a_T)$ (T<M) as in the general T-period choice problem. In general, the agent will not have to hold on to his original plan until period T. We shall assume that there is an S<T such that the agent reevaluates his plan at the end of period S. He then chooses a new T-period plan from a set of feasible choices that depends on his earlier actions. This plan is reevaluated again at the end of period 2S, a new plan is set up for the next T

periods, etc. This procedure will be described in more detail in section 4.3.

Chapter 4.3 Modelling Rolling Myopic Plans

In the following, we shall suppose that our T-period choice problem has the special form of a discrete real-valued control problem. We shall formalize the idea of rolling myopic plans and derive some basic results. The motivation for this section came from FABER/PROOPS (1990) and FABER/PROOPS/RUTH/MICHAELIS (1990) who use such plans to model the behaviour of agents in an uncertain world. Our presentation is supposed to be a systematic treatment of the planning procedure that is used in these models.

4.3.1 The Standard T-Period Control Problem

The discrete problem that our myopic agent has to solve will be simplified in one essential manner. To stay in the framework of chapter 4.1, one would have to specify the information structure. As the idea of the modelling procedure in the following is to present a simpler model of sequential decision making, such complications are not introduced. Instead, we work with completely deterministic objective functions, which can however be interpreted as being based on point expectations in the usual way.

Hence, we consider the **standard T-period control problem**, which is defined in the usual manner[10]:

Suppose $T \leq \infty$. In each period $t=0,1,2,...,T-1$, the agent has to choose a variable u_t, the **control variable**, from the real vector space R^c $(c \geq 1)$.

This choice determines the state of the system at t $(t=1,2,...,T)$, which is described by a **state variable x_t**, an element of the real vector space R^s. x_t is assumed to be given for $t=0$, x_0 is the **initial state**. For $t=1,2,...,$ the states x_t are determined recur-

[10] For an introduction to discrete control problems, cf. BELLMAN(1957) or INTRILIGATOR (1971).

sively according to $x_{t+1} = f(x_t, u_t)$, where f is a function with arguments in R^{s+c} and values in R^s, the **iteration function.** In other words, given x_0, the choice of the control u_0 determines the state x_1 as $f(x_0, u_0)$, the choice of u_1 determines $x_2 = f(x_1, u_1)$ etc.

Of course, the choice of u_t is subject to restrictions: given the initial state x_0 of the system, which is assumed to be an element of the real vector space R^s ($s \geq 1$), the choice of the control path $u := (u_0, u_1, u_2, \ldots, u_{T-1})$ is restricted to a subset $G(x_0)$ of R^{Tc}.
We shall assume that the agent maximizes an objective function $J(x_0, u_0, \ldots, x_{t-1}, u_{t-1})$ under the restrictions described above.

Hence, the problem can be summarized as

$J(x_0, u_0, \ldots, x_{T-1}, u_{T-1})$ max! subject to
(i) x_0 given (4.3.1)
(ii) $x_{t+1} = f(x_t, u_t)$ and
(iii) $(u_0, \ldots, u_{T-1}) \in G(x_0)$.

Except when otherwise mentioned, we shall assume that J is of the additively separable form $J(x_0, u_0, \ldots, x_{T-1}, u_{T-1}) = \sum_{t=0}^{T-1} I_t(u_t)$ for real-valued functions I_t. More specifically, we shall assume that $I_t = \delta^t I$ for some real-valued function I and a real number $\delta \in (0,1)$. To simplify the discussion, we shall assume that a unique optimal choice $(u_0, \ldots, u_{T-1})$ of controls exists for every initial value x_0. Because $x_{t+1} = f(x_t, u_t)$, this also determines a unique sequence $x = (x_1, \ldots, x_T)$ of states.

Economic theory abounds with problems of the type just described (cf. SARGENT 1987) and variations of it where time is taken to be continuous rather than discrete (cf. e.g. ARROW/KURZ 1970) and/or stochastic elements are added to the discussion (cf. MALLIARIS/BROCK 1982, SARGENT 1987). A few such examples will be given in the following section.

4.3.2 Examples

In this section, we shall provide examples of models that fit into the general pattern outlined in section 4.3.1.

A neoclassical growth model

We start with a standard neoclassical growth model. It is typically formulated as follows (cf. DECHERT 1984).

Find a solution to

$$V(y) = \max_{\{k_t\}} \sum_{t=0}^{\infty} \delta^t W(y_t - k_{t+1}) \text{ subject to}$$

(i) $0 \leq k_{t+1} \leq y_t = g(k_t)$,

(ii) $y_0 = y$,

(iii) $0 < \delta < 1$.

Here y_t is the per capita output of a homogeneous good that can be used as a capital good and a consumption good, k_t is per capita capital stock (and $y_t - k_{t+1}$ is the amount of the per capita output in period t that is left for consumption), W is a strictly concave one-period utility function and g is a neoclassical production function with positive first derivative and negative second derivative.

The model just sketched can be regarded as a standard T-period control problem ($T=\infty$).

To see this, one has to show that it can be written as in (4.3.1). The only problem is to show that equation (ii) of (4.3.1) can be satisfied for suitable variables x_t, u_t and a function f.

We choose $x_t = y_t$ as state variable and $u_t = y_t - k_{t+1}$ as control variable. Then $y_{t+1} = g(k_{t+1}) = g(y_t - (y_t - k_{t+1}))$ can be rewritten as

$$x_{t+1} = g(x_t - u_t). \tag{4.3.2}$$

Hence $f(x_t, u_t) = g(x_t - u_t)$ can be taken as the iteration function for the problem. With

$J(u_0, u_1, \ldots) = \sum_{t=0}^{\infty} \delta^t W(y_t - k_{t+1})$ as objective function, we see that the optimal growth problem is a standard T-period control problem ($T=\infty$).

A completely analogous formulation is possible for the case $T<\infty$.

The Neo-Austrian Model

Another model satisfying the requirements of the standard control problem was introduced by BERNHOLZ/FABER (1973) (cf. also FABER 1979, ch.5)[11]. We shall briefly summarize this model and show that it gives rise to a standard T-period control problem.

There are three commodities, a non-producible factor labour, a produced capital good and a produced consumption good. There are three linear production processes, the first two of which produce the consumption good. The third one produces the capital good according to

$$\begin{aligned}&\text{(a)}\ X_1(t) = L_1(t)/l_1,\\ &\text{(b)}\ X_2(t) = \text{Min}\,(L_2(t)/l_2, K_2(t)/k_2),\\ &\text{(c)}\ X_3(t) = L_3(t)/l_3,\end{aligned} \tag{4.3.3}$$

where for $t \in 1,\ldots,T-1$, $X_i(t)$ $(i=1,2,3)$ denotes the output, $L_i(t)$ $(i=1,2,3)$ the labour input of process i in period t, $K_2(t)$ denotes the capital input of process 2 and l_1, l_2, l_3, k_2 are positive coefficients.

While the outputs of the consumption good processes are supposed to be available in the period the process is operated, process 3 is assumed to supply the capital good after one unit of time.

The labour supply is assumed to be constant (L). The capital stock K(t) deteriorates at a constant rate c, $0 \le c \le 1$. Hence,

$$K(t+1) = (1-c)K(t)+X_3(t). \tag{4.3.4}$$

[11] For extensions of the approach the reader is referred to JAKSCH (1975), FABER (1986), STEPHAN (1989), FABER/PROOPS (1990).

Process 2 is assumed to need less labour per unit of the consumption good than process 1: $l_2 < l_1$.

We note that there is a level of capital above which further additions to the capital stock do not lead to a greater production of the consumption good with process 2. By equation (b) of (4.3.3), $X_2(t) = \text{Min}\ [K_2(t)/k_2, L_2(t)/l_2]$. As $L_2(t) \leq L$, it follows that $X_2(t) \leq L/l_2$ no matter what $K_2(t)$ is. In particular, increasing the capital stock beyond $k_2 L/l_2$ will never lead to an increase of $X_2(t)$ and hence is definitely useless.

It is therefore assumed that $K(t) \leq k_2 L/l_2$ during the periods considered.

The capital stock is required to be fully employed and equipped with labour, i.e. $K(t) = K_2(t) \leq k_2 L_2(t)/l_2$. Pure efficiency considerations imply that $K_2(t) \geq k_2 L_2(t)/l_2$. To see this, suppose $L_2(t)/l_2 > K_2(t)/k_2$. As

$$X_2(t) = \text{Min}\ [K_2(t)/k_2, L_2(t)/l_2],$$

the same output with process 2 could be achieved with $L_2(t)/l_2 = K_2(t)/k_2$, so that some labour has in fact been wasted: it could have been used for production of the consumption good instead.

Summarizing, we have

$$K(t) = K_2(t) = k_2 L_2(t)/l_2. \qquad (4.3.5)$$

We suppose that a central planning agency maximizes an aggregate welfare function

$$W(C(0),\ldots,C(T-1)) = \sum_{t=0}^{T-1} \delta^t W_0(C_t),$$

that is continuous, strictly monotonic and strictly quasi-concave.

It faces the following restrictions (t=0,1,...,T-1):

$$C(t) \leq X_1(t) + X_2(t) \qquad (4.3.6)$$

$$L_1(t) + L_2(t) + L_3(t) \leq L \qquad (4.3.7)$$

$$K_2(t+1) \leq K(t+1) = (1-c)K(t) + X_3(t). \qquad (4.3.8)$$

(4.3.6) says that consumption in period t is bounded by the amount of the consumption good that is produced in period t, i.e. the consumption good cannot be stored. (4.3.7) and (4.3.8) are factor limitations.

As it is clearly suboptimal not to use the entire labour supply and not to consume the entire production of the consumption good, (4.3.6) and (4.3.7) can be taken to be equalities. The same holds for equation (4.3.8) because of (4.3.5). Hence, we may assume

$$C(t) = X_1(t) + X_2(t) \tag{4.3.9}$$

$$L_1(t) + L_2(t) + L_3(t) = L \tag{4.3.10}$$

$$K_2(t+1) = K(t+1) = (1-c)K(t) + X_3(t). \tag{4.3.11}$$

This model can be formulated as a standard T-period model with state variable K(t) and control variable C(t). To see this, we need to show that it can be expressed as in (4.3.1). In particular, we have to show that

$$K(t+1) = g(K(t),C(t)) \tag{4.3.12}$$

for a function $g:R^2 \to R^1$.

By (4.3.4), $K(t+1) = (1-c)K(t) + X_3(t)$.
By (4.3.3) and (4.3.10),

$$X_3(t) = L_3(t)/l_3 = [L-L_1(t)-L_2(t)]/l_3. \tag{4.3.13}$$

By (4.3.3) and (4.3.9),

$$L_1(t) = l_1 X_1(t) = l_1 [C(t)-X_2(t)]. \tag{4.3.14}$$

By (4.3.3),

$$X_2(t) = \min [K_2(t)/k_2, L_2(t)/l_2]. \tag{4.3.15}$$

By (4.3.5), $K(t) = K_2(t) = k_2 L_2(t)/l_2$, so that by (4.3.3)

$X_2(t) = K(t)/k_2 = L_2(t)/l_2.$ (4.3.16)

Inserting (4.3.16) in (4.3.13), we find that

$X_3(t) = [L-L_1(t)-l_2X_2(t)]/l_3.$

Therefore, by (4.3.14) and (4.3.16),

$X_3(t) = \{L-l_1[C(t)-K(t)/k_2]-l_2K(t)/k_2\}/l_3$

and therefore, by (4.3.4),

$$K(t+1) = (1-c)K(t) + \{L-l_1[C(t)-K(t)/k_2]-l_2K(t)/k_2\}/l_3 = [(1-c)l_3k_2+l_1-l_2]K(t)/l_3k_2 + [L-l_1C(t)]/l_3,$$

so that K(t+1) is in fact representable as a function of K(t) and C(t) as desired.

Hence, the Neo-Austrian model is the standard T-period control problem

$$\sum_{t=0}^{T-1} \delta^t U(C(t)) \text{ max! } \quad \text{subject to}$$

(i) K(0) given

(ii) $K(t+1) = [(1-c)l_3k_2+l_1-l_2]K(t)/l_3k_2 + [L-l_1C(t)]/l_3$

(iii) $(C(0),...,C(T-1)) \in G(K(0))$, where G(K(0)) is the set of feasible consumption paths given the initial capital stock K(0).

4.3.3 Bellman's Principle

We will only use one simple but fundamental fact from optimal control theory which is usually referred to as Bellman's principle. In the words of the master himself, this principle reads:

"An optimal policy has the property that whatever the initial state and initial decision are, the remaining decisions must constitute an optimal policy with regard to the state resulting from the first decision." (BELLMAN 1957, p.83)

We have already used this principle in the backward recursion procedure in 4.1.5 for general T-period choice problems. We shall look into it in slightly more detail for the standard T-period control problem. To state the result in formal terms, one should first note that a standard T-period control problem with an objective function $\sum_{t=0}^{T-1} I_t(u_t)$ defines a sequence of (T-S)-period control problems (S=1,...,T):

Suppose that the optimal state and control paths for the standard T-period control problem are $(x_1,\dots,x_T)$ and $(u_o,\dots,u_{T-1})$, respectively. Then for every $S\varepsilon\{1,\dots,T\}$, one can define a (T-S)-period problem as follows.

As initial state take $y_o=x_S$. As iteration function take f as before.
Choice of controls is limited to such paths that are attainable as the last T-S controls for the original problem, given a choice sequence $(u_o,\dots,u_{S-1})$. Formally, the control set $G^*(y_o)$ is $\{(v_o,\dots,v_{T-S-1})\ \varepsilon R^{(T-S)c}\,|\,$there exists $(u_o,\dots,u_{S-1},u_S,\dots,u_{T-1})\varepsilon G(x_o)$ such that $u_S=v_o,\dots,u_{T-1}=v_{T-S-1}\}$.

As objective function take $J^*(v_o,\dots,v_{T-S-1}) = J(u_o,\dots,u_{S-1},v_o,\dots,v_{T-S-1})$, where $u_o,\dots,u_{S-1}$ are the given choices of controls in earlier periods. This reflects the fact that one wants to choose the T-S controls remaining open at time s optimal with respect to the original objective function, but has to take the first s choices as given. Clearly, J^* is maximized if and only if $\sum_{t=S}^{T-1} I_t(v_{t-S})$ is maximized.

Let us call the problem just defined **the derived (T-S)-period problem** (of a given T-period problem). Then Bellman's principle is the following proposition.

<u>Proposition 4.6:</u> If $(x_1,\dots,x_T)$ is the optimal state path for a T-period problem [with controls $u_o,\dots,u_{T-1}$], the optimal state path for the derived (T-S)-period problem is $(y_1,\dots,y_{T-S}) = (x_{S+1},\dots,x_T)$ [with controls $v_o=u_S,\dots,v_{T-S-1}=u_{T-1}$].

Note that this is just a complicated formulation of the above quotation. It says that for a path to be optimal, one has to choose the remaining variables in an optimal manner at any moment of time.

Proof: By assumption, the optimal path for the T-period problem is $x_1,\ldots,x_T$ (controls $u_0,\ldots,u_{T-1}$). Then, to get the optimal state path for the derived (T-S)-problem one has to maximize J^*. By definition, the maximum is $v_0,\ldots,v_{T-S-1}$.

Bellman's principle will be used repeatedly in the following analysis.

4.3.4 (T,S)-Plans

In the following, we shall take up the ideas of 4.2.2 and discuss rolling myopic plans. This planning procedure is modelled upon the one used by FABER/PROOPS/RUTH/MICHAELIS (1990), FABER/PROOPS (1990). It is constructed as follows.

Suppose an agent has a maximum lifetime of $M \leq \infty$. Suppose that due to lack of foresight he only has a planning horizon of $T<M$ periods (cf. section 4.2.1). He sets up a plan with horizon T in period 0, reevaluates plans after the first S choices ($S\leq T$) have been made. His planning horizon is supposed to be T as before. He repeats this procedure in period 2S, 3S, etc. Hence his plans overlap as in figure 4.5.

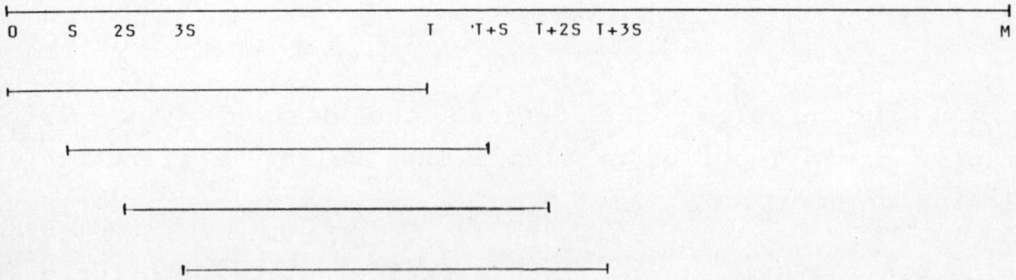

Figure 4.5: (T,S)-Plans

More specifically, suppose that in period 0 he solves a T-period control problem with an initial value x_0. Denoting the resulting state path as $x(1;0), x(2;0), \ldots, x(T;0)$, the state $x_S := x(S;0)$ is reached after S periods. From Bellman's principle, we know that if he pursues his original plan after period S, he will behave as if he was maximizing the derived (T-S)-period problem with initial value x_S. Instead, we now assume that when he reevaluates his original plan at time S with time horizon T in period S, he solves a T-period problem with initial value x_S, which gives a new optimal T-period state path that will be denoted as $x(S+1;S), \ldots, x(S+T;S)$. After another S periods, the same procedure is applied to the new path. Hence, we get a new state path $x(2S+1;2S), \ldots, x(2S+T;2S)$, which is the solution of a T-period control problem with initial value $x_{2S} := x(2S;S)$. If one repeats this procedure, one obtains a sequence of overlapping T-period plans. The state path that is actually realized is given as $x_1, x_2, \ldots = x(1;0), \ldots, x(S;0), x(S+1;S), \ldots, x(2S;S), x(2S+1;2S), \ldots$, the sequence of the initial sub-sequences (of length S) of the T-period plans. Hence the following kind of picture emerges (cf. figure 4.6).

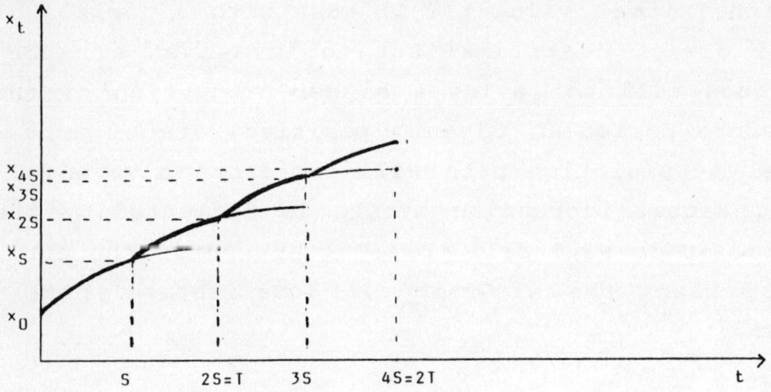

Figure 4.6: A (T, S, x_0)-path[12]

The planning strategy we just described will be called a **(T,S)-strategy**, the realized state path will be called the **(T,S,xo)-path**. Of course, the (T, S, x_0)-path does not only depend on T, S and x_0, but also on the discount rate and the function I as well as on the control space.

Taking all this as given, one may ask:

[12] In order to have a nice picture, we have substituted continuous for discrete time in this figure.

(a) What can a (T,S,x_0)-path possibly look like? and

(b) How does the nature of the path depend on T and S?

Starting with the second question, a few general remarks are helpful.

First of all, it is worth recalling from section 4.3.3 that the solution path for a standard T-period plan, though the result of a once and for all decision, may be interpreted as the result of a sequence of (T-S)-period decisions (S=0,...,T-1). Consequently, the behaviour of the path towards the end of the horizon will often show certain pathological features, so-called "end effects" which reflect the fact that towards the end of the horizon the path is equivalent to a very short-sighted path.

We illustrate this for the Neo-Austrian capital theory model of section 4.3.2. The choice of the last control variable for this problem, C(T-1), can be interpreted as the optimal choice for the 1-period problem with initial value K(T-1). But with a horizon of one period, it will always be optimal not to invest at all, because the capital good will not allow a higher production of the consumption good before period 2. Given a positive rate of depreciation, the optimal accumulation path will therefore always fall in the last period. Hence, increasing myopia is reflected by the fact that the capital stock will fall towards the end of the horizon. For a T-period plan, the situation is (qualitatively) described by figure 4.7.

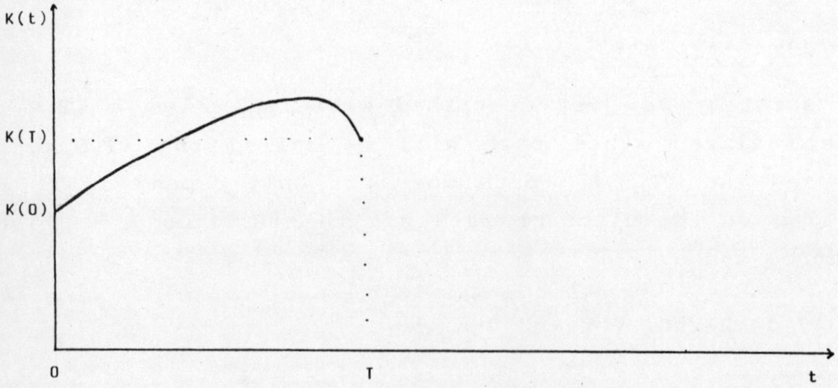

Figure 4.7: A T-Period Plan for the Neo-Austrian Model

If a (T,T)-strategy were applied to the model, a similar outcome would be observed for every section of the path. Hence, we would get the following kind of picture (cf. figure 4.8).

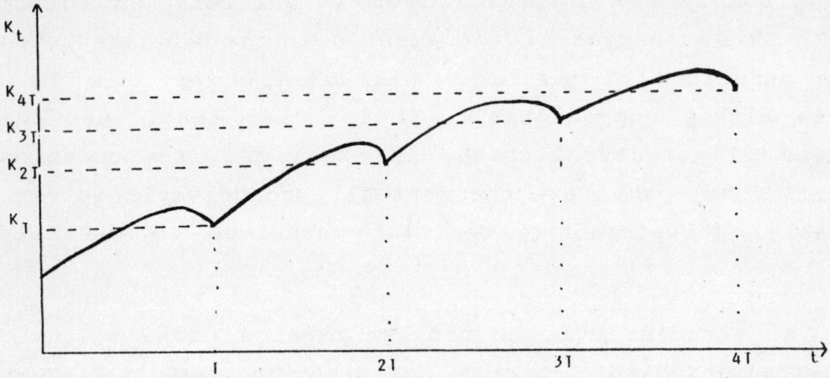

figure 4.8: A (T,T,x_0)-path for the Neo-Austrian Model

For smaller values of S (and most definitely for S=1), this kind of problem no longer occurs. Though the original plan of the agent is to behave as in figure 4.7, he does not actually carry out the last section of this plan, so that the last bit is substituted by a new plan as in figure 4.6.

End effects are therefore eliminated, simply because the planning horizon is not allowed to drop all the way down to 1 as in the case of the (T,T)-plan.

In the extreme case of the (T,1)-plan, for instance, the agent sets up a T-period plan in period 0. If he were to continue to follow this plan in period 1, he would act as if he was solving a (T-1)-period problem. Instead, he reevaluates his plan with a horizon of T periods. The same holds for periods 2,3, etc. when the original plan is equivalent to a (T-2)-plan with initial value x(2), a (T-3)-problem with initial value x(3), etc.

Summing up, the effect of moving from a (T,T)-strategy to a (T,1)-strategy is to reduce myopia and therefore to eliminate end effects.

To answer question (a), a drastic simplification is necessary. The original idea of using rolling myopic plans is that they are supposed to model the behaviour of agents who receive new information over time and possibly new information of an entirely unpredictable nature. If this openness of the agent's environment is taken seriously, the structure of the model will change over time in a manner which is highly unpredictable. It is clear that, once one admits this kind of structural change in the model, the question what kinds of (T,S,x_0)-paths are theoretically conceivable is virtually unsolvable. Therefore, we restrict ourselves to the following case:

Assumption 1: The structure of the problem remains unchanged over time so that the standard T-period decision problem the agent faces when he makes a new decision stays the same. In particular,

(a) the agent always maximizes the same utility function and
(b) if $x_{kS}=x_{lS}$ for arbitrary $k,l \in N$, it follows that $G(kS)=G(lS)$, where $G(kS)$, $G(lS)$ are the choice sets for the problem the agent faces in periods kS and lS.

In itself, this case is not interesting. The result we can derive for this case, however, though not directly applicable to more general cases, illustrates an important principle: _if_ decision situations are repeated in the same fashion, certain non-obvious regularity properties can be expected for a class of decision problems that includes familiar examples.

Assumption 1 guarantees that the T-period control problem for an agent who applies a (T,S)-strategy in period kS (k=1,2,3,...) is identical to the original T-period control problem - the only difference being that the initial value is x_{kS} instead of x_0. Hence, a (T,S,x_0)-path is not just a sequence of initial subsequences of T-period-paths, but a sequence of initial subsequences of T-period-paths for _identical_ control problems (with possibly different initial values). Hence, to understand the behaviour of the whole sequence, it suffices to investigate the original T-period control problem - it contains all relevant information.

In the following section 4.3.5 we shall give an example of this. We shall show that with relatively little information about the T-period problem we can deduce a strong result about the shape of the (T,S,x_0)-path.

4.3.5 A Monotonicity Result

The result we shall prove in this section is that, under certain assumptions on the underlying standard control problem, the path $x_0, x_1, x_2, \ldots$ can be expected to have monotonic trend, even if the solution path of the underlying T-period control problem is not monotonic itself.

More precisely, consider the sequence $x_0, x_S, x_{2S}, \ldots$ of states at the starting (and end) points of the time intervals at which plans are revised. The following proposition says that this sequence is monotonic in many cases.

<u>Proposition 4.7:</u> Suppose given a T-period control problem such that

(i) Assumption 1 of section 4.3.4 holds;

(ii) the state space is a subset of the real line;

(iii) for arbitrary initial states x_0 and y_0, $x_0 \geq y_0$ implies $x_S \geq y_S$, i.e. the optimal state at time S depends positively on the initial value.

Then the sequence $x_0, x_S, x_{2S}, \ldots$ is either monotonically decreasing or increasing.

Before proving the proposition, we start with a few words of interpretation. The proposition says that even if the state path of the T-period problem itself is not monotonic, the (T,S,x_0)-path will have a monotonic trend (cf. figure 4.9 below).

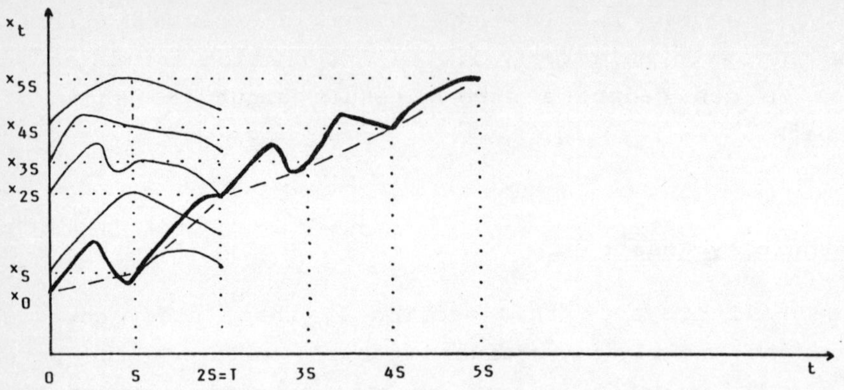

Figure 4.9: A Monotonicity Proposition

Of course, this result depends heavily on the assumptions of the proposition. If the state space is a higher-dimensional real vector space, or the T-period problem the agent faces whenever he makes a decision changes over time, or the positive dependence condition is not fulfilled, the monotonicity property need not hold. This clearly excludes many interesting models as applications, but the proposition can nevertheless be applied to some interesting models. We shall elaborate on this point after having proved the proposition.

<u>Proof:</u> We show inductively that either $x_0 \leq x_S \leq x_{2S} \leq \ldots$ or $x_0 \geq x_S \geq x_{2S} \geq \ldots$.

As the state space is the real line, the $\geq$-relation is complete, so that $x_0 \leq x_S$ or $x_0 \geq x_S$.[13]

Suppose first that $x_0 \leq x_S$. We shall start by showing that this implies $x_S \leq x_{2S}$. To see this, note that x_S is obtained as the S-th value of the state path for the T-period-problem with initial value x_0, while x_{2S} is the S-th value of the state path for the T-period-problem with initial value x_S. By assumption, $x_0 \leq x_S$, i.e. the initial value for the second problem is greater or equal than the initial value for the first problem. By assumption (iii), it follows that the S-th value for the second problem is greater or equal than the S-th value for the first problem, i.e. $x_{2S} \geq x_S$.

[13] This is of course the argument that cannot be generalized to higher-dimensional state spaces.

The same argument shows that, whenever $x_{ks} \geq x_{(k-1)s}$ ($k \varepsilon N$), it follows that $x_{(k+1)s} \geq x_{ks}$. Hence $x_0 \leq x_s$ implies that $x_0, x_s, x_{2s}, \ldots$ is monotonically increasing.

To complete the proof, one has to show that $x_0 \geq x_s$ implies that $x_0, x_s, x_{2s}, \ldots$ is monotonically decreasing, which is done in precisely the same fashion.

Summing up, if $x_0 \leq x_s$, the trend of the (T,S,x_0)-path is monotonically increasing: if $x_0 \geq x_s$, t is monotonically decreasing, so in any case it is monotonic.

<u>Corollary</u>: Under the assumptions of proposition 4.7, any $(T,1,x_0)$-path is monotonic.

<u>Proof:</u> For S=1, $(x_0, x_s, x_{2s}, \ldots) = (x_0, x_1, x_2, \ldots)$. Application of the proposition therefore shows that $(x_0, x_1, x_2, \ldots)$ is monotonic.

<u>Applications</u>

We note, without rigourously proving this claim, that under not too restrictive assumptions the proposition is applicable to both our examples in section 4.3.2.

For the neoclassical growth model, an adaptation of an argument by DECHERT (1984) is needed to show that assumption (iii) of the proposition holds. As (i) and (ii) are clearly satisfied, this is all that is required.

For the Neo-Austrian capital theory model, the crucial condition is that preferences are such that an addition to the initial capital stock will lead to higher consumption in <u>all</u> future periods. It can be shown that this condition implies assumption (iii), so that the proposition can be applied.

We note in passing that the monotonicity proposition 4.7 is applicable to the investigation of infinite horizon plans. Suppose given an infinite horizon problem with objective function

$\sum_{t=0}^{\infty} \delta^t I$. Then, by Bellman's principle, the solution path of the infinite horizon problem is equal to the solution path of the corresponding $(\infty,1)$-problem. To see this, note that Bellman's principle applied to an ∞-period problem says that at any moment S the path $x_2, x_3, \ldots$ is the solution path of the derived $\infty=(\infty-1)$-period problem, which has initial value x_1. Similarly, the path $x_3, x_4, \ldots$ has to be the solution of the derived $\infty=(\infty-2)$-period problem with initial value x_2, etc. Hence, the state path of the ∞-period problem with initial value x_0 and the $(\infty,1,x_0)$-path are identical. Now if assumptions (1) to (3) are satisfied, the $(\infty,1,x_0)$-path is monotonic. Hence, the same holds for the solution path of the infinite horizon problem.

This principle is essentially what DECHERT (1984) used when he proved that the output paths of optimal growth models as in 4.3.2 are monotonic. Given the argumentation of this section, it is not surprising that his result can not be generalized to higher dimensions, as BOLDRIN/MONTRUCCHIO (1986), DENECKERE/PELIKAN (1986) showed.

4.4 Final Remarks on the T-Period Model

In this section, we generalized the choice model of chapters 2 and 3 to T periods ($T \geq 2$).

With the exception of the digression in chapter 4.3, the purpose of chapters 2-4 was to provide a framework for the simultaneous discussion of different intertemporal choice problems. Using this framework, we investigated the effects of irreversibility and uncertainty on the optimal choice under different choice criteria.

There can be little doubt that the general model of choice developed in section 4.1 is at least sufficiently abstract to incorporate a wide variety of well known models in a general framework. On the other hand, it contains enough structure to generate interesting results.

Despite the repeated reference to economic examples, the emphasis was clearly on the understanding of the underlying structure. In the next chapter, we want to change this and see how familiar facts from the theory of money demand can be interpreted with the help of the general framework of this chapter.

Chapter 5

CONSUMPTION AND SAVINGS DECISIONS OF HOUSEHOLDS

In chapter 1, we used economic examples to get an idea how irreversibility and learning should be treated in abstract intertemporal choice models. Having investigated such models in chapters 2-4, we now proceed the other way round and show how the abstract models can be applied to a particular economic example, namely to the theory of intertemporal consumption and savings decisions of households.

The results we shall prove should not come as a great surprise. On the contrary, the economic content of most of the statements will be more or less familiar. The purpose of this chapter is not to provide new economic insights but to present familiar arguments in a coherent fashion.

To the extent that households can influence their future options they do so via their decisions to hold wealth and allocate it to different assets. A broad approach would include such intangible assets as education, but here we restrict ourselves to financial assets. In particular, this leads to the question what determines the quantity of money a household wants to hold. This is one of the most controversial issues in macroeconomic theory - not least because the effectiveness of monetary and fiscal policy is known to depend heavily on the variables that enter the money demand function and their relative importance.

The question has both theoretical and empirical aspects. Partly, different points of view on the subject of money demand arise because of the much deplored lack of microeconomic foundations in the theory of money demand. Arguably, however, the more critical points are of an empirical nature. While there is some agreement about the list of factors that should be seen as influencing the demand for money on theoretical grounds, questions that can only be settled empirically are which of the variables have a dominant influence and whether money demand can reasonably be approximated by a stable function of a small number of variables. These empirical issues are beyond the scope of this thesis. Our aim, which is directed towards theoretical questions, is more modest. We want to show how our general approach to intertemporal choice problems helps to understand the motives for the demand for money.

Many economists would subscribe to the view that some insights into money demand can be obtained from the idea that it results from an intertemporal optimization problem, in which the demand for money, non-monetary assets and consumption goods are determined simultaneously. The objective function is a utility function that depends on consumption in present and future periods; money and the other assets only enter the objective function indirectly, namely inasmuch as they influence the future consumption possibilities.

Models of this type can be used to derive properties of money demand functions via standard methods of marginal analysis (cf. NIEHANS 1978, ch.4). In this section, we shall confine ourselves to one aspect of money demand. Using an intertemporal model of consumption and portfolio choice that allows for learning, we shall ask under which conditions money will be held at all when return-bearing assets are also available. In other words, we shall give a formal treatment of motives of money demand. We shall also touch upon related issues such as motives for holding short-term assets and wealth in general. It will turn out that the general apparatus of earlier chapters is very helpful for this purpose.

5.1 Motives for the Demand for Money - Some Familiar Tenets

Even today, a discussion of motives for money demand will usually start with the three reasons KEYNES (1936) gave: the transactions motive, the precautionary motive and the speculative motive.

The first of the three reasons is based on the fact that money is needed as a means to synchronize income and expenditure streams. The second reason involves uncertainty: as the informational position of the consumer may change over time, he may realize tomorrow that he needs money to finance unexpected expenditures.

Finally, the third reason, the speculative motive, is grounded on the idea that in times when the prices of bonds are expected to fall it may be advisable to sell them at the beginning of the period of falling prices and hold cash until the end of that period. Foregone interest payments may then be outweighed by the capital gains obtained by selling the asset at a high price and buying it at a low price. From this idea and the assumption that different agents have different expectations about the future interest rate, KEYNES (1936) derived the negative dependence of money demand on interest rates.

The Keynesian arguments are not without historical precursors; the transactions motive was central to the Cambridge School (e.g. PIGOU 1917), and the interest dependency of the demand for money had also occasionally been mentioned before (cf. CANNAN 1921).

Not long before the appearance of the General Theory, HICKS (1935), in his call for an integration of monetary and value theory, formulated the main question we are going to deal with:

Why do individuals hold cash when they could also hold return-bearing assets?

Though his arguments were largely informal, HICKS already suggested the answers that postwar scholars took up. Essentially, the reasons are incomplete information and transaction costs. The idea of transaction costs was central to the models of money demand suggested by BAUMOL (1952) and TOBIN (1956). These authors argue that when the exchange of non-monetary assets for money is costly and income and expenditure streams do not coincide, agents may sometimes find it advisable to hold wealth as money if it is known that this wealth will be needed for transaction purposes relatively soon, because the foregone interest payments for such a short period may not outweigh the transaction costs that are saved by not investing into return-bearing assets. In this argument, transaction costs are fundamental; uncertainty is involved only inasmuch as it is responsible for transaction costs to occur.[1]

Another approach to money demand emphasizes the importance of incomplete information. MARKOWITZ (1952) and TOBIN (1958) considered models in which households have to decide how to allocate their exogenously given total wealth to assets that differ in the expected values and variances of their yields. Suppose the decision-maker values an asset higher the higher the expected value and the lower the variance of returns[2]. If money is considered to be a non-risky asset, it is conceivable for agents to hold money even when there are assets available that lead to higher returns, simply because the relatively low risk of money may make up for the relatively low expected rate of return.

The trouble with this argument is that, in reality, there exist assets that dominate money in the sense that they are also virtually riskless but lead to higher returns, for instance savings and time deposits. Therefore, incomplete information on its own is not a convincing reason to hold money, even if risk-aversion is postulated. Summing up, money may be held in the presence of transaction costs even when the agent is perfectly informed, but it will generally not be held if the agent is incompletely informed and there are no transaction costs. This led authors like NIEHANS (1978) and MC CALLUM/GOODFRIEND (1987) to conclude that the fundamental reason for holding money is not incomplete information, but the occurrence of transaction costs.

However, it has been argued that incomplete information nevertheless plays an important role in the understanding of motives for money demand, at least if learning is allowed to take place. To confirm this, we will give an example of a situation where an agent will only hold money if he expects to learn in the future. Roughly speaking, this is so because, if wealth is held as money,

---

1 For a detailed treatment of the reasons for the occurrence of transaction costs, the reader is referred to RICHTER (1987).

2 This is usually seen as justified for risk-averse investors, because the variance is taken as a measure of the riskiness of an asset; see however ROTHSCHILD/STIGLITZ (1970) for cautionary remarks concerning the usage of the variance as a measure of the riskiness of a random variable.

future information can be exploited more easily than if other assets are held. Investments in return-bearing assets may be reversible only at high costs, implying that portfolio rearrangements may be very expensive if the shift is not from money to other assets. It may happen that, if the agent does not expect to learn in the future (or ignores this learning possibility), he will not worry too much about this and not hold money while, if he expects to learn, he may feel more inclined to choose money because of its flexibility.

However, the usual caveat is that there are certain short-term assets which share the flexibility properties of money while leading to a positive yield that is almost certainly known. Therefore, the literature that deals with the flexibility of different assets (HIRSHLEIFER 1972, GOLDMAN 1974/1978, CHANG/HAMBERG/HIRATA 1983, JONES/OSTROY 1984) usually emphasizes that flexibility considerations are more relevant to the decision to hold such short-term assets than to the demand for money itself.

In the remainder of this chapter, all the above-mentioned reasons for money demand are discussed in the same intertemporal choice framework, which shows how the question of motives for money demand relates to more general choice-theoretic issues.

5.2 The Structure of the Model

We shall now introduce an intertemporal consumption/portfolio-model that will be the basis of this chapter.

Time is taken to be discrete with periods t=1,2,3,...,T. We consider an agent who makes his consumption and savings decisions for period 1, given expectations about future endowments, prices and preferences.

Suppose in each of the periods t=1,2,3,...,T he is equipped with an endowment vector $e_t=(e_{1t},\dots,e_{kt}) \geq 0$ of (non-storable) consumption goods.

Furthermore, there are three assets, money (m) and two non-monetary assets (b,d), of which the consumer possesses initial endowments m_0, b_0, d_0. For convenience, we assume that money yields no interest payments, though the following argument would also work with positive interest payments that are low relative to those on the other assets. Money is assumed to be the only generally accepted storable means of payment.

The non-monetary assets, which can, in most of the following, be thought of as bonds, should be regarded as yielding positive interest payments in every period. More precisely, the holder of an asset of type b(d) is entitled to a stream of interest payments in all future periods; for simplicity, we assume that he receives a constant coupon R_b (R_d) in every period until he decides to sell the asset in some period t at the going market price p_{bt} (p_{dt}). However, selling and buying these assets is only possible at positive transaction costs. Strictly speaking, all the other transactions also involve positive costs, but for simplicity, we shall ignore them.

We shall assume that transaction costs in each period are proportional to the level of transactions, with proportionality constants ß and δ ($0 \le ß, \delta$) respectively. Furthermore, we suppose that, in each period, the transactions are either all sales or all purchases. Therefore, total transaction costs in each period t are $ß|b_{t-1}-b_t|+\delta|d_{t-1}-d_t|$.

In general, we shall assume that in period 1 only the first-period prices of bonds (p_{b1}, p_{d1}) and consumption goods (p_{h1};h=1,...,k) and the first-period endowments (e_{h1};h=1,...,k) are known. As to prices and endowments in future periods, the agent is uncertain. The relevant state of the world for the agent is

$$s = ((p_2, p_{b2}, p_{d2}, e_2), \ldots, (p_T, p_{bT}, p_{dT}, e_T)),$$

where $p_t=(p_{1t}, \ldots, p_{kt})$ is the vector of consumption good prices in period t, p_{bt} is the price of bond b in period t, p_{dt} is the price of bond d in period t, $e_t=(e_{1t}, \ldots, e_{kt})$ is the endowment vector in period t.

Money and the other assets in the model are, as usual, not assumed to have an intrinsic value. The ultimate goal of the agent is to achieve a good consumption pattern; holding assets will only be regarded as useful if it allows for an improvement of this consumption pattern. Hence, only the consumption path $(c_1,\dots,c_T)$ enters the utility function. For simplicity, we also assume that the agent's utility function is additively separable, i.e. it is of the form

$$U(c_1,c_2,\dots,c_T) = \sum_{t=1}^{T} U_t(c_t)$$

for some strictly increasing spot-utility function U_t.
Hence, in the notation of chapter 4, $r_t(a_t) = U_t(c_t)$.

Here $c_t = (c_{1t},\dots,c_{ht})$ is the vector of goods that are consumed in period t.

Summarizing, the household can use his income stream in period t for:

- consumption expenditures $\langle p_t, c_t\rangle = \sum_{h=1}^{k} p_{ht}c_{ht}$,
- saving of money $m_t - m_{t-1}$,
- purchase of bonds $p_{bt}(b_t - b_{t-1}) + p_{dt}(d_t - d_{t-1})$,
- transaction cost payments $ß|b_{t-1} - b_t| + \delta|d_{t-1} - d_t|$.

These expenditures are constrained by his income stream in period t which consists of:

- receipts from the sale of his endowment $\langle p_t, e_t\rangle = \sum_{h=1}^{k} p_{ht}e_{ht}$,
- interest payments $R_b b_{t-1} + R_d d_{t-1}$.

His choice $a_t = (c_t, m_t, b_t, d_t)$ which consists of his consumption-bundle and the end of period asset stocks is therefore constrained by

$$\langle p_t, c_t\rangle + m_t + p_{bt}(b_t - b_{t-1}) + p_{dt}(d_t - d_{t-1}) + ß|b_{t-1} - b_t| + \delta|d_{t-1} - d_t| \leq m_{t-1} + R_b b_{t-1} + R_d d_{t-1} + \langle p_t, e_t\rangle \ . \qquad (5.2.1)$$

In addition, there are non-negativity constraints

$$m_t, c_t \geq 0. \qquad (5.2.2)$$

b_t and d_t may be negative, i.e. borrowing is possible, except when stated otherwise.

Finally, the information structure of the problem has to be described.
There is uncertainty as to the state of the world,

$$s = ((p_2, p_{b2}, p_{d2}, e_2), \ldots, (p_T, p_{bT}, p_{dT}, e_T)) \varepsilon (R^k{}_+ xR_+ xR_+ xR^k{}_+)^T ,$$

which will not become completely known before the end of period T.

However, at the beginning of period t (t=2,...,T), the agent gets to know the prices and endowments of that period, i.e. he receives a signal

$$y_{t-1} = (p_t, p_{bt}, p_{dt}, e_t) \varepsilon R^k{}_+ xR_+ xR_+ xR^k{}_+ .$$

As usual, the agent has a prior distribution $\Pi(s)$ on S and, for each sequence $(y_1,...,y_t)\varepsilon Y^t$ $(t\varepsilon\{1,2,...,T-1\})$, a posterior distribution $\Pi(s|y_1,...,y_t)$ on S. Furthermore, he has probability distributions $q_{yt}|y_1,...,y_{t'}$ on Y_t for each $t'<t$, $t\varepsilon\{1,...,T\}$.

The model can now be summarized as a general T-period decision problem (cf. chapter 4.1.5).

Decision Problem 5.1

$t=1,2,3,...,T.$

$a_t = (c_t, b_t, d_t, m_t) \varepsilon G_t(a_1, a_2, ..., a_{t-1}, s) \subset A_t = R^k{}_+ xR_+ xR_+ xR^k{}_+ ,$

where

$G_t(a_1,...,a_{t-1},s) = \{a_t \varepsilon A_t \,|\, (5.2.1) \text{ and } (5.2.2) \text{ hold}\},$

$s = \{(p_2, p_{b2}, p_{d2}, e_2), ..., (p_T, p_{bT}, p_{dT}, e_T)\} \varepsilon$

$S = (R^k{}_+ xR_+ xR_+ xR^k{}_+)^{T-1}$

$y_{t-1} = (p_t, p_{bt}, p_{dt}, e_t) \varepsilon Y = R^k{}_+ xR_+ xR_+ xR^k{}_+ .$

Objective function: $\sum_{t=1}^{T} r_t(a_t, s) = \sum_{t=1}^{T} U_t(c_t).$

Probability distributions:

$\Pi(s)$ on S,

$\Pi(s|y_1,\ldots,y_t)$ on S for each $t\varepsilon\{1,\ldots,T-1\}$, $(y_1,\ldots,y_t)\varepsilon Y^t$,

$q_{y_t}|y_1,\ldots y_{t'}$ on Y for each $t'<t$, $t\varepsilon\{1,\ldots,T\}$.

Note that, while the objective function is independent of the state of the world, the set of feasible paths depends on s.

One may object to the formulation of the decision problem that it only allows for finite sets of states while, in our example, it would be more natural to allow for a continuum of states. While this is arguably true, we have chosen to keep to the discrete framework of chapter 4 to avoid technicalities which do not yield substantial new insights.

Having laid out the general version of the decision problem, we shall now look at various special cases in order to deal with questions of the following type:

- Under which circumstances is the accumulation of any wealth reasonable?
- Can it be reasonable to hold wealth in the form of money when there are return-bearing assets and there is no uncertainty?
- Can it be reasonable to hold wealth in the form of money when there are no transaction costs?
- Does an additional motive for holding money arise from the fact that the agent receives information as time goes by?

5.3 Money Demand when there are no Transaction Costs

In the introductory remarks in section 5.1, we expressed the view that transaction costs are the fundamental reason for holding money in the presence of return-bearing assets.

In this section, we want to discuss more formally whether consumers hold money even when transaction costs are absent, i.e. when β and δ are 0.

We shall show that, in the model of section 5.2, when information is perfect and transaction costs are zero, money will never be held, at least if one of the assets is not subject to capital losses, i.e. if its price never declines. This is stated formally in the following proposition.

<u>Proposition 5.1:</u> Suppose the decision-maker in problem 5.1. knows the state of the world with certainty, there are no transaction costs and the price of asset b is constant over time, i.e.

(i) there exists an $s \varepsilon S$ such that $\Pi(s)=1$,

(ii) $\beta=\delta=0$,

(iii) $p_b := p_{b1} = p_{b2} = \ldots = p_{bT}$.

Then the decision-maker will never hold money, i.e. $m_t=0$ for $t=1,2,3,\ldots,T$.

<u>Proof:</u> $m_T=0$ follows immediately from the fact that any wealth that has been held until the last period will be spent, because our objective function does not include a bequest term and utility is strictly monotonic in consumption.

For $t<T$, proposition 4.5 is applicable. We need to check that for any $s \varepsilon S$ and $(a_1,\ldots,a_t)$ with $a_t=(c_t,m_t,b_t,d_t)\varepsilon G_t(a_1,\ldots,a_{t-1},s)$ and $m_t>0$ there exists an $a_t'=(c_t',m_t',b_t',d_t')\varepsilon G_t(a_1,\ldots,a_{t-1},s)$ that is at least as flexible as a_t and satisfies $r_t(a_t') > r_t(a_t)$.

To obtain an a_t' of the above type, one should proceed as follows. Choose $m_t'=0$. Compared to the original choice a_t, one can therefore use m_t additional units to spend on bonds and consumption goods in period t. In fact, we shall show that one can buy enough bonds to obtain an a_t' (with $m_t'=0$) that is at least as flexible, and still have some money left over to buy additional consumption goods, so that $r_t(a_t')>r_t(a_t)$.

Ceteris paribus, reducing the money stock from m_t to 0 means that future options are reduced. To make up for this reduction, additional bonds have to be held. To determine the extra amount of bonds, db_t, that is needed as a compensation for giving up the money stock m_t, one has to make sure that the sum of the value of this extra amount ($p_b db_t$) and the interest payments ($R_b db_t$) equal the size of the money stock originally held, i.e.

$(p_b + R_b) db_t = m_t$.

Hence, choose

$db_t = m_t / (p_b + R_b)$.

To buy these additional bonds,

$p_b db_t = p_b m_t / (p_b + R_b) < m_t$

units of money are needed.

Assuming, without loss of generality, that the price of consumption good 1 in period T is 1, the remaining

$m_t - p_b m_t / (p_b + R_b) = R_b m_t / (p_b + R_b)$

units of money can be used to buy $R_b m_t / (p_b + R_b)$ units of consumption good 1.

Therefore,

$$a_t' = [c_t', m_t', b_t', d_t'] =$$
$$[(R_b m_t / (p_b + R_b), 0, \ldots, 0) + c_t, 0, b_t + m_t / (p_b + R_b), d_t]$$

is feasible if a_t is.[3]

Clearly, $r_t(a_t') > r_t(a_t)$ because $r_t(a_t) = U_t(c_t)$, $c_t' > c_t$ and U_t is strictly increasing in c_t.

To complete the proof, we have to show that $G(a_1, \ldots, a_{t-1}, a_t', s) = G(a_1, \ldots, a_{t-1}, a_t, s)$. Because the set of options in periods t+2,...,T only depends on the choice of a_{t+1}, it suffices to show that $G_{t+1}(a_1, \ldots, a_{t-1}, a_t', s) = G_{t+1}(a_1, \ldots, a_{t-1}, a_t, s)$.

This can be seen as follows. On the one hand, without transaction costs, the budget restriction for period t+1 is

[3] This can also be checked directly by inserting a_t' for a_t in (5.2.1) and bearing in mind that this inequality is satisfied by a_t.

$$\langle p_{t+1}, c_{t+1}\rangle + m_{t+1} + p_{d(t+1)}(d_{t+1}-d_t) - R_d d_t - \langle p_{t+1}, e_{t+1}\rangle \le m_t + R_b b_t - p_b(b_{t+1}-b_t) \qquad (5.3.1)$$

after a choice of $(a_1, \ldots, a_{t-1}, a_t)$. On the other hand, the budget restriction after a choice of $(a_1, \ldots, a_{t-1}, a_t')$ is

$$\langle p_{t+1}, c_{t+1}\rangle + m_{t+1} + p_{d(t+1)}(d_{t+1}-d_t') - R_d d_t' - \langle p_{t+1}, e_{t+1}\rangle \le m_t' + R_b b_t' - p_b(b_{t+1}-b_t'). \qquad (5.3.2)$$

These inequalities are identical: the left hand sides are equal because $d_t = d_t'$ and the right hand sides are equal because from and $b_t' = b_t + m_t/(p_b+R_b)$ and $m_t' = 0$, one obtains

$$m_t' + R_b b_t' - p_b(b_{t+1}-b_{t'}) =$$
$$R_b[b_t + m_t/(p_b+R_b)] - p_b[b_{t+1} - b_t - m_t/(p_b+R_b)] =$$
$$[(R_b+p_b)/(R_b+p_b)]m_t + (R_b+p_b)b_t - p_b b_{t+1} =$$
$$m_t + R_b b_t - p_b(b_{t+1}-b_t).$$

Therefore, a choice such that money demand is positive cannot be optimal, which proves the proposition.

It can be shown that, instead of assuming away uncertainty altogether, it is sufficient to assume that there is a non-monetary asset that is not subject to capital losses and yields a positive interest rate with certainty. In reality, there usually are assets which can reasonably be described in this manner, namely savings and time deposits. Hence, there is little to support the view that there is a reason to hold money when there are no transaction costs, except perhaps the expectation of capital losses.

5.4 Transaction Costs

In section 5.3, we have seen that, in the absence of transaction costs, money will not be held under reasonable assumptions on the nature of the available assets.

Transaction costs are therefore necessary for money to be held. We shall now show that the same is not true for incomplete information: as long as there are transaction costs, it may well be reasonable to hold money even when the state of the world is known with certainty.[4]

However, we shall show that, while incomplete information is not a necessary condition for money to be held, it may provide an additional motivation for doing so. The idea is that the agent may expect to learn more about the future as time goes by: for instance, this additional knowledge could make it desirable to either rearrange the portfolio in order to adapt to shifts in interest rates or to liquidate assets in order to use them for purchases of consumption goods in periods of unexpectedly low income. If all wealth is held in the form of long-term (high-interest) assets, these activities may be prohibitively expensive because such assets can usually not be redeemed before maturity without interest losses. An agent who expects to learn about shifts in interest rates may therefore wish to keep himself flexible by holding money even though this means foregoing interest payments.

This argumentation fits into the pattern of the preceding chapters. In general, the choices of agents who consider learning possibilities (Bayesians) will differ from the choices of those who do not. According to general principles, however, the recognition of learning possibilities can only lead to a choice of money if holding a long-term asset is not at least as flexible. If long-term, high-interest assets could be transformed into money at no costs, such assets would clearly be more flexible than money: the high interest that is earned by holding bonds in period t would give additional future options without taking away any options. When there are transaction costs, however, deciding to hold one non-monetary asset means making some future options inaccessible, in particular those involving a high stock of the alternative non-monetary assets. Therefore, with transaction costs, money may have a "flexibility advantage".

The purpose of this section is to illustrate these ideas by means of two examples. In the first one, money is held because of transaction costs in a world without uncertainty. In the second one

[4] Again, this statement is familiar, but it is usually proved in a different framework (cf. BAUMOL 1952, TOBIN 1956).

(cf. section 5.4.1), money would not be held merely because of transaction costs, but the expectation of new information in connection with transaction costs is enough to induce the agent to hold money. Before going into details, we note that the argument becomes slightly more complex when assets are included that yield positive interest and are almost as liquid as money. This will be discussed in more detail in section 5.4.2.

5.4.1 Holding Money in the Absence of Uncertainty

To give an example of a situation where a consumer holds money in the absence of uncertainty, it is sufficient to consider an economy with one consumption good and one bond, say b.

Intuitively, one would expect the consumer to hold money if, on the one hand, consumption in the not too distant future can only be financed by using up wealth that was built up in period 1 and if, on the other hand, transaction costs are high relative to the interest rate on bonds so that it is not worth holding bonds for short periods.

The first condition will be guaranteed by (5.4.4), (5.4.5) and (5.4.6) below, the second one by (5.4.2). Assumptions (5.4.1) and (5.4.3) are not necessary, but simplify the argumentation.

We now list the assumptions we shall use.

Firstly, suppose that

$$p_1 = p_2 = 1. \qquad (5.4.1)$$

Furthermore, suppose that the nominal interest rate, R_b, is smaller than the transaction cost factor ß, i.e.

$$R_b < ß. \qquad (5.4.2)$$

To show that expected capital losses of the bond are not the reason to hold money, we assume that

$$p_b := p_{b1} = \ldots = p_{bT}. \qquad (5.4.3)$$

Moreover, the agent is assumed not to inherit any assets from earlier periods, i.e.

$$m_0 = b_0 = 0, \tag{5.4.4}$$

and he is not allowed to go into debt, i.e.

$$b_t \geq 0 \text{ for } t=1,\dots,T. \tag{5.4.5}$$

Furthermore, suppose the problem is such that in period 2 the optimal quantity of the consumption good, c_2, is greater than the endowment e_2. For instance, this will be the case if $e_1>0$, $e_2=0$ (or low compared with e_1) and preferences for consumption in period 2 are not excessively weak. In fact, we have to assume slightly more than $c_2>e_2$, namely that

$$c_2 - e_2 > R_b e_1/p_b. \tag{5.4.6}$$

This is to be interpreted as follows. Even if the agent sells his entire first-period endowment e_1 to buy bonds, he could only buy e_1/p_b units. Hence, the interest payments he receives if he sells his entire endowment in period 1 is $R_b e_1/p_b$. Thus, (5.4.6) says that the agent cannot finance his entire excess consumption in period 2 with the interest payments on bonds that were purchased in period 1. If the agent does not hold money in period 1, he will therefore have to sell bonds in period 2 to finance his consumption.

<u>Proposition 5.2:</u> If assumptions (5.4.1)-(5.4.6) are satisfied, the agent will hold money in period 1, i.e. $m_1>0$.

<u>Proof:</u> We apply proposition 4.5. To this end, it suffices to show that, if $a_1=(c_1,m_1,b_1)\varepsilon A_1$, $a_2 \varepsilon G(a_1)$, $m_1=0$, there exist $a_1'=(c_1',m_1',b_1')\varepsilon A_1$, $a_2'=(c_2',m_2',b_2')\varepsilon G(a_1')$ such that

$$r_1(a_1) < r_1(a_1'),\ r_2(a_2) = r_2(a_2') \tag{5.4.7}$$

and

$$G(a_1',a_2') = G(a_1,a_2), \tag{5.4.8}$$

contradicting the optimality of a_1.

In fact, we shall show that, if $a_1 \varepsilon A_1$ with $m_1=0$, $a_2 \varepsilon G(a_1)$, there exists $a_1' \varepsilon A_1$, $a_2' \varepsilon G(a_1')$ such that $c_1 < c_1'$ and $a_2'=a_2$. This implies (5.4.7) because
$c_1 < c_1' \Rightarrow r_1(a_1) < r_1(a_1')$ and $a_2 = a_2' \Rightarrow r_2(a_2) = r_2(a_2')$

and (5.4.8) because, as the budget constraint for periods 3,4,... depends on a_1, a_2 only inasmuch as they influence m_2 and b_2, $a_2'=a_2$ implies $G(a_1', a_2') = G(a_1, a_2)$.

Because $m_1=0$, it follows from (5.4.4), (5.4.5) and (5.4.6) that to finance his excess consumption $c_2 > e_2$, the agent has to buy bonds in period 1 and sell some of them in period 2, i.e.

$a_1 = (c_1, 0, b_1)$; $a_2 = (c_2, m_2, b_2)$; $b_2 < b_1$.

To find (a_1', a_2') such that $c_1' > c_1$ and $a_2'=a_2$, reduce b_1 to $b_1'=b_2$ units. Hence, while for the original paths $b_1 - b_2$ units of bonds were sold in period 2, no such sales take place for the new path a'. This implies that, if consumption and wealth in period 2 is to remain unchanged, i.e. $a_2 = a_2'$, $(p_b + R_b - ß)(b_1 - b_2)$ units of the consumption in period 2 that were financed through the sale of bonds now have to be financed with money ($p_b(b_1 - b_2)$: value of the bonds; $R_b(b_2 - b_1)$: interest earned in period one; $ß(b_1 - b_2)$: transaction costs).

But the reduction of bonds by $(b_1 - b_2)$ units gives $p_b(b_1 - b_2) > (p_b + R_b - ß)(b_1 - b_2)$ units of money, where the inequality follows from (5.4.2). Therefore,

$$\varepsilon := p_b(b_1 - b_2) - (p_b + R_b - ß)(b_1 - b_2) = (ß - R_b)(b_1 - b_2) > 0$$

additional units can be used for consumption good purchases in period 1.

By (5.4.1), $p_1=1$, so that, using the ε units of money to buy consumption goods, one obtains

$$a_1' = (c_1', m_1', b_1') = (c_1 + \varepsilon, (p_b + R_b - ß)(b_1 - b_2), b_2);$$
$$a_2' = (c_2, m_2, b_2).$$

Clearly, $c_1 < c_1'$ and $a_2'=a_2$, so that it cannot be optimal to choose (a_1, a_2) if (a_1', a_2') is feasible.

The way a_1' and a_2' were constructed, they can be expected to be feasible given that a_1 and a_2 are feasible. But for the sake of completeness, we now check this explicitly. The reader who thinks feasibility is obvious can move on to the end of the proof.

Firstly, we have to show that a_1' satisfies (5.2.1) if a_1 does. Bearing in mind that $m_0=b_0=0$ and that we have no asset d, this inequality reads

$$p_1 c_1'+m_1'+p_b b_1'+\beta b_1' \leq p_1 e_1 .$$

Inserting $a_1' = (c_1',m_1',b_1') = (c_1+\varepsilon,(p_b+R_b-\beta)(b_1-b_2),b_2)$ gives

$$p_1(c_1+\varepsilon)+(p_b+R_b-\beta)(b_1-b_2)+p_b b_2+\beta b_2 \leq p_1 e_1 . \qquad (5.4.9)$$

From $p_1=1$ and the definition of ε it follows that $p_1(c_1+\varepsilon)= c_1+(\beta-R_b)(b_1-b_2)$. Hence, (5.4.9) is seen to be equivalent to

$$c_1+(\beta-R_\beta)(b_1-b_2)+(p_b+R_b-\beta)(b_1-b_2)+p_b b_2+\beta b_2 \leq p_1 e_1$$

or, equivalently,

$$c_1 + p_b b_1 + \beta b_2 \leq p_1 e_1 . \qquad (5.4.10)$$

This certainly holds: a_1 is feasible and therefore

$$p_1 c_1 + p_b b_1 + \beta b_1 \leq p_1 e_1 ,$$

so that (5.4.10) follows from $p_1=1$ and $b_1>b_2$.

Inserting a_2' into (5.2.1) for t=2 gives

$$p_2 c_2' + m_2' + p_b(b_2'-b_1') + \beta|b_1'-b_2'| \leq m_1' + R_b b_1' + \langle p_2 , e_2 \rangle .$$

From $(c_1',m_1',b_1') = (c_1+\varepsilon,(p_b+R_b-\beta)(b_1-b_2),b_2)$, $(c_2',m_2',b_2') = (c_2,m_2,b_2)$, we get

$$p_2 c_2 + m_2 \leq (p_b+R_b-\beta)(b_1-b_2) + R_b b_2 + p_2 e_2$$

or, equivalently,

$$p_2 c_2 + m_2 \leq (p_b-\beta)(b_1-b_2) + R_b b_1 + p_2 e_2 . \qquad (5.4.11)$$

The feasibility condition for a_2 is

$$p_2 c_2 + m_2 \leq R_b b_1 + p_2 e_2 .$$

A necessary condition for a to be optimal is that $p_b \geq ß$ (otherwise the sale of bonds would incur losses that could be avoided by not selling). Together with $b_1 > b_2$, the feasibility condition for a_2 therefore implies (5.4.11).

Hence, if (a_1, a_2) is feasible, so is (a_1', a_2'). This fills the last gap in the proposition.

We have shown that it is conceivable for economic agents to hold money in the presence of assets yielding positive interest simply because it is more costly to exchange other assets for consumption goods. Obviously, the choice of the assumptions of our example has been guided by convenience rather than desire for generality. There are only two points that really matter. Firstly, the benefits from the purchase of bonds outweigh the losses from transactions only in the long run. Secondly, preferences and income streams are such that, in some periods, money that is earned will be spent soon afterwards so that it is not worth purchasing assets with this money.

We finish this section by showing how uncertainty can provide additional incentives to hold money or, more precisely, money or assets that can be sold without interest penalty.

5.4.2 Holding Money to Stay Flexible

As in section 5.4.1, we suppose that there is only one consumption good. However, we now require three assets.

Two of them, b and d, are supposed to be long-term commitments that are modelled upon those assets that can only be sold prior to maturity if certain interest losses are accepted. As an example, consider time or savings deposits, which banks liquidate before maturity only at extra costs (cf. ASHAUER 1988). The third asset, m, we shall call money. It has the same properties as before (generally accepted means of payment with zero interest rate).

Before we start the formal work, we remind the reader of the object of this section. We want to show that if money competes with uncertain, illiquid (long-term) assets, it is conceivable that agents who ignore flexibility considerations would hold long-term assets, while those who care about flexibility prefer to hold at least some money, because they want to avoid having to pay liquidation fees in situations where they would like to react to new information with portfolio rearrangements.

This result would have to be modified in a world with close substitutes for money, i.e. short-term securities that guarantee a known positive yield even if they are sold before maturity at short notice (e.g. the "Bundesschatzbrief" in Germany, cf. ANDREAS 1988, p.994). Such assets usually give lower interest rates than long-term assets but higher interest rates than money. We shall not include such assets in our model, but the reader will notice that if they were included, a similar argument as the following would show that flexibility considerations can be an argument for holding such short-term assets instead of holding long-term assets rather than an argument for holding money instead of long-term assets (cf. CHANG/HAMBERG/HIRATA 1983).

As we have noted earlier, one reason to hold money is the fact that it can be used directly for purchases of consumption goods (unlike the other two assets, which have to be transformed into money first, which involves positive transaction costs). To investigate whether other reasons could induce a consumer to hold money, we shall modify our model slightly and abstract from transaction costs in the traditional sense of brokerage fees, effort, etc. However, we assume that one type of transaction is only possible at positive costs which are explained by the above reasoning: borrowers are only willing to accept the liquidation of long-term assets before maturity if they are conceded a certain interest reduction.

In such a setting, one would expect a Bayesian agent to hold money, say, in period 1, if

(a) his initial wealth and/or his first-period income are high enough that he wishes to hold some kind of asset in period 1,
(b) first-period returns on the long-term assets are relatively low (so that foregoing those returns does not involve too high an interest loss),
(c) liquidation costs are relatively high so that holding long-term assets for short periods is not worthwhile and
(d) the agent knows relatively little about the future returns of the two assets but expects to learn more about them.

When (a)-(d) are satisfied, it seems conceivable that, while the best strategy for an expected utility maximizer who disregards flexibility considerations would be to hold only long-term assets in every single period, a Bayesian agent would prefer to start by holding money for some relatively short period of time and wait before he decides on one or the other of the two assets. In the following, we shall show that such configurations exist.

To this end, we can still use the decision problem 5.1, at least after some minor reformulations and reinterpretations which affect the transaction cost terms. As mentioned earlier, we want to abstract from transaction costs except for payments that have to be made when long-term assets are liquidated before their maturity date. We shall assume that the maturity date in our model is T. Therefore, whenever a long-term asset is liquidated before period T, payments have to be made. For simplicity, we assume that these payments are proportional to the desired reduction of the stock (though a more realistic approach would be to let the payments depend on the number of periods until maturity). Therefore, if agents choose $b_t < b_{t-1}$, they have to pay a "liquidation fee" $ß(b_{t-1}-b_t)$; $0 \leq ß \leq 1$. If, however, $b_t \geq b_{t-1}$, no liquidation fees have to be paid. Generally, we can therefore write liquidation costs as $\max\ [ß(b_{t-1}-b_t),0]$ and correspondingly as $\max\ [\delta(d_{t-1}-d_t),0]$ for the asset d.

Therefore, one has to exchange the terms $|ß(b_{t-1}-b_t)|$ and $|\delta(d_{t-1}-d_t)|$ in (5.2.1) for $\max\ [ß(b_{t-1}-b_t),0]$ and $\max\ [\delta(d_{t-1}-d_t),0]$ respectively, so that the new budget restriction is

$$\langle p_t, c_t \rangle + m_t + p_{bt}(b_t - b_{t-1}) + p_{dt}(d_t - d_{t-1}) + \max [ß(b_{t-1} - b_t), 0] + \max [\delta(d_{t-1} - d_t), 0] \leq m_{t-1} + R_b b_{t-1} + R_d d_{t-1} + \langle p_t, e_t \rangle. \qquad (5.4.12)$$

We now make simplifying assumptions. Firstly, we suppose that asset prices are constant over time and known with certainty. However, the interest payments in periods 2,3,...,T are no longer assumed to be constant and known when the first choice is made: they depend on a state of the world which does not become known until the end of period 1. Whatever the state, however, the interest rate is expected to be positive with certainty from period 2 onwards. Furthermore, the interest rates in period 1, R_{b1} and R_{d1} are assumed to be known.

For simplicity, we assume that there are only two states s^1, s^2. We write $R_{bt}(s^1)$ for the interest rate in period t (t=1,2,...) for asset b in state i (i=1,2) and correspondingly for asset d.

Summing up,

(a) $S = \{s^1, s^2\}$ (two states of the world),

(b) $R_b = R_{bt} = R_{bt}(s^1) > 0$; $R_{dt} = R_{dt}(s^1) > 0$ for t=1,2,...=T
(positive and state-dependent interest rates),

(c) R_{b1} and R_{d1} are known, (5.4.13)

(d) $p_b := p_{b1} = p_{b2} = ... = p_{bT} = p_d := p_{d1} = p_{d2} = ... = p_{dT}$
(constant and identical asset prices).

Except for (b), these assumptions are necessary only to make the calculations tractable, there is no economically obvious reason why they should be necessary for the desired statement to hold.

Furthermore, we assume that

(a) $\Pi(s^1) = q_{y1} > 0, \Pi(s^2) = q_{y2} > 0$
(positive probabilities of both states of the world)

(b) $R_{bt}(s^1) > R_{dt}(s^1)$ for t=2,...,T, (5.4.14)

(c) $R_{bt}(s^2) < R_{dt}(s^2)$ for t=2,...,T,

(d) $ß, \delta > 0$ (positive liquidation costs).

Hence, there is a positive probability that a person who possesses asset b is better off than an agent who possesses agent d (and vice versa).

Finally, suppose that our decision problem is such that

$$\langle p_t, e_t \rangle > \langle p_t, c_t \rangle \text{ for } t \epsilon \{1,\ldots,T-1\}, \tag{5.4.15}$$

i.e. income from the sale of goods exceeds consumption expenditures in the first T-1 periods. Such problems clearly exist: For instance, if the agent is well endowed with goods in early periods but expects little income in period T[5], while at the same time he wishes to have a relatively smooth consumption pattern, (5.4.15) will be satisfied.

An immediate consequence of (5.4.15) is that saving is positive in each of the periods $t \epsilon \{1,\ldots,T-1\}$ so that

$$m_t > m_{t-1} \text{ or } b_t > b_{t-1} \text{ or } d_t > d_{t-1}. \tag{5.4.16}$$

We are now ready to show that the (Non-Bayesian) expected utility maximizer will not hold money in period 1 in our example.

<u>Proposition 5.3:</u> For the agent who ignores future information, $m_1 = 0$ whenever (5.4.13),(5.4.14),(5.4.15) are satisfied.

<u>Proof:</u> By contradiction.
Suppose that $m_1 > 0$ for the optimal path $a = (a_1, a_2, \ldots, a_T)$ with $a_t = (c_t, m_t, b_t, d_t)$; $t=1,2,\ldots,T$.

(i) To begin with, suppose further that $m_t \geq m_1$ for each $t \epsilon \{2,\ldots,T-1\}$. We shall show that there exists an alternative feasible path a' which is preferred to path a.

To see this, alter the first-period choice a_1 by reducing m_1 to 0 and buying m_1/p_b units of the asset b, while leaving consumption in period 1 unchanged. Suppose that these additional m_1/p_b units are held until the end of the period T-1, which reduces the money demand in each of the periods by m_1 - this reduction is possible because, by assumption, $m_t \geq m_1$ in these periods.

---

[5] For instance, T can be interpreted as old age.

On the other hand, in each of the periods $t=1,...,T-1$ additional interest is earned, namely $R_{bt}(s^1)m_1/p_b$. Suppose, to begin with, that this interest is held as money in periods $t=2,3,...,T$ so that the money stock is increased by $R_{b1}m_1/p_b$ in period 2,
by $(R_{b1}+R_{b2}(s^1))m_1/p_b$ in period 3,...,
by $(R_{b1}+R_{b2}(s^1)+...+R_{b(T-1)}(s^1))m_1/p_b$ in period T.

Furthermore, suppose that in period T the agent redeems the additional m_1/p_b unit bonds he has been holding since period 1, which gives him m_1 units of money. Because he has held the unit bonds until the maturity date, liquidation does not involve any interest penalty. Summing up the changes in period T, we get a money stock $m_T+(R_{b1}+R_{b2}(s^1)+...+R_{b(T-1)}(s^1))m_1/p_b$.

Now define
$\varepsilon:= (R_{b1}+R_{b2}(s^1)+...+R_{b(T-1)}(s^1))m_1/p_b > 0$
and suppose that the agent consumes this additional income in period T instead of holding it as money. Assuming, without loss of generality, that $p_T=1$, it follows that $c_T'=c_T+\varepsilon$, while $m_T'=m_T$.

Furthermore, the sale of asset b has brought back the stock of asset b to the level in the original example, $b_T'=b_T$.

By construction, therefore,

$$a_1' = (c_1, 0, b_1+m_1/p_b, d_1),$$
$$a_2' = (c_2, m_2-m_1+R_{b1}m_1/p_b, b_2+m_1/p_b, d_2),$$
$$...,$$
$$a_t' = (c_t, m_t-m_1+R_{b1}m_1/p_b+...+R_{b(t-1)}m_1/p_b, b_t+m_1/p_b, d_t),$$
$$...,$$
$$a_{T-1}' = (c_{T-1}, m_{T-1}-m_1+R_{b1}m_1/p_b+...+R_{b(T-2)}m_1/p_b, b_{T-1}+m_1/p_b, d_{T-1}),$$
$$a_T' = (c_T+\varepsilon, m_T, b_T, d_T).$$

$c_1'=c_1,...,c_{T-1}'=c_{T-1}$ and $c_T'>c_T$ imply

$r_1(a_1')+...+r_T(a_T') > r_1(a_1)+...+r_T(a_T)$, independent of s.

While it is intuitively clear that a' is feasible if a is, we have not given a strict proof yet. As the calculations are slightly tedious and not very illuminating, we have deferred them to the appendix.

Once it is clear that a' is feasible, it follows that a path with $m_1>0$ cannot be optimal if $m_t \geq m_1$ for each $t\varepsilon\{2,...,T-1\}$.

(ii) Now suppose there exists $t\varepsilon\{2,...,T-1\}$ such that $m_t<m_1$. Then clearly there exists $s\varepsilon\{2,...,T-1\}$ such that $m_s<m_{s-1}$. But then from (5.4.16), $b_s>b_{s-1}$ (or $d_s>d_{s-1}$; in which case the following argument carries over analogously). This cannot be optimal: changing the portfolio composition by reducing m_{s-1} to $m_{s-1}-\alpha$ by buying α/p_b additional units of asset b in period s-1 (where α is sufficiently small so that $m_{s-1}-\alpha\geq 0$ and $b_{s-1}+\alpha/p_b \leq b_s$) gives additional interest payments ($\alpha R_b/p_b$), but does not cause additional liquidation costs.

Therefore, if a path is to be optimal, $m_t \geq m_1$ in each of the periods $t\varepsilon\{2,...,T-1\}$. But we have seen that in this case $m_1=0$.

This finishes the proof of proposition 5.3.

We now show that, under the assumptions made so far, the agent, even though he will not hold money if he ignores future information, may do so when he takes this information into account.

<u>Proposition 5.4:</u> There exist parameter constellations satisfying (5.4.13)-(5.4.15) so that the Bayesian agent who optimizes according to chapter 4.1.5 will choose money in period 1.

<u>Proof:</u> By (5.4.1c), $b_1>0$ or $d_1>0$ or $m_1>0$. We need to check that there are parameter constellations satisfying (5.4.13), (5.4.14), (5.4.15), for which a path $a_1 = (c_1,0,b_1,d_1)$ with $b_1>0$ cannot be optimal for the agent who takes information into account[6].

We start with a parameter constellation that satisfies (5.4.13), (5.4.14) and (5.4.15) except for (5.4.13b): we suppose that $R_{b1}=R_{d1}=0$ so that (5.4.13b) only holds for t=2,...,T. Of course, this is not supposed to be an economically reasonable assumption; it will be dispensed with in the process of the proof.

---

6 The proof that $m_1=0, d_1>0$ cannot be optimal is analogous.

Then suppose a_1' is obtained from a_1 by selling b_1 and holding money instead, i.e.

$$a_1'=(c_1',m_1',b_1',d_1')=(c_1,p_b b_1,0,d_1).$$

We will show that

$$r_1(a_1) + V(a_1) < r_1(a_1') + V(a_1'). \qquad (5.4.17)$$

Intuitively, this is clear; as we are assuming that b and d pay no interest in period 1, holding these assets instead of money does not open any additional future options, while the fact that b and d can only be sold at positive transaction costs means that some future options are given up. Therefore, one should expect a_1' to be preferred to a_1.

As a first step towards a proof of (5.4.17), note that

$$G(a_1,s^i)\subset G(a_1',s^i);\ i=1,2.$$

This holds because $m_1=0$ and $R_{b1}=R_{d1}=0$ imply that $G(a_1,s^i)$ is given by the restriction

$$\langle p_2,c_2\rangle + m_2 + p_b(b_2-b_1) + p_d(d_2-d_1) + \max[\delta(d_1-d_2),0] - \langle p_2,e_2\rangle \le -\max[\beta(b_1-b_2),0], \qquad (5.4.18)$$

while $G(a_1',s^i)$ is given by

$$\langle p_2,c_2\rangle + m_2 + p_b b_2 + p_d(d_2-d_1) + \max[\delta(d_1-d_2),0] - p_b b_1 - \langle p_2,e_2\rangle \le 0. \qquad (5.4.19)$$

Bearing in mind that $R_{b1} = 0$, it is clear that (5.4.19) is satisfied whenever (5.4.18) is. Hence, $G(a_1',s^i)\supset G(a_1,s^i)$.

Therefore,

$$q_{y1} \max_{a_2 \varepsilon G(a_1, s1)} v(a_2, y^1) \leq q_{y1} \max_{a_2 \varepsilon G(a_1', s1)} v(a_2, y^1); \tag{5.4.20}$$

$$q_{y2} \max_{a_2 \varepsilon G(a_1, s2)} v(a_2, y^2) \leq q_{y2} \max_{a_2 \varepsilon G(a_1', s2)} v(a_2, y^2) . \tag{5.4.21}$$

Furthermore, the second inequality is strict, i.e.

$$q_{y2} \max_{a_2 \varepsilon G(a_1, s2)} v(a_2, y^2) < q_{y2} \max_{a_2 \varepsilon G(a_1', s2)} v(a_2, y^2) . \tag{5.4.22}$$

For suppose in period 1 the agent receives signal y^2. Because of 5.4.13(b) (which holds for t=2,...,T) and 5.4.14(c),(d), an agent who holds asset d at the beginning of period 2 will not switch to asset b if he receives the signal y^2, because the higher interest payment gives higher future income without higher costs today. Therefore, if the first-period choice was a_1 (and hence $b_1=0$), the optimal second-period choice a_2 in $G(a_1, s^2)$ will involve $b_2=0$. Hence, if (5.4.21) were an equality, the optimal choice b_2' in $G(a_1', s^2)$ would also have to be optimal in $G(a_1, s^2)$ and hence it would have to be such that $b_2'=0$.

But from $b_1'>0$ and $b_1=0$ it follows that, if $b_2'=0$, $\max[\beta(b_1'-b_2'),0] > \max[\beta(b_1-b_2'),0]$. Hence, for any element (c_2, m_2, b_2, d_2) that satisfies $b_2'=0$ (which is necessary to be optimal in $G(a^1', s^2)$, there exists an element of $G(a_1, s^2)$ that allows greater c_2 and is otherwise equal (because transaction costs are saved). Therefore, there is no element in $G(a_1', s_2)$ that can be optimal in $G(a_1, s^2)$, i.e

$$\max_{a_2 \varepsilon G(a_1, s2)} v(a_2, y^1) < \max_{a_2 \varepsilon G(a_1', s2)} v(a_2, y^2) .$$

Inequality (5.4.22) then follows immediately from $q_{y2}>0$ (cf. 5.4.14b).

From $r_1(a_1) = r_1(a_1')$, inequalities (5.4.20) and (5.4.22) and the definition of $V(a_1)$, it then follows that $V(a_1')>V(a_1)$.

Now $r_1(a_1)+V(a_1)$ depends continuously on $(R_{bt}(s^1), R_{dt}(s^1))$. Hence (5.4.17) is still true after a sufficiently small perturbation of parameters such that $R_{b1}>0, R_{d1}>0$; i.e. such that the unreasonable assumption that $R_{b1}=R_{d1}=0$ no longer holds.

Therefore, there exist parameter constellations satisfying (5.4.13)-(5.4.15), where only the Bayesian agent will hold money, which proves the proposition.

From proposition 5.3 and 5.4, we get the following casually formulated proposition.

Proposition 5.5: Flexibility considerations can make an agent turn from long-term assets to more liquid short-term asset, e.g. money.

The model we just dealt with is one of the typical cases mentioned at the very end of chapter 3.5: holding money is not more flexible than holding long-term assets in a rigourous sense. While the fact that it is easier to reallocate wealth if it is held as a short-term security is advantageous from the point of view of flexibility, the foregone interest payments clearly have a negative influence on flexibility.

Therefore, the JONES-OSTROY theorem which, to recall, can be crudely formulated as "greater uncertainty implies a more flexible choice" cannot be applied.

Nevertheless, we have shown that "though the principle that greater uncertainty leads to more flexible choices ... is not generally valid, the more fundamental principle that a change in the degree of uncertainty will somehow change the optimal behaviour of the agent remains unaffected" (cf. p. 105).

We note in passing that the considerations of the JONES/OSTROY-type are applicable to a slightly different question. One may ask how the expectation of additional information affects the total wealth that is held. Here, one can use the fact that, if total wealth is higher for one path than for the other, it is clearly more flexible.

More precisely, if $a_1 = (c_1, m_1, b_1, d_1)$, $a_1' = (c_1', m_1', b_1', d_1')$ are efficient and $m_1 \geq m_1'$, $b_1 \geq b_1'$, $d_1 \geq d_1'$, then a_1 is at least as flexible as a_1'. Therefore, we know that, if the conditions of the JONES/OSTROY-theorem hold, an increase in uncertainty will favour a_1', i.e. will lead to a tendency towards increased savings.

The lower today's consumption level, the greater the wealth one can carry over to future periods and the greater the future options for consumption and accumulation of wealth. Therefore, higher saving allows a more appropriate response to future information.

We can now summarize this chapter.

The main reason why money is held in the presence of interest-bearing assets is the fact that it is the only universally accepted means of payment, so that in the presence of transaction costs it may sometimes not be advisable to turn money into interest-bearing assets if need for consumption good purchases in the not too distant future is anticipated. The occurrence of transaction costs makes the problem more "irreversible" in the terminology of chapter 3.1. In situations where, without this additional irreversibility, one would like to hold bonds, it may be advisable to hold money if the irreversibility is present. Incomplete information does not play a significant role in this argument.

What is more, under realistic assumptions, there is no other reason why incomplete information should induce agents to hold money. The argument that money is held because other assets, though promising a higher return, are riskier, is limited by the existence of assets that are similarly riskless but promise a higher return. Therefore, it can merely be used to explain the demand for such assets, but not necessarily for money.

Flexibility considerations can explain the demand for money relative to interest-bearing assets in a world without close substitutes for money. If there are such short-term assets, however, that lead to a positive return that is more or less known in advance, and if these events can even be sold without interest losses, the argument no longer goes through. In a realistic setting, flexibility considerations can therefore only explain why agents might hold short-term assets in the presence of long-term assets that yield higher interest rates.

Appendix:

Proof of Proposition 5.3: It remains to be shown that a_1' is feasible if a is.

Inserting a_1' into the budget restriction (5.4.12) gives

$$\langle p_1, c_1'\rangle + m_1' + p_b(b_1'-b_0) + p_d(d_1'-d_0) + \max[\delta(d_0-d_1'),0] + \max[ß(b_0-b_1'),0] \le m_0 + R_b b_0 + R_d d_0 + \langle p_1, e_1\rangle. \qquad (A5.1)$$

By definition, $a_1'=(c_1',m_1',b_1',d_1') = (c_1,0,b_1+m_1/p_b,d_1)$, so that (A5.1) reads

$$\langle p_1, c_1\rangle + 0 + p_b(b_1+m_1/p_b-b_0) + p_d(d_1-d_0) + \max[\delta(d_0-d_1),0] + \max[ß(b_0-b_1-m_1/p_b),0] \le m_0 + R_b b_0 + R_d d_0 + \langle p_1, e_1\rangle$$

or, equivalently,

$$\langle p_1, c_1\rangle + m_1 + p_b(b_1-b_0) + p_d(d_1-d_0) + \max[\delta(d_0-d_1),0] + \max[ß(b_0-b_1-m_1/p_b),0] \le m_0 + R_b b_0 + R_d d_0 + \langle p_1, e_1\rangle. \qquad (A5.2)$$

(A5.2) differs from the budget restriction for a_1 only in the last term on the left hand side (cf. 5.4.12). Instead of $\max[ß(b_0-b_1),0]$, we now have $\max[ß(b_0-b_1-m_1/p_b),0]$.

From $ß(b_0-b_1-m_1/p_b) \le ß(b_0-b_1)$, it follows that the budget restriction for a_1 implies inequality (A5.2) and, hence, the feasibility of a_1'.

For t=2,...,T-1, inserting a_t' in (5.4.12) gives

$$\langle p_t, c_t'\rangle + m_t' + p_b(b_t'-b_{t-1}') + p_d(d_t'-d_{t-1}') + \max[ß(b_t'-b_{t-1}'),0] + \max[\delta(d_t'-d_{t-1}'),0] \le m_{t-1}' + R_b b_{t-1}' + R_d d_{t-1}' + \langle p_t, e_t\rangle. \qquad (A5.3)$$

By definition, $a_t'=(c_t',m_t',b_t',d_t') = (c_t, m_t-m_1+R_{b1}m_1/p_b+\ldots+R_{b(t-1)}m_1/p_b, b_t+m_1/p_b, d_t)$, so that (A5.3) reads

$$\langle p_t, c_t\rangle + m_t - m_1 + R_{b1}m_1/p_b + \ldots + R_{b(t-1)}m_1/p_b + p_b(b_t + m_1/p_b - b_{t-1} + m_1/p_b) + p_d(d_t - d_{t-1}) + \max[(b_t + m_1/p_b - b_{t-1} - m_1/p_b), 0] + \max[\delta(d_t - d_{t-1}), 0] \le m_{t-1} - m_1 + R_{b1}m_1/p_b + \ldots + R_{b(t-2)}m_1/p_b + R_{b(t-1)}(b_{t-1} + m_1/p_b) + R_{d(t-1)}d_{t-1} + \langle p_t, e_t\rangle$$

or, equivalently,

$$\langle p_t, c_t\rangle + m_t + p_b(b_t - b_{t-1}) + p_d(d_t - d_{t-1}) + \max[\beta(b_t - b_{t-1}), 0] + \max[\delta(d_t - d_{t-1}), 0] \le m_{t-1} + R_{b(t-1)}b_{t-1} + R_{d(t-1)}d_{t-1} + \langle p_t, e_t\rangle,$$

which is the budget constraint for a_t.

As the last step of the proof, we show that a_T' is feasible if a_T is.

The budget constraint for period T is simpler because there are no interest penalties (T is the maturity date). For a_T', the constraint is

$$\langle p_T, c_T'\rangle + m_T' + p_b(b_T' - b_{T-1}') + p_d(d_T' - d_{T-1}') \le m_{T-1}' + R_{b(T-1)}b_{T-1}' + R_{d(T-1)}d_{T-1}' + \langle p_T, e_T\rangle. \qquad (A5.4)$$

By definition, $a_T' = (c_T', m_T', b_T', d_T') = (c_T + \varepsilon, m_T, b_T, d_T)$, so that (A5.4) reads

$$\langle p_T, c_T + \varepsilon\rangle + m_T + p_b(b_T - (b_{T-1} + m_1/p_b)) + p_d(d_T - d_{T-1}) \le m_{T-1} - m_1 + R_{b1}m_1/p_b + \ldots + R_{b(T-2)}m_1/p_b + R_{b(T-1)}(b_{T-1} + m_1/p_b) + R_{d(T-1)}d_{T-1} + \langle p_T, e_T\rangle.$$

Because $p_T = 1$ and ε was defined as $R_{b1}m_1/p_b + \ldots + R_{b(T-1)}m_1/p_b$, this is equivalent with

$$\langle p_T, c_T\rangle + m_T + p_b(b_T - b_{T-1}) + p_d(d_T - d_{T-1}) \le m_{T-1} + R_{b(T-1)}b_{T-1} + R_{d(T-1)}d_{T-1} + \langle p_T, e_T\rangle,$$

the budget constraint for a_T.

This fills the last gap in the proof of proposition 5.3.

EPILOGUE

The goal of this study was to present an analytical framework that is capable of dealing with the behaviour of economic agents who receive information over time. We saw that in the presence of irreversibility it is not only advisable to adjust to such information once it has been received; in addition, flexibility considerations should already be made before the information is received. In the framework we studied, several economic phenomena can be seen to be compatible with rational behaviour. For instance, the desire of firms to abstain from investment in particularly uncertain times or to invest into "flexible" equipment may turn out to be optimal in this framework. Similarly, households are more likely to hold money or short-term assets in a world where they expect to receive additional information in the future than in a world where knowledge does not improve over time.

The results we obtained can be extended in various directions. For instance, a possible approach would appear to be the application of the results of this study, in particular those about the comparative statics of uncertainty, to general equilibrium models. An appropriate framework to deal with agents basing their decisions on expectations about future information is the temporary equilibrium model (cf. GRANDMONT 1986). It seems conceivable that in such a framework "market laws" can be derived: using the results of chapter 3 one can investigate under which circumstances the equilibrium consumption in period 1 declines if uncertainty rises.

Whatever the extensions of the model that one introduces, it is useful to bear in mind the principal limitations of the approach. We shall concentrate on the fundamental assumption of the model that, despite the agent's uncertainty about the state of the world, he completely understands the structure of the optimization model he is facing (or at least behaves as if he understood this structure). Of course, no reasonable economist would claim that such an assumption is realistic in general. The best one can hope for is that, to answer some questions, the usage of this unrealistic assumption does not give misleading conclusions. It is only in this sense that the approach of this study can be justified as an aid to the understanding of <u>some</u> economic phenomena that arise in a dynamic context. However, it seems highly likely that to obtain a deeper understanding of other economic phenomena, the very fact that agents do <u>not</u> understand the structure of the problem they are facing may be of some explanatory potential. When agents are ignorant in such a fundamental fashion, it is not obvious what "optimal" behaviour should be. But the absence of a clearly defined optimal behaviour does not mean that resulting actions are completely erratic.

For instance, HEINER (1983) argues that agents who lack the "competence" to solve difficult problems can reasonably be assumed to apply rule-governed, quasi-instinctive behaviour instead of optimization. He claims that assuming such rule-governed behaviour can actually give more definite explanations of economic regularities than assuming optimization. Recalling the developments in mathematical economics in the last twenty years, such a claim can hardly be considered as particularly bold. Given the impressive production of indeterminateness results in such fields as general equilibrium theory and growth theory,[1] it is at least clear that, in many contexts, optimization is too vacuous a concept to provide definite explanations. Of course this does not imply that such problems would not occur with alternative approaches. Inderterminateness may already occur when it comes to adequate substitutes for optimization as a fundamental principal of economic model-building: there is no obvious clearly defined, single principle that could take the place of optimization. Instead of searching for such a principle, it may be advisable to be more modest and restrict oneself to the search for stylized facts about sequential decision-making.

---

[1] To name only a few such indeterminateness results: the non-uniqueness of market equilibria in exchange economies; the results of SONNENSCHEIN (1973), DEBREU (1974) and MANTEL (1974) on the indeterminateness of market excess demand functions; the indeterminacy of accumulation paths in optimal growth models (cf. BOLDRIN/MONTRUCCHIO 1986).

To this end, the investigation of so-called choice anomalies (FREY/EICHENBERGER 1989) could be helpful. It would appear that such systematic deviations from "rational" economic behaviour can provide clues as to regularities in the behaviour of agents who do not completely understand the decision problem they have to solve. For instance, the status quo bias observed by SAMUELSON/ZECKHAUSER (1988) could be a useful general principle. These authors found out that in choice problems where some alternatives are framed as status quo, agents tend to choose such alternatives more often than one should expect on the basis of economic rationality arguments. The status quo character of an alternative gives it a particular attractiveness to most decision makers. One possible explanation would be that, lacking a precise understanding of the nature of the problem, agents stick to earlier choices as a guide for their present choices. We do not want to overemphasize the apparent irrationality of such behaviour: as has been argued before, the rationality concept is sufficiently flexible to be made compatible with a great variety of behavioural patterns; the standard fashion to deal with "choice-theoretical anomalies" is to extend the concepts of economic theory in a manner that allows to deal with apparent counterexamples to optimality as special cases of more general optimization behaviour. We do not argue that this procedure is illegitimate. However, it is conceivable that important insights are obscured by the ongoing search for "rational" explanations for apparently "irrational" behaviour. Instead of pushing the optimality principle to its limits, it may be more fruitful to use assumptions about the way people cope with their ignorance as structural elements in a dynamic microeconomic theory.

For instance, status quo preference can be interpreted as a kind of "subjective irreversibility". Though present choice may leave a variety of future options open, it may form future preferences in such a way that, from a subjective point of view, very few future options are compatible with present choice. This appears to be a general principle: in a dynamic context, there are strong links between present and future behaviour which restrict the choice sequences that agents are likely to choose. Studying such links more closely may help to improve the understanding of economic processes.

Summing up, the theory of sequential economic decision making should be extended in such a way that rationality arguments are just one element; in addition, the explanatory potential of human ignorance needs to be investigated. It has to be recognized that "dynamic economics" should really be treated as "foggy economics" (HEY 1979, p.233). Admittedly, this study was almost exclusively about "nice-weather economics", as the more conventional counterpart of "foggy economics" might be called. For the time being, the reader is asked to make do with the simple excuse that the path to "foggy economics" is somewhat foggy itself.

REFERENCES

ALLAIS, M. (1953), "Le Comportement de l'Homme Rationnel Devant le Risque, Critique des Postulats et Axioms de l'Ecole Americaine," Econometrica 21, 503-546.

ANDREAS, K. (1988), "Kapitalmarkt," in : N. Kloten and J.H. v.Stein (eds.), Geld-, Bank- und Börsenwesen, Poeschel Verlag, Stuttgart.

AOKI, M. (1990), "Towards an Economic Model of the Japanese Firm," Journal of Economic Literature 28, 1-27.

ARROW, K.J. (1968), "Optimal Capital Policy with Irreversible Investment," in: J.N. WOLFE (ed.), Value, Capital and Growth, Papers in Honour of Sir John Hicks, Edinburgh University Press, Edinburgh.

ARROW, K.J. (1988), "Summary," in: P.Anderson, K.J. Arrow and P.Zarembka (eds.), The Economy as an Evolving Complex System, Addison-Wesley, Reading, Mass.

ARROW, K.J. and A.C. FISHER (1974), "Environmental Preservation, Uncertainty and Irreversibility," Quarterly Journal of Economics 88, 312-320.

ARROW, K.J. and L.HURWICZ (1972), "An Optimality Criterion for Decision-Making under Ignorance," in: C.F. CARTER and J.L. FORD (eds.), Uncertainty and Expectations in Economics, Basil Blackwell, Oxford.

ARROW, K.J. and M. KURZ (1971), Public Investment, The Rate of Return and Optimal Fiscal Policy, Johns Hopkins University Press, Baltimore.

ASHAUER, G. (1988), "Geld- und Kapitalanlageleistungen," in: N. Kloten and J.H. v.Stein (eds.), Geld-, Bank- und Börsenwesen, Poeschel Verlag, Stuttgart.

BALDWIN, C.Y. (1982),"Optimal Sequential Investment when Capital is not Readily Reversible," The Journal of Finance 37, 763-782.

BAUMOL, W.J. (1952), "The Transactions Demand for Cash: An Inventory Theoretic Approach," Quarterly Journal of Economics 66, p. 545-556.

BELLMAN, R. (1957), Dynamic Programming, Princeton University Press, Princeton, N.J.

BERNANKE, B.S. (1983), "Irreversibility, Uncertainty and Cyclical Investment," Quarterly Journal of Economics 98, 85-106.

BERNHOLZ, P. (1967), "Erwerbskosten, Laufzeit und Charakter zinstragender Forderungen als Bestimmungsgründe der Geldnachfrage der Haushalte," Zeitschrift für die gesamte Staatswissenschaft 123, 9-24.

BERNHOLZ, P. and M. FABER (1973), "Technical Productivity of Roundabout Processes and Positive Rate of Interest. A Capital Model with Depreciation and n-Period Horizon," Zeitschrift für die gesamte Staatswissenschaft 129, 46-61.

BESSANT,J. and B.HAYWOOD (1986), "Flexibility in Manufacturing Systems," OMEGA International Journal of Management Science 14, 465-473.

BOLDRIN, M. and L. MONTRUCCHIO (1986), "On the Indeterminacy of Capital Accumulation Paths," Journal of Economic Theory 40, 26-39.

BROWN, D. and L. LEWIS (1981), "Myopic Economic Agents," Econometrica 49, 359-368.

BÜHNER,R. (1986), "Arbeitseinsatz und Arbeitsstrukturierung in flexiblen Fertigungsystemen," WISU 15, 69-74 (1986).

CABALLERO, R.J. (1991), "On the Sign of the Investment-Uncertainty Relationship," American Economic Review 81, 279-288.

CANNAN, E. (1921), "The Application of the Theoretical Apparatus of Supply and Demand to Units of Currency," Economic Journal 31, 453-461.

CHANG,W.W., D. HAMBERG and J. HIRATA (1983), "Liquidity Preference as Behaviour toward Risk is a Demand for Short-Term Securities - Not Money," American Economic Review 73, 420-427.

CHEW, S.H. and L. EPSTEIN (1989), "A Unifying Approach to Axiomatic Non-Expected Utility Theories," Journal of Economic Theory 49, 207-240.

DAMANPOUR, F. and W.M. EVAN (1984), "Organizational Innovation and Performance: The Problem of 'Organizational Lag'," Administrative Science Quarterly 29, 392-402.

DASGUPTA, P. (1982), The Control of Resources, Basil Blackwell, Oxford.

DASGUPTA, P. and G.M. HEAL (1979), Economic Theory and Exhaustible Resources, Nisbet, Cambridge.

DEBREU, G. (1974), "Excess Demand Functions," Journal of Mathematical Economics 1, 15-23.

DECHERT, W.D. (1984), "Does Optimal Growth Preclude Chaos? A Theorem on Monotonicy," Zeitschrift für Nationalökonomie 44, 57-61.

DENECKERE, R. and S. PELIKAN (1986), "Competitive Chaos," Journal of Economic Theory 40, 13-26.

EBERWEIN, R.-D. (1989), Organisation flexibel automatisierter Produktionssysteme, Physica-Verlag, Heidelberg.

EICHHORN,W. and A. VOGT (1990), "Gemeinsames bei der Messung von Ungleichheit, Streuung, Risiko und Information," Mitteilungen der Schweizerischen Vereinigung der Versicherungsmathematiker, 53-73.

EISNER, R. and R.H. STROTZ (1963), "Determinants of Business Investment," in Commission on Money and Credit: Impacts of Monetary Policy, Prentice-Hall, Eaglewood Cliffs.

ELLSBERG, D. (1961), "Risk, Ambiguity and the Savage Axioms," Quarterly Journal of Economics 75, 643-49.

EPSTEIN, L. (1980), "Decision Making and the Temporal Resolution of Uncertainty," International Economic Review 21, 269-283.

FABER, M. (1979), Introduction to Modern Austrian Capital Theory, Springer-Verlag, Berlin, Heidelberg, New York, London, Paris, Tokyo.

FABER, M. (ed.) (1986), Studies in Austrian Capital Theory, Investment and Time, Springer-Verlag, Berlin, Heidelberg, New York, London, Paris, Tokyo.

FABER, M., R. MANSTETTEN and J.PROOPS (1990), Humankind and the World: An Anatomy of Ignorance and Surprise, Discussion Paper Nr. 159, University of Heidelberg.

FABER, M., H. NIEMES and G. STEPHAN (1987), Entropy, Environment and Resources. An Essay in Physico-Economics, Springer-Verlag, Berlin, Heidelberg, New York, London, Paris, Tokyo.

FABER, M. and J.L.R. PROOPS (1990), Evolution, Time, Production and the Environment, Springer-Verlag, Berlin, Heidelberg, New York, London, Paris, Tokyo.

FABER, M., J.L.R. PROOPS, P. MICHAELIS and M. RUTH (1990), "Economy-Environment Interactions in the Long Run," Ecological Economics 2, 27-55.

FABER, M. and G. WAGENHALS (1988), "Towards a Long-Term Balance between Economics and Environmental Protection," in: W.Salomons and U.Förstner (eds.), Environmental Management of Solid Waste, Dredged Materials and Mine Tailings, Springer-Verlag, Berlin, Heidelberg, New York, London, Paris, Tokyo.

FISHER, A.C. and W.M. HANEMANN (1987), "Quasi-Option Value: Some Misconceptions Dispelled," Journal of Environmental Economics and Management 14, 183-190.

FISHBURN, P.C. (1985), Nonlinear Preference and Utility Theory, Johns Hopkins University Press, Baltimore & London.

FREY, B.S. and R. EICHENBERGER (1989), "Zur Bedeutung entscheidungstheoretischer Anomalien in der Ökonomik," Jahrbücher für Nationalökonomie und Statistik 206, 81-101.

FUSS,M.C. and D. McFADDEN (1978),"Flexibility versus Efficiency in ex ante Plant Design," in: M.C.FUSS and D.McFADDEN (eds.), Production Economics: A Dual Approach to Theory and Applications, North-Holland, Amsterdam.

GERWIN, D. (1985), "Organizational Implications of CAM," OMEGA International Journal of Management Science 13, 443-451.

GOLDMAN, S.M. (1974), "Flexibility and the Demand for Money," Journal of Economic Theory 9, 203-222.

GOLDMAN, S.M. (1978), "Portfolio Choice and Flexibility: The Precautionary Motive," Journal of Monetary Economics 4, 263-279.

GOULD, J.P. (1968), "Adjustment Costs in the Theory of Investment of the Firm," Review of Economic Studies 35, 47-55.

GRANDMONT (1986), "Temporary Equilibrium Theory," in: K.J. ARROW and M.D. INTRILIGATOR, Handbook of Mathematical Economics, North-Holland, Amsterdam etc.

HAMMOND, P.J. (1976), "Changing Tastes and Coherent Dynamic Choice," Review of Economic Studies 43, 159-73.

HANEMANN, W.M. (1989), "Information and the Concept of Option Value," Journal of Environmental Economics and Management 16, 23-37.

HEAL, G.M. (1973), The Theory of Economic Planning, North-Holland, Amsterdam etc.

HEINER, R.A. (1983), "The Origin of Predictable Behaviour," American Economic Review 73, 560-595.

HENRY, C. (1974), "Investment Decisions under Uncertainty: The Irreversibility Effect," American Economic Review 64, 1006-12.

HEY, J.D. (1979), Uncertainty in Microeconomics, Martin Robertson, Oxford.

HICKS (1935), "A Suggestion for Simplifying the Theory of Money," Economica 2, 1-19.

HIRSHLEIFER, J. (1972), "Liquidity, Uncertainty and the Accumulation of Information," in: C.F.CARTER and J.L.FORD (eds.), Uncertainty and Expectations in Economics: Essays in Honour of G.L.S. Shackle, Blackwell's, Oxford.

HIRSHLEIFER, J. and J.G. RILEY (1979), "The Analysis of Uncertainty and Information - An Expository Survey," Journal of Economic Literature 17, 1375-1421.

HOOVER, K.D. (1990), The New Classical Macroeconomics, Basil Blackwell, Oxford.

INTRILIGATOR, M.D. (1971), Mathematical Optimization and Economic Theory, Prentice Hall, Eaglewood Cliffs.

IRVIN, G. (1978), Modern Cost-Benefit Methods, Macmillan, London and Basingstoke.

JAKSCH, H.J. (1975), "Die Mehrergiebigkeit längerer Wege in einem linearen Vielsektormodell," Zeitschrift für die gesamte Staatswissenschaft 131, 92-105.

JORGENSON, D.W. (1967), "The Theory of Investment Behaviour," in: R. FERBER (ed.), Determinants of Investment Behaviour, Universities-National Bureau Conference Series, No. 18, Columbia Press, New York.

JONES, R. and J.M. OSTROY (1984), "Flexibility and Uncertainty," Review of Economic Studies 51, 13-32.

KEYNES, J.M. (1936), The General Theory of Employment, Interest and Money. Macmillan, London.

KEYNES, J.M. (1957), Treatise on Probability, Mac Millan, London.

KNIGHT, F.H. (1921), Risk, Uncertainty and Profit, Houghton Mifflin, Boston/New York.

KOCH, H. (1982), Integrierte Unternehmensplanung, Gabler, Wiesbaden.

KOOPMANS, T.C. (1960), "Stationary Ordinal Utility and Impatience," Econometrica 28, 287-310.

KOOPMANS, T.C. (1964), "On Flexibility of Future Preferences," in: M.W. SHELLY et al.(eds.), Human Judgements and Optimality, New York.

KREPS, D. (1979), "A Representation Theorem for Preference for Flexibility," Econometrica 47, 565-578.

KREPS, D. (1988), Notes on the Theory of Choice, Westview Press, Boulder,Colorado.

KYDLAND, F.E. and E.C. PRESCOTT (1977), "Rules rather than Discretion: The Inconsistency of Optimal Plans," in : R.E. LUCAS and T.J. SARGENT (eds.), Rational Expectations and Econometric Practice, Allen & Unwin, London.

LAFFONT, J.J. (1989), The Economics of Uncertainty and Information, MIT Press, Cambridge, Mass. and London.

LUCAS, R.E. (1967), "Adjustment Costs and the Theory of Supply," Journal of Political Economy 75, 321-334.

MACHINA, M. (1982), "Expected Utility Analysis without the Independence Axiom," Econometrica 50, 277-323.

MACHINA, M. (1987), "Choice under Uncertainty: Problems Solved and Unsolved," Journal of Economic Perspectives 1, 121-54.

MACHINA, M. (1989), "Dynamic Consistency and Non-Expected Utility Theory Models of Choice under Uncertainty," Journal of Economic Literature 27, 1622-1668.

MAIER, G. (1984), Rohstoffe und Innovation, Verlagsgruppe Athenäum/Hain/Hanstein, Königstein.

MAKOWSKI, L. (1989), "Keynes's Liquidity Preference Theory: A Suggested Reinterpretation," in: F.HAHN (ed.), The Economics of Missing Markets, Information and Games, Clarendon Press, Oxford.

MALLIARIS, A.G. and W.H. BROCK (1982), Stochastic Methods in Economics and Finance, North-Holland, Amsterdam, New York, Oxford, Tokyo.

MANTEL, R. (1974), "On the Characterization of Aggregate Excess Demand," Journal of Economic Theory 7, 348-353.

MARKOWITZ, H. (1952), "Portfolio Selection," Journal of Finance 7, 77-91.

MARSCHAK, J. and K. MIYASAWA (1968), "Economic Comparability of Information Systems," International Economic Review 9, 137-74.

MARSCHAK, T. and R. NELSON (1962), "Flexibility, Uncertainty and Economic Theory," Metroeconomica 14, 42-58.

MARTIRENA-MARTEL, A.M. (1971), "Optimal Inventory and Capital Policy under Certainty," Journal of Economic Theory 3, 241-253.

MASKIN, E. (1979), "Decision Making under Ignorance with Implications for Social Choice," Theory and Decision 11, 319-337.

MC CALLUM, B.T. and M.S. GOODFRIEND (1987), Money, in: J. EATWELL, M. MILGATE, P. NEWMAN (eds.), The New Palgrave, A Dictionary of Economics, Mac Millan, London.

MC DONALD, R. and D.R. SIEGEL (1986), "The Value of Waiting to Invest," Quarterly Journal of Economics 101, 707-728.

MENGES, G. and S. HUSCHENS (1984), "The Information Problem in Decision Making," Theory and Decision 16, 45-58.

MILLER, J.R. and F. LAD (1984), "Flexibility, Learning and Irreversibility in Environmental Decisions: A Bayesian Approach," Journal of Environmental Economics and Management 11, 161-172.

MILLS, D.E. and L. SCHUMANN (1985), "Industry Structure with Fluctuating Demand," American Economic Review 75, 758-767.

NICKELL, S.J. (1974a), "On the Role of Expectations in the Pure Theory of the Firm," Review of Economic Studies 41, 1-20.

NICKELL, S.J. (1974b), "On Expectations, Government Policy and the Rate of Investment," Economica 41, 241-255.

NICKELL, S.J. (1977), "Uncertainty and Lags in the Investment Behaviour of Firms," Review of Economic Studies 44, 249-263.

NICKELL, S.J. (1978), The Investment Decisions of Firms, Cambridge University Press, Cambridge.

NIEHANS, J. (1978), The Theory of Money, Johns Hopkins University Press, Baltimore.

PERSSON, M., T.PERSSON and L.E.O. SVENSSON (1987), "Time Consistency of Fiscal and Monetary Policy," Econometrica 55, 1419-1432..

PIGOU, A.C. (1917), "The Value of Money," Quarterly Journal of Economics 32, 38-65.

PINDYCK, R.S. (1988), "Irreversible Investment, Capacity Choice and the Value of the Firm," American Economic Review 78, 969-984.

RASMUSEN, E. (1989), Games and Information, Basil Blackwell, Oxford.

RICHTER, R. (1987), Geldtheorie, Springer-Verlag, Berlin, Heidelberg, New York, London, Paris, Tokyo.

ROTHSCHILD, M. and J.E. STIGLITZ (1970), "Increasing Risk I: A Definition," Journal of Economic Theory 2, 225-243.

SAMUELSON, W. and R. ZECKHAUSER (1988), "Status Quo Bias in Decision Making," Journal of Risk and Uncertainty 1, 7-59.

SARGENT, T.J. (1987), Dynamic Macroeconomic Theory, Harvard University Press, Cambridge.

SHACKLE, G.L.S. (1958), Time in Economics, North-Holland, Amsterdam.

SINN, H.W. (1980), Ökonomische Entscheidungen bei Ungewißheit, J.C.B. Mohr (Paul Siebeck), Tübingen.

SONNENSCHEIN, H. (1973), "Do Walras' Identity and Continuity Characterize the Class of Community Excess Demand Functions?", Journal of Economic Theory 6, 345-354.

STACKELBERG, H. v. (1939), "Beitrag zur Theorie des individuellen Sparens," Zeitschrift für Nationalökonomie 9,167-200.

STEPHAN, G. (1988), A Neo-Austrian Approach to Computable Equilibrium Models: Time to Build Technologies and Imperfect Markets, Schweizerische Zeitschrift für Volkswirtschaft und Statistik 124, 49-63.

STEPHAN, G. (1988a), Minderschätzung zukünftiger Bedürfnisse: Zur Formalisierung eines psychologischen Phänomens, Jahrbücher für Nationalökonomie und Statistik 205, 348-362.

STEPHAN, G. (1989), Pollution Control, Economic Adjustment and Long-Run Equilibrium, Springer-Verlag, Berlin, Heidelberg, New York, London, Paris, Tokyo.

STIGLER, G. (1939), "Production and Distribution in the Short Run," Journal of Political Economy 47, 305-28.

STOCK, J.H. and D.A. WISE (1990), "Pensions, the Option Value of Work, and Retirement, Econometrica 58, 1151-1160.

STROTZ, R. (1955/56), "Myopia and Inconsistency in Dynamic Utility Maximization," Review of Economic Studies 23, 165-180.

TOBIN, J. (1956), "The Interest-Elasticity of Transaction Demands for Cash," Review of Economics and Statistics 38, 241-247.

TOBIN, J. (1958), "Liquidity Preference as Behaviour Towards Risk," Review of Economic Studies 25, 65-86.

UNGERN-STERNBERG, T.v. (1990), "The Flexibility to Switch between Different Products," Economica 57, 355-369.

USATEGUI, J.M. (1990), "Uncertain Irreversibility, Information, and Transformation Costs," Journal of Environmental Economics and Management 19, 73-85.

VISCUSI, W.K. (1988)," Irreversible Environmental Investment with Uncertain Benefit Levels," Journal of Environmental Economics and Management 15, 147-157.

WEISBROD, B.A. (1964), "Collective-Consumption Services of Individual-Consumption Goods," Quarterly Journal of Economics, 78, 471-477.

WILDEMANN, H. (1984), "Investitionsplanung und Wirtschaftlichkeitsrechnung für eine flexible Produktionstechnik," unpublished notes, Passau.

WILDEMANN, H. (1987), "Betriebswirtschaftliche Wirkungen einer flexibel automatisierten Fertigung," Betriebswirtschaftliche Forschung und Praxis, 1987, p.209-224.

WODOPIA, F.J. (1986), Intertemporale Produktionsentscheidungen: Theorie und Anwendung auf die Elektrizitätswirtschaft, Verlagsgruppe Athenäum/Hain/Hanstein, Königstein.

Vol. 360: P. Stalder, Regime Translations, Spillovers and Buffer Stocks. VI, 193 pages . 1991.

Vol. 361: C. F. Daganzo, Logistics Systems Analysis. X, 321 pages. 1991.

Vol. 362: F. Gehreis, Essays In Macroeconomics of an Open Economy. VII, 183 pages. 1991.

Vol. 363: C. Puppe, Distorted Probabilities and Choice under Risk. VIII, 100 pages . 1991

Vol. 364: B. Horvath, Are Policy Variables Exogenous? XII, 162 pages. 1991.

Vol. 365: G. A Heuer, U. Leopold-Wildburger. Balanced Silverman Games on General Discrete Sets. V, 140 pages. 1991.

Vol. 366: J. Gruber (Ed.), Econometric Decision Models. Proceedings, 1989. VIII, 636 pages. 1991.

Vol. 367: M. Grauer, D. B. Pressmar (Eds.), Parallel Computing and Mathematical Optimization. Proceedings. V, 208 pages. 1991.

Vol. 368: M. Fedrizzi, J. Kacprzyk, M. Roubens (Eds.), Interactive Fuzzy Optimization. VII, 216 pages. 1991.

Vol. 369: R. Koblo, The Visible Hand. VIII, 131 pages.1991.

Vol. 370: M. J. Beckmann, M. N. Gopalan, R. Subramanian (Eds.), Stochastic Processes and their Applications. Proceedings, 1990. XLI, 292 pages. 1991.

Vol. 371: A. Schmutzler, Flexibility and Adjustment to Information in Sequential Decision Problems. VIII, 198 pages. 1991.